Foreword

The Hidden Places Series

This is an established collection of travel guides which covers the U.K and Ireland in 16 titles.

The aim of the books is to introduce readers to some of the less well known attractions of each area whilst not ignoring the more established ones.

We have included in this book a number of hotels, inns, restaurants, various types of accommodation, historic houses, museums, and general attractions which are to be found in this part of the country, together with historical background information.

There is a map at the beginning of each chapter with line drawings of the places featured, along with a description of the services offered.

We hope that the book prompts you to discover some of the fascinating "Hidden Places" which we found on our journey, and we are sure the places featured would be pleased if you mentioned that our book prompted your visit.

We wish you an enjoyable and safe journey.

The
Hidden Places of the
Thames & Chilterns

CONTENTS

The
HIDDEN PLACES

THAMES & CHILTERNS

Front Cover:
The Thames at Henley
by PAUL BENNETT

Acknowledgements

The Publishers would like to thank the following for their assistance in the production of this book: ;Deborah , and Jean for Administration. Joanna, Gerald and Sarah for Writing. Nigel, Peter, for research. Sue Wyatt for editing, Simon at Graphix for the maps.
ALL MAPS COPYRIGHT MAPS IN MINUTES
RH Publications 1996

OTHER TITLES IN THE HIDDEN PLACES SERIES

Ireland
Scotland
Wales
The Lake District
The Welsh Borders
Northumberland & Durham
Lancashire, Cheshire and the Isle of Man
Yorkshire
Devon and Cornwall
Dorset, Hampshire, I.O.W
Somerset, Avon, Glos, Wilts.
East Anglia
The Heart of England
The South East
(ORDER FORM AT BACK OF BOOK)

© M & M Publishing Ltd. 118 Ashley Rd .Cheshire. U.K. WA14 2UN

CHAPTER ONE

West Berkshire

Basildon Park

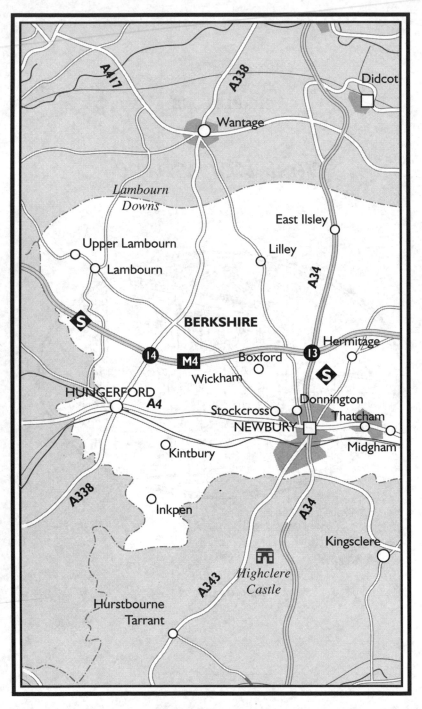

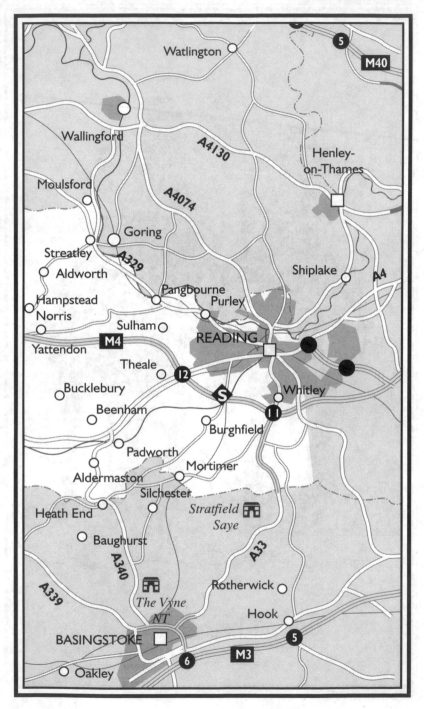

Lambourn

West Berkshire

Most people catch their first view of Berkshire hurtling down the M4 motorway towards London and passing the 'Welcome to Berkshire' signs prior to Membury services which lies just over the border.

However, coming off at the next junction, No 14, and heading along the A4 towards Hungerford, one is rewarded with a far morepleasant journey than travelling along the M4 which, by taking much of the traffic, leaves this formerly very busy road a lot quieter. To the north, a string of racehorses can often be seen galloping across the Lambourn Downs.

LAMBOURN

Set in the heart of the beautiful West Berkshire Downs, Lambourn is one of the most celebrated racehorse training centres in Europe. The immediate area is home to over 30 trainers, as well as to a concentration of related services, including veterinary surgeons, laser and solarium facilities, saddlers and racehorse transporters. The **Lambourn Trainers Association** is an organisation of trainers based in the Valley of the Racehorse who have come together to promote the exceptional facilities of Lambourn to racehorse owners and the public at large. The Association is chaired by Peter Walwyn, a renowned figure within the racing industry who has trained almost 2000 winners in Europe and America, and who has twice been UK champion trainer. His yard at Windsor House in the heart of Lambourn is one of the best-equipped in the area, having its own superb equine swimming pool and all-weather gallop in addition to the magnificent natural facilities provided by the surrounding downland landscape. Situated just a few miles north west of junction 14 on the M4, Lambourn is ideally located for access to the motorway system and Britain's major racecourses. Its close proximity to London and Heathrow Airport also means that owners from the capital and all over the world lie within easy reach.

In recent years, members of the Association have been opening their yards to visitors. Guided tours beginning at 10am and lasting approximately two hours are offered daily, except Sundays and Bank Holidays. Trainers are on hand to answer questions on the training of thoroughbred racehorses, and visitors are able to see the horses in their stables, at exercise on the gallops, or perhaps even having a swim in an equine pool. On Good Friday, the Association holds its annual open day, when over 30 training stables throw open their gates to visitors. As well as tours of the stables, there are a number of ancillary attractions, including live music, refreshments and a number of horse-related events. The charge for touring the training stables at any time of year is £5 per person plus VAT, with proceeds going towards a charity which raises money for stable lads' housing. For further information on the activities of the Lambourn Trainers Association, please contact the office of Peter Walwyn on 01488 71347.

LAMBOURN

VALLEY OF THE RACEHORSE

Lambourn Trainers Association, Windsor House, Lambourn Tel: 01488 71347 Fax: 01488 72664

In **Lambourn** village itself whether you are a horse fan or not there is plenty to keep the visitor amused and occupied. The village has a fine medieval church for example, and do look out for the old almshouses, and the ancient village cross.

There is some beautiful countryside around here, with tiny villages tucked away, yet so close to the motorway and London.

With its central location in this picturesque village, **Lodge Down** offers its guests luxury accommodation. Set in its own spacious grounds, this Country House has a good size swimming pool, tennis court and a 'Ride' just outside the immediate gardens, where racehorses are regularly exercised. As Lambourn is one of the most famous racehorse training centres in the country, John and Sally Cook, your hosts for the duration of your stay, can arrange visits to local stables and the Cheltenham, Newbury and Ascot race meetings.

Lodge Down has achieved the English Tourist Board grade and the AA 4Q selected Awards for excellence and offers its visitors a warm and friendly welcome to this stylish family home. There are three en-suite guest bedrooms, each having been comfortably furnished and individually decorated to a very high standard.

For those wishing to stay a little longer, John and Sally also provide a cosy self-contained flat that boasts superb views over the gardens, woods and downs that surround this scenic property. The accommodation consists of one double-bedded room, one single-bedded room, a kitchen, bathroom with separate toilet and a light and airy sitting room complete with colour TV. Bunk beds and a cot are available if needed and the tennis court and swimming pool can be used in season.

Located just off the B4000 on your right as you pass through Lambourn, Lodge Down is less than one hour from Heathrow and is ideally situated for exploring Stonehenge, Bath and the glorious Cotswolds.

Lodge Down, Lambourn Tel/Fax 01672 540304

HUNGERFORD

This is very much racing country, with courses at Lambourn, Newbury, Windsor and Ascot and there are several hotels in West Berkshire that do special racing weekends for visitors. One of these is **The Bear Hotel** in **Hungerford**, one of the oldest and best known former coaching inns which lies at the junction of the A4 with the A338. Although it has an impressive Georgian frontage, the building actually dates back to 1494 or possibly even earlier. At one time it formed part of the manor of Chilton Foliat and was gifted by Henry VIII to five of his six wives in turn. It was here on 7th December 1688 that a meeting between William of Orange and representatives of his father-in-law James II, resulted in the end of the House of Stuart, following the flight of James II to France.

Situated on the southern slopes of the Kennet Valley, Hungerford is an old market town on the old Bath Road, once a very busy coaching route.

The town prospered during the early 19th Century with the opening of the Kennet and Avon Canal in 1810 and by 1840 boasted no less than eight coaching inns, but after the opening of the railway in 1847, the coach and canal traffic dwindled and Hungerford became once more a quiet market town.

Each year on the second Tuesday after Easter, residents of Hungerford continue an ancient tradition known as the Hocktide Festival or 'Tutti Day' ('Tutti' means 'bunch of flowers'), which was originally used as a means of collecting an early form of 'council tax'. During this colourful event, two men carrying a two metre pole decorated with ribbons and flowers would go from household to household collecting the 'tax'. To ease the burden of their visit, they would share a drink with the man of the house, give him an orange and kiss his wife before collecting the penny payment! This tradition has continued ever since, although nowadays without the payment of a penny.

The delightful **Tutti Pole** occupies a handsome 16th Century house at the end of Hungerford High Street. This charming tearoom and restaurant takes its name from the flower covered pole carried around the village on Tutti Day (15 days after Easter Monday) as part of an ancient municipal custom. The walls are decorated with photographs of the celebrations and a replica Tutti Pole can be seen in the window. Proprietors Barbara and Norman Barr serve delicious morning coffees, home-cooked lunches and afternoon teas in an atmosphere which is relaxed and attentive. In summer, customers can also sit in the delightful walled patio at the rear.

The Tutti Pole, 3 High Street, Hungerford Tel 01488 682515

Provided it is not the height of the season, it is usually fairly easy to park in Hungerford and there is an abundance of lovely antique and craft shops to browse amongst.

From here you can stroll down to the bridge which crosses the Kennet and Avon canal and watched the brightly coloured boats as they slowly

8

make their way through the water. A boat trip from here is a peaceful, leisurely way of viewing the beautiful scenery of the Kennet Valley.

Marshgate Cottage Hotel is a delightful family-run establishment lying at the end of a secluded lane within a mile of Hungerford town centre. This friendly small country hotel occupies a delightful rural location next to the Kennet and Avon Canal, and to Freeman's Marsh with its meandering trout streams and abundant wildlife.

The beautifully-appointed guest bedrooms are located in a tastefully-designed addition to a 17th-Century thatched cottage. The rooms are all at ground level and are equipped with private shower and toilet, colour TV, direct-dial telephone, radio and tea/coffee making facilities.

Resident owner Mike Walker has created a relaxed and cheerful atmosphere which is particularly attractive to the young-at-heart. The interior is pleasantly decorated in modern country style, with bare-brick walls, exposed timber beams and mellow pine furniture.

Marshgate Cottage adjoins a Site of Special Scientific Interest and provides the perfect base for walkers, cyclists and bird-watchers. For those preferring to browse in antique shops, a 15-minute stroll along the towpath of the Kennet and Avon Canal leads to the centre of Hungerford.

Marshgate Cottage Hotel, Marsh Lane, Hungerford Tel 01488 682307 fax 01488 685475

Situated just a few minutes' drive from junction 14 on the M4, **Fishers Farm** at Shefford Woodlands is a 600-acre cereal and sheep farm which offers superb bed and breakfast accommodation. An elegant traditional farmhouse built of mellow red brick, it is set in its own extensive garden within quarter of a mile of the ancient Roman road of Ermine Street.

The large drawing room has an oak-beamed ceiling and a blazing log fire in winter, and the three guest bedrooms are spacious, beautifully-decorated and equipped with private bathrooms, either en suite or

Only 400 yards away is the Kennet and Avon Canal, a picturesque stretch of water regularly used by narrow boats and barges, with many a nautical group being seen making their way up the lane for a visit to the Coach and Horses. Chris and Glynis can also direct you to some excellent bed and breakfast accommodation in the surrounding area if you wish to stay a little longer in this charming hamlet.

The Coach and Horses, Bath Road, Midgham Tel 01734 (01189 from 1997) 713384

ALDERMASTON

It was in this tranquil village that the William pear was first propagated in 1840 by the then village schoolmaster John Staid, although it was then known as the Aldermaston pear. A cutting of this plant is believed to have been given to Australia where it is called the Bartlett pear.

Aldermaston's **Church of St. Mary the Virgin** still retains much of its original 12th Century structure and has a splendid Norman door. This lovely church provides the setting for the York Mystery Cycle, nativity plays dating from the 14th Century which are performed annually in beautiful contemporary costume with period music including a piece written by William Byrd. Lasting a week, the plays attract visitors from far and wide.

Outside under the yew tree in the churchyard lies the grave of Maria Hale, formerly known as the Aldermaston witch. She was said to turn herself into a large brown hare and although the hare was never caught or killed, at one time a local keeper wounded it in the leg and from then on it was noticed that Maria Hale had become lame!

Close to the village there is a delightful canalside walk along **Aldermaston Wharf** leading to **Aldermaston Lock**, a Grade II listed structure of beautifully restored 18th Century scalloped brickwork. At

16

the Wharf you will also find the Information and Visitor Centre with its canal exhibition, picnic area and shop.

More recent history has seen the famous protest marches of the1950s outside the Atomic Research Establishment, which, rather mysteriously, is not to be found on Ordnance Survey Maps.

At the nearby village of **Beenham** which boasts its own vineyard, a pleasant afternoon can be spent wandering through the grounds of **Beenham House**, the Regency home of Professor and Mrs. Gerald Benney. The grounds extend to some 21 acres and feature old Lebanon cedars, oaks and hornbeams. There are spectacular views across the park and the Kennet Valley and a proportion of the small admission charge is donated to St. Mary's Church, Beenham.

To the west of Beenham are the attractive villages of **Bradfield** and **South End** which lie very close to the lovely **Bucklebury Estate**, a real haven for walkers, with over two square miles of mixed woodland criss-crossed with public footpaths. Home to a wealth of bird and animal life, this is a nature lover's paradise.

THEALE

Following the A4 out of Beenham towards Reading, the road leads into the centre of **Theale**, a delightful town which was once a regular stopping-off point for travellers on this old coaching route. The main street is a listed town centre thoroughfare.

The dominant feature of the town is its 19th Century Church, **Holy Trinity**. A splendid piece of architecture, the exterior closely resembles that of Salisbury Cathedral, particularly at the west front where two pinnacled towers stand either side of an arched tower leading into the church.

Another interesting building here is the fine **Oast House** which stands at the back of the old Theale Brewery buildings and which can be seen by following the public footpath from the eastern end of the High Street towards the rear of the buildings.

The **Fox and Hounds Restaurant and Inn** is easily reached from the M1 intersection with the A4 Reading to Newbury Road, taking Station Road. The land on which this inn now stands was leased in 1846 to a Jesse Stroud (Innkeeper) by the then Earl of Shrewsbury and Waterford. Old documents show that soon after that date the original Fox and Hounds was built. Recent modernisation has retained the old world charm and character with oak beams and blazing log fires in the winter. Don and Sue Guppy have been resident hosts at the Fox and Hounds for two and a half years now and have a good local trade, usually an indicator of the success of an establishment.

They provide quality food in a congenial atmosphere with a full menu available at both lunchtimes and in the evenings, as well as hot and cold lunchtime snacks and daily specials. Sue looks after all the cooking, and no doubt it is her ability to produce really tasty and freshly prepared dishes that keeps the customers coming back time and again for more. The special Sunday Roast is particularly recommended and booking is advised.

Don's speciality is looking after his cellar; Wadsworths fine ales are on tap and there's a choice of eight real ales regularly available. Outside is a very pleasant beer garden with a children's play area.

The Fox and Hounds is located in an area described as Rambler's Paradise, with many scenic walks in the vicinity. Opposite is a bird sanctuary which offers an interesting opportunity to see these lovely little creatures at close quarters. Children and pets under control are welcome. Call in and sample the hospitality.

The Fox and Hounds, Sunnyside, Theale Tel 01734 302295

The River Pang rises at East Ilsley and flows into the Thames at Pangbourne. At least, it did until the upper reaches dried up during the drought years of 1989 to 1991. But it was not just the lack of rainfall that caused the damage, it was the abstraction of water at Compton to pump to Didcot. Various organisations, notably the Pang Valley Conservation Trust and the NRA (National Rivers Authority), created such a lobby that Thames Water was forced to alter its abstraction policy. Less pumping at Compton, together with heavy rainfall, resulted in water levels in the Pang being higher than for several years.

The future of the Pang Valley is largely in the hands of those who manage and farm the land. With an initial focus on the land close to the River Pang, the **Pang Valley Countryside Project** is working with farmers wishing to conserve and enhance their land. The Project is advising on farm conservation plans, the major objective being to co-ordinate work across the Valley. This is enabling the creation of wildlife and landscape corridors which are linking farms and habitats. Farmers do receive advice and help with grant applications for conservation work.

The Project has started groups of volunteers to help farmers with the labour intensive tasks, such as: pond clearance, tree planting, hedge laying, coppicing and footpath clearance. Readers can help with their ideas, views and support, and by demonstrating that the community cares about their environment. Your commitment is vital to ensure that the Pang Valley Countryside Project is a success. In future the Project will run events. Your financial support will be vital to ensure success. Corporate Sponsorship would be especially welcome.

The Project is building on the work of the Pang Valley Conservation Trust and the Farming and Wildlife Advisory Group (FWAG), and has five broad aims:

* To conserve and enhance the existing landscape and wildlife habitats of the Pang Valley
* To promote environmentally responsible farming practises throughout the project area
* To improve and promote enjoyment of the Pang Valley
* To promote an understanding of the need to integrate agriculture, conservation forestry and public access in the countryside
* To promote environmental education

Walk Access Points:

1. In Pangbourne - Pangbourne Meadows on the Thames. Nearby Car Park A - Walk for All Ages
2. Moor Copse Car Park - A Woodland Nature Reserve - An Ancient Woodland Walk along the River Pang at Sulham and Tidmarsh
3. Rushall Manor Farm - In the Heart of the Pang Valley near Bradfield
4. Pot Kiln Pub at Frilsham - Car Park and Circular Walk into the Valley
5. Bucklebury Common - Near Upper Bucklebury - Park car and walk onto Lowland Heathland, one of Britain's Rarest Habitats
6. Bell at Aldworth - Car Park onto the Ridgeway + Berkshire Downs

Woodland Crafts and Skills

The ancient broadleaved woodlands of Berkshire have become fragmented and suffer from neglect. These woodlands would once have been intensively managed producing firewood and timber products.

Modern forestry tends to regard small farm woodlands as being uneconomic and consequently these woods fall into decline. As a result many species which have evolved to take advantage of the cyclical changes within a woodland caused by man's activities are also declining.

CUTTING WILLOW

The project is restoring management to those woodlands where this effort will produce the greatest conservation benefit, in particular relatively recently coppiced woodland. Any woodland managed by the Project will have a balanced management plan based on the needs of the individual wood. Where specific requirements have not been identified, diversity of structure within a wood will be the priority. To encourage and ensure that this management occurs, the Project has established a group of coppice and woodland workers who undertake the work and utilise the timber to make a variety of products.

Coppice Products: Made by local craftsmen from local woodlands. These hurdles are ideal as fencing or garden screens. They combine a traditional rustic look with practicality. Hurdles act as effective wind barriers and screens; by allowing air through they are less likely to be blown down.

Alternatively a continuous woven fence made from hazel could be constructed to your specification. Hurdles are made six ft in length but varying heights can be made to order. Gate hurdles, besom brooms, bean poles, hazel stakes and hedgelaying binders are also available. Buy your products direct from the craftsmen and help encourage rural employment and the responsible management of the local woodland. Availability depends on the season.

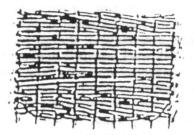

Hazel hurdles - Made by local craftsmen from local woodlands

Charcoal - This year Pang Valley Charcoal will produce more than 15 tonnes of high quality charcoal. If you are concerned about your environment and enjoy a barbecue you should be using British Charcoal. Why? Pang Valley Charcoal is *not* the product of rainforest and mangrove swamp clearance and is not transported half way round the world. Local employment is created and a traditional craft is being maintained. It is claimed that Pang Valley Charcoal burns hotter and lasts longer than imported charcoals. The charcoal lights easily saving costly firelighters and fuel.

Courses - The Project is organising a series of courses throughout the summer months. These are alternative weekend breaks that will give an insight into woodland crafts. No previous experience of woodworking is necessary and all tools will be provided.

Longbow Making - Create a working English Longbow from a piece of locally grown ash. Learn to make *woven hazel hurdles* in the setting of an historic farm museum near Witney.

Harness the simple rhythm of the pole lathe to produce *dibbers, rounders bats, candlesticks, rattles* and perhaps a *three-legged stool* from locally grown wood. Discover **randing, waling and slewing** as you make and take home your own baskets from a variety of native grown willows. Learn individually or as Corporate Groups, camping or in B&B accommodation. Enjoy the experience of the countryside combined with learning skills with a difference.

Environmental Education

The John Simonds Trust for Education in the Countryside is based at Rushall Farm, Bradfield, and has been catering for large numbers of school children. The Pang Valley is now an accepted educational resource

READING

And so from here we travel to the busy town of **Reading**. It was in the old town gaol that Oscar Wilde languished and wrote his famous 'Ballad of Reading Gaol' during his two years' hard labour.

Despite being a modern business community and thriving shopping centre, Reading still features many buildings of historic and architectural interest. In the centre of the town, the **Forbury Gardens** were formerly the grounds of **Reading Abbey** and today provide an attractive oasis for the public to enjoy, with the dominant feature being the famous **Maiwand Lion**, an enormous stone sculpture weighing some 16 tons! To the south east of the lion, a smaller yet very important memorial is the Celtic Cross which was erected in 1901 in memory of King Henry I, founder in 1121 of the Abbey. Today only the ruined shell of the Abbey can be seen lying to the south east of Forbury Gardens and featuring the remains of the Church's south transept, the Chapter House, Refectory and Dormitory. Housed within the restored **Town Hall**, the **Museum of Reading** is well worth a visit. It provides a detailed history of the town from Saxon times to the present day, with various exhibitions and galleries including one housing a facsimile of the Bayeux Tapestry. It is also noted for the display of Roman remains from the abandoned town of Silchester, or Calleva.

Those with an interest in canals should make their way to **Blake's Lock Museum**, refurbished in recent years, which tells the story of inland waterways in the area.

One of Berkshire's Treasure Troves is to be found just a short distance from the centre of Reading at Spencers Wood. The tranquil setting of the Foxhill 'World of Carriages' Visitor Centre is home to one of the biggest collections of horse drawn carriages to be seen in the UK, and visitors express amazement that such a collection exists. Over 150 carriages, which have been collected by one family over a 40-year period, are on display representing all forms of life as far back as the Romans. From station bus to stately carriage, from hansom cabs to hearses, a whole world of transport evolution unfolds before you. A recent arrival is the sleigh used in the film 'Santa Clause - The Movie' starring Dudley Moore.

Children are as fascinated by the carriages as they are by the horses and other animals that they meet on a visit to Foxhill. Many of these horses are film and television stars in their own right and Larry the ram is a firm favourite for all ages. Whilst visiting Lambs Farm, mums and dads can relax in a peaceful countryside setting and enjoy a refreshing cup of tea or coffee whilst keeping a watchful eye on their offspring burning off their energy in the children's play area, which overlooks the grazing fields. For the more energetic, riding lessons could be the order of the day, with lessons available throughout the week. If you already have riding skills, why not pop down for a hack?

Whatever your age, whatever your mood, Foxhill is a centre which has something for all the family, and it is Reading's nearest 'out-of-town' attraction, so why not make a visit soon; you will be amazed at what you find. Foxhill 'World of Carriages' is on the B3349 Basingstoke Road, Spencers Wood.

Foxhill Carriages and Stables Ltd, World of Carriages Collection, Basingstoke Road, Spencers Wood, Reading Tel 0118 988 3334 Fax 0118 988 5516

One thing to beware of when exploring Reading is that its one-way road system can have you driving round in circles if you don't know where you are going, so be warned!

Goring Lock

CHAPTER TWO

East Berkshire

Windsor Castle

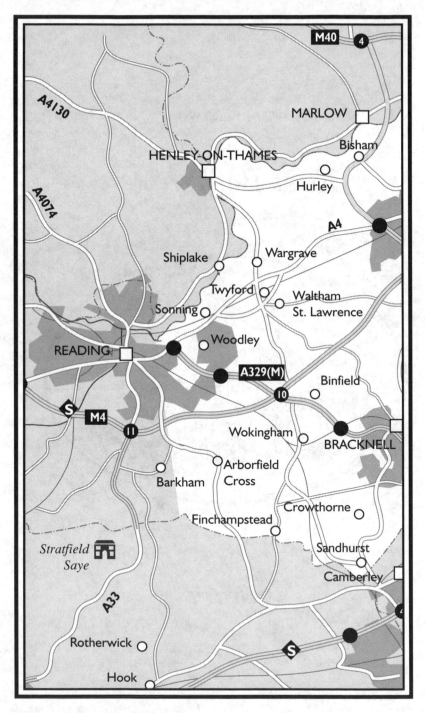

MARLOW

M40 4

Bisham

HENLEY-ON-THAMES

Hurley

A4130

A4074

A4

Shiplake

Wargrave

Twyford

Waltham
St. Lawrence

Sonning

Woodley

READING

A329(M)

Binfield

10

S M4

Wokingham

BRACKNELL

11

Arborfield
Cross

Barkham

Crowthorne

Finchampstead

Sandhurst

Stratfield
Saye

Camberley

A33

4

Rotherwick

S

Hook

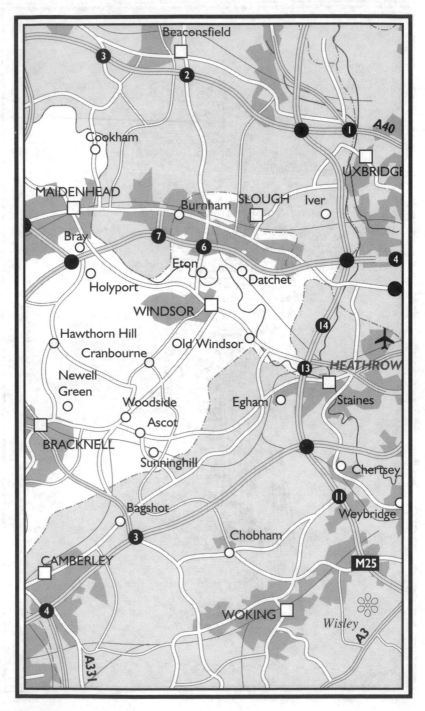

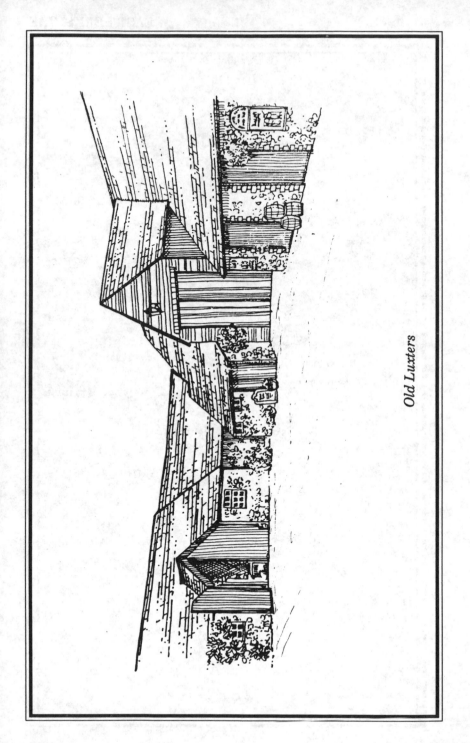

Old Luxters

CHAPTER TWO

East Berkshire

SONNING

We begin this chapter just outside Reading off the A4 at **Sonning**. The eleven-arched brick bridge over the river here is one of the oldest on the upper Thames and is so narrow that traffic has to cross it single file. The ground climbs steeply away from the bridge on this side of the river, and the village's main road is lined with flower-bedecked old houses and fine inns. Close by is the famous **Sonning Cutting**, a deep and steep-sided man-made gorge through which runs the main Paddington to Bristol railway line, a grand monument to brute manpower, having been cut almost exclusively by hand.

We now make our way south-east from Reading towards Wokingham and turn off to explore **Barkham**, the oldest village in the locality which receives a mention in the Domesday Book and which once formed the boundary of Henry VIII's hunting forest. Today this attractive village is still surrounded by beautiful woodland and countryside, home to badgers, deer, foxes and a variety of birds. Despite the development of modern housing estates in the outlying areas, Barkham has successfully retained its individuality and character, little changed over the centuries.

A short diversion north-east, skirting Wokingham brings us to **Binfield**. Be sure to look out for the **Jack O'Newbury Inn**, situated just past the Post Office on the outskirts of the village. This 17th Century pub mustn't be missed. In the times of Henry VIII the very beautiful inn used to be a very popular stop-over point for travellers going to and from the Windsor Forest which lies between Newbury and London. Today you will find the pub just as favoured by passing trade and locals alike. Your hosts Jean and Mick Lowes will ensure that your welcome is a warm and genuine one. Crackling log fires burn brightly in the grates on those wintry evenings and the scenic and spacious beer garden proves very popular in the summer months, as it boasts a superb view over the surrounding forests.

A good selection of home-made food is served at lunchtime and in the evenings, with an ever-changing blackboard filled with daily specials for your delectation. The Jack O'Newbury also has a large skittle alley available if you enjoy the sport, and you can even hire the entire alley and hold a function there if you so wish.

Traditional ales are kept in perfect condition by Mick's magic hands and a comprehensive range of spirits, lagers and bottled drinks is always available. To the rear of the inn you will find a large car park for your convenience and in the gardens there is an excellent play area to keep the children occupied while you sit, relax and soak up the friendly atmosphere that pervades throughout this welcoming pub.

Jack O'Newbury, Terrace Road, North Binfield Tel 01344 54881

BRACKNELL

Further east, **Bracknell** offers a wealth of activity and excitement for sporting enthusiasts, including **Coral Reef**, an amazing water world with a tropical paradise theme and even its own pirate ship! Bracknell's modern Sport and Leisure Centre is one the largest in the country and is a popular meeting place as well as providing comprehensive sporting facilities.

ASCOT

From here it is not far to **Ascot**, famous of course for its horse racing and 'Royal Ascot' where everyone turns out to compete for the 'most eccentric outfit and floppy hat' award, the prize being brief exposure on the television.

Older than the Ascot Racecourse, **The Royal Berkshire Hotel** began life as The Oaks. Built in 1705 for Charles Churchill, son of the first Duke of Marlborough, the house has blossomed over the centuries. From 1846 the house was owned by Robert Blane who had a distinguished career in the army and became commander of Bath. He remained at the Oaks until Mrs Entwistle took over in 1880. Following the military tradition Major Guy Aubyn lived in the house from 1911 until the arrival of Colonel Horlick at the beginning of the First World War. Colonel Horlick (of malted drink fame) did much to improve the estate, adding one of the first private swimming pools and the Walled Garden. His family remained at the house, now known as Little Paddocks, until they felt it too large to manage and it was offered to the Barclay School for partially sighted girls, which was evacuated from Brighton in 1941. It remained a school until 1969 and several guide dog graves complete with epitaphs can still be found close to the tennis courts.

Ladbroke Hotels purchased the estate in 1985 and the Mansion was totally refurbished with replumbing, rewiring and reroofing. The existing 52 bedrooms were reduced to 40, and whilst the interior panelling remained the same, it was coated in grey scumble to echo the contemporary colour themes throughout the building. A much more modern feel was given to the interior using the arts of drag, stipple and marbling which brought the house to life. Further radical changes took place during 1986 and the Hotel now boasts 63 en-suite bedrooms, including six suites, two of which have four-poster beds. Sporting facilities abound with hard tennis courts, croquet, squash, saunas, a Roman style indoor swimming pool and a small gym.

The Hotel is ideally situated only 25 miles from central London, 12 miles from London Heathrow Airport and seven miles from Windsor, reached by leaving the M25 at Junction 23 and following the A30 for approximately four miles. After turning right at the traffic lights opposite Wentworth Golf Club on to the A329 signposted Ascot, continue along this road for one and a half miles, and the Hotel will be seen on the right hand side.

The Royal Berkshire, London Road, Sunninghill, Ascot Tel 01344 23322

WINDSOR

The beautiful Royal town of **Windsor** is most notable for its **Castle** which covers 13 acres and is the largest one in Britain. A popular tourist spot, magnificent Windsor boasts a wealth of delightful pubs and restaurants and shopping here is a sheer delight, with a variety of wonderful shops set inside beautiful buildings and dotted down narrow cobbled streets and pedestrianised walkways.

The town centre is always busy so it is best to park outside the centre and walk in to browse at your leisure. During the summer months the area around the castle is circled by wooden benches which seem to be permanently occupied. To absorb fully the history and magic of Windsor takes far more than a day.

From the castle the long tree-lined walk offers magnificent views of the town and its surroundings. The changing of the guard is a daily event during the summer months.

The town which has given its name to the Royal Family owes its existence to this fortress which dominates the area from its high hill above the Thames, and remains today the largest inhabited Castle in the world.

The settlement of Windelsora was used for centuries by Saxon Kings hunting in the forest and the conquering Normans followed suit, building the first fortress four miles upstream from the Saxon settlement. The site was chosen by William the Conqueror, who built a fort of earthworks and wooden defences. It soon became an important Castle, a town growing around it. Henry I held court here, its defensive position giving him protection from the hostile Saxons, but not until until Henry II's reign were the first stone buildings built, providing a home for kings and queens for nearly nine hundred years.

Open to the public are the **Precincts**, the **State Apartments** and **Queen Mary's Doll's House**, and they attract visitors from the world over.

The sixteen magnificent State Apartments hold a remarkable collection of furniture, porcelain and armour. The carvings of Grinling Gibbons are everywhere, the walls adorned with a plethora of masterpieces, especially those by Van Dyck and Rembrandt.

In the amazing Doll's House, built by Sir Edwin Lutyens, everything works, right down to the dewdrop sized lightbulbs. Built to a scale of one inch to one foot famous artists, craftsmen and writers all contributed to this gift to Queen Mary, presented in 1924. The detail is breathtaking, linen in the pantry is initialled and the cars in the garage can manage 20,000 m.p.g.

George III, Windsor Great Park

St George's Chapel, the Chapel of the Order of the Garter, was begun in the reign of Edward IV and completed by Henry VIII. Until the recent devastating fire it was the setting of the ceremonious annual service of the Sovereign and Knights Companion of the Order. Restoration has of course begun, but it will be the turn of the millennium before we can once again admire this marvel of medieval architecture.

Today's Windsor is largely Georgian and Victorian, though there are far older buildings. **Windsor Parish Church** dates from 1168, though it was rebuilt in 1820, and its register records the burial of Charles I. The **Three Tuns Hotel** was built in 1518 and in St Albans Street is the 17th Century home of Nell Gwynne, mistress of Charles II. Just a mile from the castle is **Clewer Parish Church**, built in the 11th century, which features a tomb with Saxon lettering and a Saxon font.

Behind Castle Hill and Church Lane there are plenty of narrow cobbled streets to explore, all lined with fascinating 17th and 18th Century buildings. There are also several other attractions worth seeking out whilst you are here.

The Guildhall, begun in 1689 by Sir Thomas Fitz and finished by Wren, today houses an exhibition of local history from the palaeolithic period to the present day. There is also a notable collection of royal portraits from the time of Elizabeth I and a series of dioramas showing historical events at Windsor from earliest times to the celebration of George III's Jubilee celebrations of 1809.

In the old buildings of **Central Station** is a firm visitors' favourite, Madame Tussaud's Royalty and Empire Exhibition. Undoubtedly the most impressive display here depicts Queen Victoria's Diamond Jubilee celebrations with a full-sized replica of the Royal Train and a theatre presentation!

If you have an interest in the military the **Household Cavalry Museum**, at Combermore Barracks, is considered one of the finest in the country. Exhibits, including uniforms, weapons, horse furniture and armour, help trace the history of the regiment from the Monmouth Rebellion of 1685 right up to the present day.

Rocking Horse House is a large, traditional Victorian villa that has retained much of its original character, features and charm. You are guaranteed a warm and friendly welcome from your hosts, the Stanton family, and it is their unique blend of hospitality that keeps guests returning year after year. Each of the spacious twin and double rooms, some en-suite, include colour TV, tea and coffee making facilities and feature traditional Victorian fireplaces. The outside of Rocking Horse House boasts small but delightful gardens with colourful window boxes in the summer months.

The guest house is named after the superb full size rocking horse given by the owner Guy to his wife Claire as a wedding present. Several other horses have since joined the ever-expanding collection, some from abroad when Guy and Claire sailed their own yacht around the world!

While it is located close to the town centre, Rocking Horse House is far enough away from the hustle and bustle to offer quiet and relaxing accommodation and easy access by car or on foot. Indeed, Windsor's train stations are within easy walking distance as are several good eating houses.

Children are welcome and flexible arrangements can be made to suit early airport departures from Heathrow, which is just 8 miles away, or to meet the requirements of visitors on business. Smoking is restricted.

We feel that Rocking Horse House offers some of the best Town House accommodation in Berkshire whilst being an ideal base for those touring the surrounding countryside.

Rocking Horse House, 88 St Leonard's Road, Windsor Tel/Fax 01753 853984

To the south of the Castle is **Windsor Great Park**, 4800 acres of Royal Park that include parkland, woods and magnificent gardens. The **Long Walk** stretches from the towers of Windsor to **Snow Hill**, a distance of three miles. Up on Snow Hill stands a huge bronze of George III on horseback, erected in 1831. During his reign Thomas Sandby and his brother laid out the two-mile long lake of **Virginia Water**, with its fine cascade. On the banks of the lake stand a group of Roman columns brought from Tripoli. During her reign Queen Anne added the three mile ride to Ascot.

There are several lodges in the park, including **Cumberland Lodge**, named after 'Butcher' Cumberland of Culloden. From here the famous **Rhododendron Walk** stretches for a mile to **Bishop's Gate**, where the poet Shelley once stayed. In 1931 Eric Savill started work on the **Savill Gardens**, laid out to show rhododendrons, magnolias, cherries and camellias to their best advantage. Beside the ponds and streams grow primulas, irises and lilies, there are beds of roses, rock plants and alpines - almost every manner of plant found in English gardens. The **Valley Garden**, near Virginia Water, is similar, and the **Kurume Punch Bowl** is a magnificent amphitheatre of thousands of Japanese Kurume azaleas.

ETON

To the north west of Windsor lies **Eton** which can be reached either by car, via a scenic boat trip or across the pedestrian bridge over the river. Perhaps best known for its public school, we recommend a visit here.

The famous **Eton College** was founded in 1440 as a Collegiate Church with a Grammar School. Still seen today as the epitome of the public school, it has educated a string of famous names, and still retains many now anachronistic traditions that have made it famous. Of the original school only the College Hall and the kitchen survive, most of the rest dating from the 15th Century. The west range of the cloisters, the great gatehouse, and Lupton's Tower were added in the early 16th Century, and the Upper School was built in about 1690.

The Henry VI, High Street, Eton Tel 01753 670134

Here on the High Street you will discover **The Henry VI**, an old town pub, renamed after the founder of Eton College situated nearby, and no doubt with a most interesting history. In 1996 it was fully and carefully refurbished to retain its original character. As you enter the Henry VI you will be greeted by a warm and friendly ambience within a traditional setting of open fires and the buzz of conversation. In the bar you'll find a good range of cask conditioned ales and an excellent bar menu with a vast choice of sandwiches. The main menu features steaks and grills, with a further selection of home cooked food and desserts displayed on the blackboard. Outside there is a large beer garden which allows good circulation and a pleasant way to meet new friends or just soak up the atmosphere while enjoying good food and drink.

HOLYPORT

Not far from Eton just off the A330 is **Holyport**, a delightful Conservation Village which boasts one of only 17 Real Tennis courts in the country still in use today. Originating in the 13th Century, Real Tennis was the predecessor of lawn tennis as we know it today and it attracted the interest of Henry VIII who had a luxury court, still to be seen, built at Hampton Court Palace.

Every year on the first Saturday in June, the residents of Holyport awake to find their village green bursting with life as marquees, stalls and a central merry-go-round are set up for the wonderful summer fair. Locals enjoy the challenge of traditional fairground games such as shove halfpenny and bowling for the pig, and groups of burly men compete in a gruelling tug of war. Children enjoy horse-drawn trailer rides to the background music of the merry-go-round while their parents browse among the various craft stalls. It's 'quiet please' as the Master of Ceremonies announces the winner of the Miss Holyport contest and other prizewinners. Then it's time for the popular Beer Race where a group of fit young men, starting at the Belgian Arms, run from pub to pub downing half a pint of ale at each one before running back to the finishing line outside The Lodge on the green. By mid-morning on Sunday, it all seems like a dream, with the village back to normal until the next June.

In Holyport there is wonderful accommodation at **Moor Farm**, a beautiful 700-year-old Manor. Tucked down a rose-lined pathway, it enjoys a peaceful rural location which belies its closeness to the M4 motorway. Proprietors Chris and Gillian Reynolds have worked hard to maintain the farm's original charcter and the beamed ceilings and antique furniture emphasise this, creating a cosy atmosphere of old world charm. This continues in the guest rooms which are equally tastefully furnished and provide every modern comfort, each with private facilities.

For those preferring self-catering, there are also four first-class converted Courtyard Cottages for use by non-smokers, one on the ground floor being particularly suitable for disabled visitors. These have been converted from timber-framed Georgian stables and barns.

Moor Farm B &B and Self-Catering, Holyport, nr Maidenhead Tel 01628 33761

BRAY

Further north towards Maidenhead is the pretty village of **Bray**, made familiar to many by the 18th Century ballad 'The Vicar of Bray', a satirical tale of a clergyman who changed his religion and political persuasion according to the monarch in power at the time, thereby apparently outliving Charles II, James II, William and Mary, Queen Anne and George I.

MAIDENHEAD

Beehive Manor is, by any account, an exceptional and beautiful medieval building dating back to the 1500s. Set in pleasant mature gardens of just under one acre where paths wind among camellias, ceanothus and a whole variety of other flowers, this Tudor house exudes great charm and history. A Japanese film crew who visited were hardly able to believe their eyes! Strange carved heads greet you at the front door, whilst the wisteria-clad walls and the attractive lattice-paned windows complete the scene of this traditional English manor.

Run by two delightful sisters Barbara Barbour and Sue Lemin, the bed and breakfast accommodation here is truly in the grand manner. Three spacious and tastefully decorated guest rooms have en-suite or private facilities and, as in all the rooms, an arrangement of fresh flowers as well as the 'fatal attraction' of chocolates by the bed! Befitting a house of such history, breakfasts are something of a banquet, served at a large oak refectory table and with a choice of Finnan haddock, hot smoked Cornish mackerel or a traditionally cooked breakfast including home-made lemon curd, marmalade and local honey. The rooms are light and sunny with lots of stained glass, oak beams and linenfold panelling. A 32ft long oak panelled drawing room with television is for use by guests.

At one time in the last century the house became an inn called The Dog and Partridge. Subsequently it was a farmhouse and bakery before reverting to a private residence. In the 20th Century it has been lived in by a countess, a millionaire (who subsequently became bankrupt and moved in to live with his butler and cook!) and during the last war the manor was let to the Duke of Manchester.

Beehive Manor is a wonderful spot to stay and you will be warmly greeted upon your arrival with a cup of tea or coffee; late arrivals are offered a glass of sherry. Both Barbara and Sue are a mine of information about the many sights in the vicinity. Windsor, Henley, Ascot and Hampton Court are all nearby. From Maidenhead station, just over a mile away, a frequent train service will have you in London in 30 minutes for shopping, galleries or exhibitions, or, if a theatre appeals, the trains run an all night service to take you back to Maidenhead afterwards. A local pub serves excellent evening meals.

Beehive Manor has the top AA listing for B&B, 5QQQQQ 'Premier Selected' and features in the WHICH Guide to B&B - listed as one of the '20 favourites' of the Editor.

Beehive Manor, Cox Green Lane, Maidenhead Tel 01628 20980

On the western outskirts of Maidenhead, just off the A4, is the **Courage Shire Horse Centre**. Set amidst pleasant countryside the Centre has a fine collection of these lovely gentle creatures. The Centre was established to create interest in the breed and to help ensure their survival. The timber-built stables contain a coach house for the show drays and boxes where the horses can be seen.

In the display room are many rosettes and shining horse brasses, as well as a static exhibition of the ancient craft of coopering or barrel making. There is also a farriers shop and around the Centre is a collection of farm carts and agricultural equipment.

Opposite stands a famous coaching inn, once called The Coach and Horses, but now renamed the **Shire Horse Inn**, whose deeds go back some 300 years.

Just to the south of Maidenhead, situated just off the A4 at Hare Hatch in the centre of the pretty village of **Waltham St Lawrence**, **The Bell** is a traditional and very inviting Inn which dates back to circa 1400. Run by Steve and Dee for the past 25 years, The Bell has an interesting and chequered history, with the original building being little changed since its purchase by Ralph Newberry in 1596. The cellar was excavated in the early 19th Century and the floor of the small room above, now called the Noggin, was raised. This Noggin is rather like a snug and still has its original wooden floors, open log fire and a definite air of mystery in this cosy and comfortable room. When renewing the dining room floor an old well was discovered which has been retained as a special feature though with the addition of a glass top so that no accidents can occur when the beer is flowing!

Speaking of beer, this Free House is home to many well kept traditional ales with Steve supplying a changing Guest Beer on a regular monthly basis. The two large gardens to the side and rear of the Inn have won several awards for their incredible flower displays including 'Royal Borough in Bloom' and 'Local Garden in Bloom' prize winners. Home cooked food is served every lunchtime and on Tuesday to Saturday evenings from 7.00pm - 9.30pm with an ever-changing selection of 'Daily Specials', though Fridays are always traditional 'Fish and Chips' days.

The Bell, Waltham St Lawrence Tel 01189 341788

COOKHAM

To the north of Maidenhead is the village of **Cookham**. Anyone familiar with the paintings of Stanley Spencer may recognise parts of the village. He was born here and based much of his work on local scenes. The **Stanley Spencer Gallery** and the house where he was born stand in the High Street. The **Bell and Dragon** pub here was open for business in the 15th Century, and there is an old lettered sign on the wall nearby warning 'All fighting to be over by 10 o'clock'.

The ancient ceremony of **Swan Upping**, the annual marking of the Queen's swans, starts here in early July, and the boatyard by the bridge belongs to the Queen's Swan Master.

Close by on the river is **Bisham**, a little Thames-side village haunted by a ghost and a curse. The ghost is said to be that of Lady Elizabeth Hoby, a lady-in-waiting to Elizabeth I. It is said you can catch brief glimpses of her at **Bisham Abbey**, once in the possession of the Knights Templar.

The curse was laid by the last Abbot of Bisham, who vowed that no family should succeed to the abbey lands, and indeed, the Vansittarts, who lived there, never succeeded in a direct line, all the eldest sons dying prematurely. The **Abbey**, open only by appointment, now belongs to the Sports Council.

Close by, the Hoby family, including Lady Elizabeth, lie buried under a fine alabaster monument in All Saints Church.

Back on the road again, we follow signs for the ancient village of **Hurley** which was once the site of a priory, the fragmented remains of which can still be seen.

HENLEY-ON-THAMES

We finish our tour of Berkshire in **Henley-on-Thames**, upriver from Hurley. The town is renowned in society circles for its prestigious annual **Regatta**, held in July. The first inter-varsity race took place here in 1829 and within a decade the event was enjoying royal patronage. The graceful 18th Century bridge in Henley is appropriately decorated with faces of Father Thames and the goddess Isis.

Apart from the boating available throughout the summer and the pleasant walks along the tow paths, there are lots of interesting shops, inns and tea-shops in the town. Most of the inns are old coaching houses with yards that were once the scene of bull and bear fights.

Since opening in 1995, **Henley Needlecrafts** has established itself as a comprehensive one-stop supplier of threads, ribbons and sewing accessories of every description. With over 80 different suppliers, the shop has everything anyone might need for hand sewing, embroidery, quilting and tapestry. It also offers friendly helpful service in an atmosphere where customers are welcome to browse. The staff are accessories of every description. With over 80 different suppliers, the shop has everything anyone might need for hand sewing, embroidery, quilting and tapestry. It also offers friendly helpful service in an atmosphere where customers are welcome to browse. The staff are happy to order items that are not in stock, and offer a postal forwarding service. Henley Needlecrafts also run special classes for those keen to improve their skill at needlepoint and cross stitching, and organise a series of exhibitions during the summer.

Henley Needlecrafts, 13 Reading Road, Henley-on-Thames Tel / Fax 01491 410840

An excellent place to stop for lunch or an evening meal is **Ye Olde Bell Inn**, a traditional olde worlde pub situated in the town centre.

Ye Olde Bell Inn, 20 Bell Street, Henley-on-Thames Tel 01491 573883

This classic public house offers the weary traveller the perfect excuse to sit, rest awhile and maybe try a glass of real ale or sample some of the

Sunday lunchtime, though be aware that a reservation is preferred as the pub gets very popular at mealtimes! The atmosphere is welcoming and informal, with plenty of locals available to add some colour to this quality English pub.

Situated in one of the most luxurious areas of Henley-on-Thames, **The Rise** offers a level of luxury and splendour for the most discerning guest. The accommodation is on a bed and breakfast basis with full use of the guest lounge and dining room. There are three light and airy double bedrooms, all of which are en-suite with colour television and tea and coffee making facilities. Your host is Shelagh Stanbridge, who has owned and personally run the business for over three years, extending a very warm and friendly welcome to every guest and providing all the comforts of a home from home.

Offering informal and luxurious accommodation, The Rise is the perfect location for those professional persons who are away from home but wish to maintain their own high standards. Additionally the historic town of Henley-on-Thames with its beautiful riverside walks, public houses and restaurants is but a five-minute walk away. You will also find that the M40 and M4 motorways are approximately 15 minutes by car, giving the business person a fast and easy access for travelling.

The Rise, Rotherfield Road, Henley-on-Thames Tel 01491 579360

First-class bed and breakfast accommodation within three minutes' walk of Henley town centre, the railway station and the River Thames can be found at **Amervyn House** in St Marks Road. Resident owner Caroline Ely offers a warm welcome, comfortable overnight accommodation for one or more nights and an excellent English breakfast in this spacious Victorian home. The three centrally-heated guest bedrooms all have tea/coffee-making facilities, colour televisions and hot and cold running water. One also has en-suite facilities and another

47

a shower. Amervyn House is English Tourist Board approved, 1 Crown and Commended.

Amervyn House, 4 St Marks Road, Henley-on-Thames Tel 01491 575331 Fax 01491 411747 Email 100742.2530@COMPUSERVE.COM

If peace and quiet is what you are after then we suggest that you look no further than **The Laurels**. Offering superb bed and breakfast accommodation in any of the three spacious and bright bedrooms, you can guarantee a relaxing stay in this friendly atmosphere. Owned and run by an Australian couple, The Laurels has the distinct feel of a real home from home. It comes as no surprise to find out that visitors from all over the world return year after year to sample the excellent hospitality.

The Laurels, 107 St Marks Road, Henley-on-Thames Tel 01491 572982

Although situated in a quiet, tree-lined location, The Laurels is only a few minutes' walk from the pretty town, which offers plenty of shops, pubs and riverside walks to keep you entertained. There are also off-road parking facilities for all guests and some charming gardens at the rear of the establishment where you can sit out and enjoy a drink or let the children play for a while in this relaxing retreat.

The Swiss Farm International Camping Site is to be found only a few minutes' walk from Henley's Regatta course and on the very edge of the magnificent Chiltern Hills. The site amenities include a small but very comprehensive shop where you can purchase all your groceries, and a licensed social club which is just the place to enjoy a long, cool drink on those balmy evenings.

Swiss Farm International Camping Site, Marlow Road, Henley-on-Thames Tel 01491 573419

This area of outstanding natural beauty is the perfect location for this superb campsite that offers a large selection of caravans to suit your every requirement. Functional design is evident in the kitchen with everything where you would expect to find it, including a full size gas cooker. Relax in the spacious lounge with its fitted carpets and large picture windows; the generous seating arrangement allows you to enjoy a meal in comfort. A full size shower unit is installed in the bathroom, as well as washbasin and WC, and all gas and electricity is included in the price.

There is fishing available on site in the large lake and also a full size children's play area with a games room and food bar to help keep visitors entertained.

Located in some of the most peaceful surroundings yet central to all local amenities you will find **Ledard**. This large, well-appointed Victorian house has been owned and personally run by Irene and Alan Howard for the past five years, and you can expect a very warm greeting from this friendly couple.

Offering some excellent budget bed and breakfast accommodation, Ledard has three light and airy bedrooms, all of which are private and offer all the usual facilities. Every morning a continental or Full English breakfast, which is a feature of this establishment (and guaranteed to set you up for the rest of the day!) is served in the pleasant surroundings of the dining room.

Ledard, 8 Rotherfield Road, Henley-on-Thames Tel 01491 575611

There are gardens to the rear of the property, perfect for your pets or children, or a ten-minute walk will bring you to the bustling town of Henley where you can explore the many shops at your leisure.

Set amongst some of the most picturesque Chiltern countryside, **Old Luxters**, also called the **Chiltern Valley Winery and Brewery**, is a well-established winery and brewery producing over 200,000 bottles annually and has achieved over 50 trophies, awards and commendations in blind-tasted national and international competitions. They have also revived the tradition of farm-brewed Real Ales. The finest malted barleys are brewed to the brewery's own special blend to create a flavour that is packed with depth and rich aroma, so do feel free to sample these delicious brews.

Also part of this prestigious establishment is **Luxter's Gallery** which is housed in a large Chiltern barn which has been commended for its restoration in 1990. Exhibitions are held in this opened beamed building, by artists from the UK and abroad. This beautiful gallery also provides an unusual venue for opera, corporate events, conferences, private receptions and film and photographic location work. In addition to this, David Ealand, the owner of Old Luxters for the last 16 years, hosts regular dinners, wine evenings, tours and tutored tastings. So if you are travelling through Hambleden, be sure to drop into Old Luxters and experience first hand the idyllic atmosphere that pervades throughout these old and rustic buildings.

Old Luxters, Hambleden, Henley-on-Thames Tel 01491 638330 Fax 01491 638645

There are many wonderful 'hidden places' in this lovely county and we have listed just a few. By following our meandering route, we hope you will discover a few 'gems' of your own.

North Cherwell Country

Banbury Cross

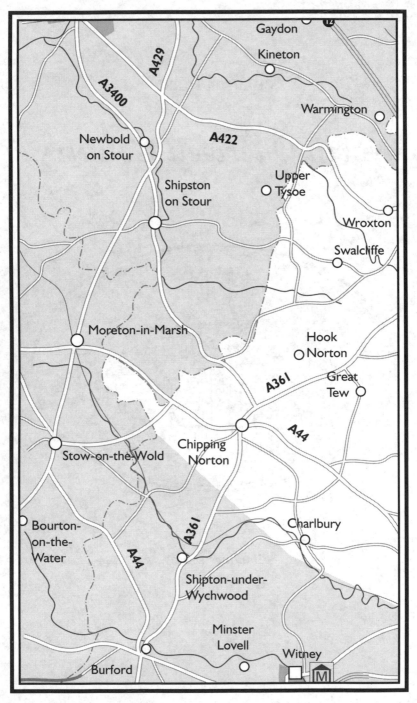

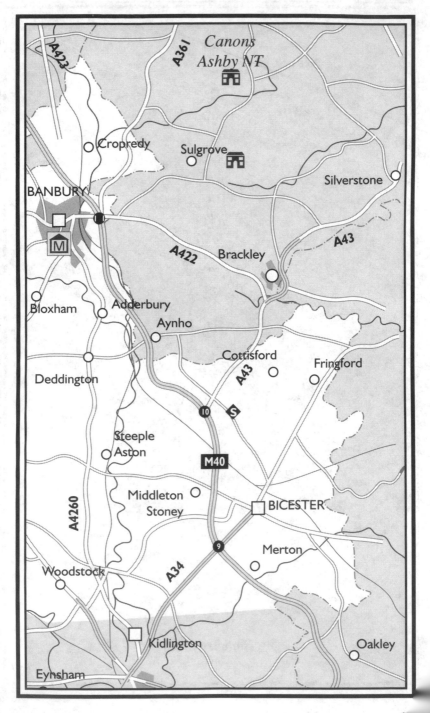

Banbury Cross

North Cherwell Country

We begin our exploration of Oxfordshire in the rich farming country on clay soil between Oxford and the Midlands. Flora Thompson, whose Lark Rise to Candleford gives us a wonderful evocation of a Victorian childhood in a farm labourer's home, was born and grew up in this area.

Her description of the landscape is not very flattering, speaking of arable fields 'bare, brown and windswept for eight months out of the twelve'. 'Only for a few weeks in later summer,' she continued, 'had the landscape any real beauty. Then the ripened cornfields rippled up to the doorsteps of the cottages and the hamlet became an island in a sea of dark gold.'

She was a little hard, maybe, on this green and gentle countryside. Even if it is not dramatic enough for your taste, you will surely find ample compensation in its towns, villages and houses.

MERTON

We start just south of Bicester in the village of **Merton**. The Church is an interesting one even for this area, a happy hunting ground for those who appreciate churches as beautiful buildings, for the history they encapsulate, or just enjoy the quiet, as Philip Larkin once put it, of 'a serious house on serious earth'.

It was originally built in the Decorated style characteristic of the 14th Century, and has later Perpendicular additions. What you see now is much reduced from its original plan, both the north aisle and the spire having fallen victim to the mischances of time.

To the west of the Church is a **Tithe Barn** with a thatched roof, which probably dates back to the 15th Century, and the village also has some attractive old houses.

Just to the south of Merton lies **Otmoor**, a completely flat landscape covering some six square miles. It was formerly marshland where people lived by fishing, fowling and peat-cutting. It was drained in the 19th Century but remains remote, somehow rather eerie. The M40 motorway now cuts a swathe through where a Roman road once passed very close to Merton.

BICESTER

For our next destination we pick up the A41 for **Bicester**. As the name suggests, this was an area of Roman settlement, the 'cester' part of the name coming from the Old English 'ceaster' which, in turn, comes from the Latin 'castra' meaning a military camp. The A421 follows the characteristic straight course favoured by the imperial road engineers to the north-east while away south and west ran Akeman Street, to the now vanished Roman town of Alchester at **Wendlebury**, just south of Bicester.

Bicester's attractions are not only historical. It is a pleasantly bustling place with a triangular market 'square' around which houses of different ages, including some half-timbered 16th and 17th Century examples together with two coaching inns, make a pleasant ensemble. To complete the scene there is a large Church, with the unusual dedication to St Edburg and a solid-looking battlemented tower.

Around the town are several small villages each with their own attractions and hidden places.

Until quite recently the quiet of this corner of rural Oxfordshire was regularly broken by the roar of the U.S. Air Force planes at RAF Upper Heyford, and there was the added chance surprise of meeting one of the service personnel in his or her 'Yank Tank' American car on the narrow lanes.

MIDDLETON STONEY

Close to the former RAF base at Upper Heyford is **Middleton Stoney** nestling alongside the B430 equidistant between junctions 9 and 10 on the M40 in the delightful countryside of Oxfordshire.

The Jersey Arms, Middleton Stoney Tel 01869 343234, fax 01869 343565

The Jersey Arms is within easy reach of Oxford. The inn has the discreet charm and ambience of a long-established English coaching inn. Privately owned and managed by Helen and Donald Livingston, The Jersey Arms has all the character one associates with granite lintels, log fires and old beams, with traditional comfort to ensure that you are cosseted during your stay at this delightful hotel. The 16 rooms are out of this world, all with private access and the usual facilities. They have been converted from the stables and blacksmithy that once surrounded the courtyard. The blacksmith suite still houses the old forge and chimneys, or you could stay in the Lily Langtry suite, reminiscent of times past with a delightful four-poster bed.

The cosy and intimate restaurant has won many awards and is Egon Ronay recommended. This is a very friendly place and a warm welcome awaits you. This is certainly somewhere you will want to return to time and time again.

Our next stop is to visit **Fringford**, **Cottisford** and **Juniper Hill**, immortalised as 'Candleford', 'Fordlow' and 'Lark Rise' by Flora Thompson, whose comments on the local landscape we quoted at the beginning of this chapter. This is actually the wrong order in which to visit them, as she lived in Juniper Hill, went to school in Cottisford and worked at the Post Office in Fringford.

Coming from the south, we first reach the place where Flora began her adult life. Her employer, called Miss Lane in the book, was obviously a capable businesswoman of a type we don't expect to have lived in Victorian times. She was both the village postmistress and ran the village smithy, so that at one end of the 'long, low white house which might have been taken for an ordinary cottage' there was a board 'which informed the public that the building was CANDLEFORD GREEN POST AND TELEGRAPH OFFICE'. And at the other end was a board which read 'DORCAS LANE, SHOEING AND GENERAL SMITH'. Both are now gone, and the building is a private house.

From Fringford we take the minor road north to **Cottisford**, where Flora Thompson, and 'Laura' her fictional self, went to school. The school, which she describes as a 'small grey one-storied building' with 'one large classroom which served all purposes' and which had a two roomed cottage for the schoolmistress built on one end, is now also a private house, as is the way in villages nowadays. The schoolmistress must have had her work cut out, for we are told that the average attendance was about 45 and she taught all classes simultaneously, helped only by monitors - ex-scholars of about twelve who were paid a shilling a week.

We now turn north for **Juniper Hill,** following the road along which Laura and her schoolmates 'straggled, in twos and threes and in gangs, their flat, rush dinner baskets over their shoulders and their shabby little coats on their arms against rain'. Her description of life in the hamlet is one of hardship, and we would see it as one of poverty and unbelievable limitations. But Flora Thompson insists that Lark Rise should not be seen 'as a slum set down in the country'. The people whose lives she records 'were not unhappy, and, though poor, there was nothing sordid about their lives'.

Flora Thompson's own life was rather an unhappy one. She wrote constantly but success came only very late in her life. She seems to have been rather a lonely person and when recognition finally came to her she felt it had come to late to give her any pleasure.

AYNHO

Coming out onto the B4031 we turn west to **Aynho,** a charming village built of warm cream stone and famous for its apricot trees, to see **Aynhoe Park House** (the house has an 'E' though the village does not). This attractive mansion was originally built in the 16th Century and extensively altered by Sir John Soane in the 17th.

Soane was an interesting man, the son of a Berkshire builder and one of the most original of English architects. In spite of this he lacked confidence in himself and some people see this reflected in his rather complicated designs, which are deeply romantic though superficially neo-classical. He eventually became a professor of the Royal Academy and died in 1837. The house is in the centre of the village and is still lived in, though a few rooms are open to the public.

DEDDINGTON

Next we take the B 4031 across the valley of Cherwell to **Deddington.** If you follow in our footsteps and think you see something familiar about this peaceful village, it is probably because you saw it being 'demolished' by a runaway crane in the BBC television adaptation of Tom Sharpe's Blott on the Landscape. The damage was, of course, all cleverly faked and Deddington still retains its character as a thriving medieval market town with its large central square, Town Hall and Church.

The earthworks of **Deddington Castle,** in the care of English Heritage, are well worth a leg-stretching walk. The extensive earthworks enclose a large outer and small inner bailey. Excavations which were carried out found that the inner bailey contained remains of a 12th Century curtain wall, a hall and a small rectangular keep. These were covered again after the excavation and are no longer visible.

From Deddington turn north onto the A423 to head for our next destination.

ADDERBURY

Adderbury is just off the A423 road and **Adderbury House**, built of dark local ironstone in 1624, was the home of John Wilmot, 2nd Earl of Rochester, after his marriage to Elizabeth Malet, a wealthy heiress, in 1667. Rochester was a gallant soldier and a poet of genius who wrote the lovely lines 'When wearied with a world of woe, To thy safe bosom I retire, Where love, and peace, and truth does flow, May I contented there expire'. However, the words do not seem to have been totally sincere as in fact he was a notorious libertine who spent most of his time at court hoping for preferment from the king. Alexander Pope also stayed in the house in 1739.

Coach and Horses, The Green, Adderbury Tel 01295 810422

Situated overlooking the village green and only a few hundred yards from the local church you will find **The Coach and Horses** which has proved itself to be a very convenient and friendly watering hole. This old coaching house has been owned and run by Noreen and Tony for the past 11 years and is a real credit to their ability to make you feel at home from the moment you step through the door. This warm and busy pub has plenty of atmosphere with locals and visitors to the area mixing together in the generously sized bar area. If you would like some entertainment, then there is a Pool room available where you can knock around a few balls whilst enjoying a pint or two of Tony's excellent ale.

Food is served at lunchtimes and evenings and can be eaten in either the bar or in the attractive restaurant. The menu is varied and delicious with daily specials a regular occurrence. You can expect the usual pub fayre as well as a wide selection of meals that have a more substantial nature. When the weather is warm you can take your drink outside onto the patio area in the front of the pub that proves to be very popular on those long, hot summer afternoons.

The Coach and Horses has the most idyllic setting in this small and pretty village and offers any traveller a warm and friendly welcome.

Morgans Orchard Restaurant has gathered momentum over the last three years and has gained an enviable reputation as the quality and service has become well known. Chris Morgan is an international chef of high acclaim and his menus are extensive and wide-ranging to suit all types of occasions. Party nights, dinner parties and private functions are catered for in a professional and friendly manner.

The bed and breakfast accommodation is nicely presented and comfortable with television and central heating. An aperitif may be enjoyed in the intimate reception bar and an extensive wine list is provided which includes New World wines.

Morgans Orchard Restaurant, Twyford Gardens, Adderbury Tel 01295 812047

Open for both lunches and evening meals, Morgans is certainly the place to dine and enjoy your special celebrations. The front of the building has hanging baskets and painted milk churns which cascade with flowers. Chris and his wife Carol have won the 'Cherwell in Bloom' '1st Prize in its Class' and the colour and presentation add to this pretty venue. They look forward to greeting you and will make your visit one to remember.

BANBURY

What everyone has heard in the famous nursery rhyme about **Banbury**, our next stop, is that it has a Cross. And so it has, in Horsefair, built in 1859 to commemorate a previous one which was demolished during the Civil War by the Puritans, for whom Banbury also used to be famous. The ever-so-slightly comic figures around the base of the present Cross, of Queen Victoria, Edward VII and George V were added in 1914.

There was a time when 'a Banbury man' was a name for a bigot. A comic poem of 1638 contains the lines 'To Banbery came I, O prophane one, Where I saw a Puritan one, Hanging his cat on Monday, For killing a mouse on Sonday.'

Banbury was also at one time famous for its cheeses, which were only about an inch thick. This gave rise to the expression 'thin as a Banbury cheese'. The town's other legendary claim to fame is its cakes, made of spicy fruit pastry. These can still be bought, and very good they are too.

The **Church** nearby is unusual, a classical building which was described at the time of its building as 'being more like a gaol than a Christian temple'. This is rather unkind - the warm-coloured stone and hefty pillars are a pleasantly eccentric touch in the middle of a businesslike town. The original architect was S P Cockerell, though the tower and portico were completed in 1818-22 by his son, C R Cockerell. The style reflects the strong influence on English architecture of Piranesi's Views of Rome, using massive shapes and giving stone the deliberately roughened appearance which comes from the technique known as rustication.

The successors of the Banbury Puritans have a much more modest place of worship, the **Friends Meeting House**, built in 1751 with a classical porch added in 1820, in Horsefair.

A wander round Banbury's streets is very varied and rewarding. There are also lots of interesting old houses and shops to linger over. The **Museum**, also in Horsefair, tells the story of the development of Banbury and district.

Situated within sight of the famous Banbury Cross and the beautiful St Mary's Church, **Elisabeth The Chef** is a charming Tea Room and Restaurant that offers the guest the best in snacks and delicious meals. Sue Wootton is your superb hostess and has become well known in the surrounding area for her gorgeous home-made fayre which can be either eaten in the attractive dining area or taken away to be consumed at your leisure. The bright and airy dining room is clean and comfortable with wicker chairs and silk flowers on every table. The walls are covered in paintings with plenty of plants and greenery in every corner adding to the feeling of space and lightness.

There is a large display cabinet at the end of the room where you will find a staggering display of home-made cakes and Elisabeth The Chef cream cakes which you can select and enjoy at your leisure. The menu is wide and varied, ranging from lunchtime snacks to all day breakfasts, cream teas and hot meals. Why not sample the delicious 'Vegetable Lasagne' or the 'Lightly Dusted Haddock Fillets' each with a full selection of accompaniments, and for dessert there is a selection of ice creams or a slice of Sue's home-made cake. Sue also caters for special occasions, with the cakes being prepared and decorated by Elisabeth The Chef.

Elisabeth The Chef, 4/5 North Bar Street, Banbury Tel 01295 250507

This charming tea room is located next to an ample-sized pay and display car park, so make sure that you have enough time to sample all the culinary delights that Elisabeth The Chef have to offer.

Winston's Hotel, 65 Oxford Road, Banbury Tel 01295 270790

Winston's is a family-run Private Hotel with both a friendly homely atmosphere and appreciation of business people's needs. The hotel aims to provide the tourist, holidaymaker and business person alike with the comfort and facilities found in larger establishments but with a friendliness and high standard which will make you want to return. You will certainly receive a lovely welcome from Elizabeth the owner and her staff, who showed us around her very comfortable establishment.

All rooms are centrally heated and have private facilities en-suite. All rooms have their own colour televisions with satellite and video channels and provision for tea and coffee making as well as direct dial telephones. Although the hotel does not offer evening meals, they do offer bar meals in the small licensed bar. There are many and varied restaurants within five minutes' walk and Elizabeth will be happy to help with recommendations. There is ample parking space at the rear of the hotel which is easily located on Oxford Road, itself in turn only five minutes from Junction 11 on the M40 motorway.

The convenient situation of this hotel makes it an ideal base from which to explore, being on the fringe of the beautiful Cotswolds and within easy reach of many places of interest such as Shakespeare's country, Warwick and Broughton Castles, Blenheim Palace and George Washington's family birthplace.

Those of you who have a taste for industrial archaeology will not want to miss seeing something of the surviving Victorian buildings around the Oxford Canal, built in 1769. Banbury is still a thriving industrial centre and it seems difficult to believe now that canals were once at the cutting edge of transport technology. This one was conceived as part of a grand system of linking canals which would connect the Severn, Mersey, Thames and Trent. But then the railways took over and the canals became an irrelevance. Now they have been rediscovered as great places for recreation with an increasing number of people taking to the water in colourful narrow boats and other craft.

SULGRAVE

Many Americans make the pilgrimage to the area to visit **Sulgrave Manor**, ancestral home, from 1539, of the family of George Washington. It is situated 7 miles north-eastwards out of Banbury, close to the village of the same name, and is a charming small manor house, where enormous care has been taken to give an impression of the home of a successful man in Elizabethan times.

Although it is true that George Washington knew nothing about it, there is a connection. His family originated in Washington in County Durham, where their existence is recorded in the 12th Century.

The family then migrated to Lancashire, before Lawrence Washington moved south in about 1530 to Northampton, where he made a small fortune as a wool merchant. As a seal of his success he bought the manor of Sulgrave in 1539 and built the house soon afterwards.

The house has been extended over the years, but the heart remains as Lawrence built it and it is possible to imagine the prosperous wool merchant, his wife and their eleven children, entertaining their guests in the hall. The furnishings have been chosen carefully to reflect the period of the house and its general ambiance has been just as carefully fostered to give a real feeling for the way it was lived in.

CROPREDY

Inspired by Banbury's Civil War history (its castle endured two sieges, was then pulled down and the material used to repair damage to the town), we make our way through **Culworth** and **Wardington** to **Cropredy Bridge**, the site of a battle won by the Royalist armies in 1644. The Church in the village contains some relics of the conflict.

FARNBOROUGH

We now continue westwards on to the site of the **Battle of Edge Hill**, through **Farnborough**, pausing to look at **Farnborough Hall**, a mid-18th Century classical house, which has some very fine plasterwork and a terrace walk with temples and an obelisk. It is in the care of the National Trust.

A few miles beyond Farnborough and off the B 4086 is the village of **Radway**. It was here in 1642 that the armies of the King and Parliament faced each other for the first time. The Royalist cavalry charged and broke straight through the Parliamentary lines. But instead of pressing home their victory they carried on galloping allowing the Parliamentary foot soldiers to regroup. The first battle of the English Civil War is therefore best regarded as a draw. The scene is now so peaceful that it is hard to look towards Edge Hill and the village, and visualise the Royalist cavalry sweeping down on the Parliamentarian foot soldiers, standing firm with their pikes.

There is a small museum dedicated to the battle at Farnborough Hall, which has examples of arms and armour as well as models and dioramas.

Before leaving the area of Edge Hill stop to see **Upton House**, a 17th Century house, built of local stone, with extensive gardens including terraces planted with herbaceous plants above a pool set in a deep valley.

The real glory of the house, however, is its art collection, which includes Brussels tapestries, Sevres porcelain and Chelsea figurines, 18th Century furniture and some 200 paintings, among which are to be found

masterpieces of the British, Dutch, Flemish, French, German, Italian and
Spanish schools. This is a rendezvous art lovers must not fail to keep.

We now turn west towards **Middle** and **Upper Tysoe** for a glimpse
of **Compton Wynyates**, a fairy-tale vision of a red brick Tudor mansion
in a green valley. In an area where the great glories are the stone
buildings, the warm pink brick of the house seems particularly attractive.
It is also in total contrast to Farnborough and Upton. No classical notions
of symmetry went into its building, only the needs of the time and an
innate sense of what was fitting. It has been described as 'the most
glorious of Tudor jumbles' and that seems a very apt description. The
house is not open to visitors, but the view from the road of this most
picturesque English house is worth the trip.

WROXTON

Returning toward Banbury we pause at the pretty village of **Wroxton**.
Here cottages built of local brown stone, many of them with a thatched
roof, cluster around the **Abbey**, a lovely 17th Century house built on the
site of a Priory, where you can wander in the gardens and the grounds,
restored as an 18th Century park.

Nearby **Broughton Castle**, a moated 14th Century mansion, has been
owned by the same family since 1451. It has an interesting medieval
Chapel and Gatehouse and there are some fine Elizabethan additions,
including plaster ceilings, panelling and fireplaces. Here too there are
Civil War memories, for the house has a secret room where leaders of the
Parliamentary side made their plans.

Take a look at the Church which is just next to the castle. It has an
unusual stone chancel screen and, as you might expect from the tour of
the house, there are six centuries of monuments and 'hatchments' -
diamond-shaped wooden panels painted with coats of arms which were
hung in churches after the funerals of members of aristocratic families.

SWALCLIFFE

From Broughton we meander west along the B4035 to **Swalcliffe**.
This historic village contains lots of fascinating buildings, many thatched,
and a fine Church, **St. Peter and St. Paul**, which was built by the Normans
in the 11th Century and incorporates architectural styles from then until
the 15th Century.

HOOK NORTON

Continuing south from Swalcliffe and keeping to the unclassified
roads brings us to the curiously named **Hook Norton**, well know to Real
ale buffs for its traditional beers.

Hook Norton Victorian Tower Brewery

If you are in need of some alcoholic refreshment, look no further than **The Gate Hangs High Inn**, with its stone walls smoothed by time, low beamed ceilings, open fire in the bar and a friendly, country welcome from your hosts Stuart, Joyce and Susannah. Originally a Drover pub, The Gate Hangs High is also thought to have been a Toll House. Possibly this is where the wonderful name comes from, as cattle and horses had to be paid for but geese and ducks were allowed to pass free under the gate.

During the warm summer months the Inn's gardens offer an ideal setting from which to sample the wide selection of real ales, or mull over the sumptuous menus that are packed with reasonably-priced and delicious home cooking. The a la carte menu, featuring Hook Norton pate and toast, is comprehensive and includes a range of char grilled steaks. Set Sunday lunches are available throughout the year, so popular that an early booking is recommended to avoid disappointment. The Bar Menu offers plenty of tasty dishes including Blackboard specials, vegetarian meals and a selection of home-made sweets.

The Gate Hangs High, Hook Norton Tel 01608 737387

Although The Gate Hangs High caters for the more mature diners and special occasion dinners, children are welcomed in the Inn. With an extensive list of over 55 wines and all the delicious cooking, visitors are often tempted to stay, which those who have their own caravans can do, as Stuart and Joyce have facilities in their own grounds.

BLOXHAM

On our way to our next destination we pass through **Bloxham**, on the A361. Pause here to look at its **Museum** of village life, an interesting collection of local bygones.

The Red Lion Inn in Bloxham is a handsome building which dates back to around 1810. Situated on the main A361 road through the village, the inn has long been popular with locals and visitors alike. For the past 12 years, under the ownership of Paul and Carol Cooper, its reputation for serving fine ales and excellent food has deservedly grown, and the pub now attracts visitors from a wide radius.

This is very much a traditional style pub, in both its appearance and the warmth of atmosphere that pervades. If you get a chance, try to book a table for one of the 'Speciality Nights', when for a modest amount you can enjoy a superb set four-course meal which has been specially 'themed' to tie in to a particular event or location. As an added bonus, a 'Courtesy Carriage' service is provided for parties of four or more diners within a ten-mile radius of Bloxham. This service is free of charge and enables everyone in the party to thoroughly enjoy the selection of fine wines and ales which accompany the menu. Be sure to phone for full details of the service and forthcoming events. A fine 'Hidden Place' which is well worth a visit.

The Red Lion Inn, Bloxham Tel 01295 720352

GREAT TEW

Continuing south, turn at the B4022 towards the unforgettable village of **Great Tew**. The village has long been considered one of the most picturesque villages in the Cotswolds, with its honey-coloured thatched houses nestling in a fold of beautifully landscaped hillside.

The village looks so much a natural part of the landscape now that it is interesting to learn that it was deliberately made to look more picturesque in the early 19th Century. At this time villages were often demolished by the landowners to whom they belonged, so as not to spoil the view from the 'great house', but here the cottages were improved and trees planted.

The house in this case was **Great Tew Park**, on rising ground to the south of the village. The house we see now is mostly 19th Century, although the stables are earlier, about 1700. However, its 17th Century predecessor, somewhat to the north of the present building, was a gathering place for the intellectuals of the day, including the authors Abraham Cowley, Edmund Waller and Ben Jonson and scholars from Oxford. Of this house only the garden walls remain.

The village Church is also well worth a visit, and particularly the brass monument to John and Alice Wilcotes dating from 1410, showing the medieval couple reclining under intricate canopies. Completely different in style is the monument, by the sculptor Francis Chantrey, to Mary Anne Boulton who died in 1829, which depicts her very naturally, seated on a chaise longue.

STEEPLE ASTON

Travelling now eastwards on minor roads to rejoin the busy world again at the A4260, turn south to **Steeple Aston**.

One does not often think of smiling at a monument in a Church, but Jennifer Sherwood's description of the memorial to Sir Francis Page and his wife, in the Oxfordshire volume of the Buildings of England series, is intriguing. Could it really be technically superb and look ridiculous? You may well agree. The figures are life-size and obviously portraits, with Sir Francis, who was a Judge, in his legal robes and his wife in her nightdress. The monument is the work of Henry Scheemakers and was commissioned in 1730. The couple had a house in the village which was demolished in the last century.

The Red Lion in South Street is what could be called a true community pub. Conversation is encouraged by the ambience of the place - you will find no wallpaper music and no juke box here - even the landlord, Colin Mead, loves to strike up a conversation.

The Red Lion, South Street, Steeple Aston Tel 01869 340225

The Red Lion is Egon Ronay recommended and is a Mecca for anyone who enjoys fine wines and good food. Margaret is the chef and she produces excellent food for bar snacks or a full meal. The food is also very good value; whatever price is shown against a main course dish is the all-inclusive price for a three-course meal with coffee. The wine list would make any wine lover drool with a range of over 100 wines. Most are French but the selection covers several continents from Australia to America with plenty in between!

The history of the Red Lion is interesting. The building dates from the mid-17th Century but the inn was created in the latter half of the last century out of old stabling and a house which was formerly the inn itself.

The building was restored in 1972 and has an intimate bar and small dining room which has been carefully furnished to evoke the best traditions of an Old English Pub. If you are a connoisseur of fine malt whisky take a look at the selection here! The dining room only seats 20 and it is advisable to book in advance. Food is served Tuesday to Saturday evenings.

To the front of the Red Lion is a delightful floral/patio terrace and a flagpole which flies various flags on National days. This establishment is visited by people from all over the world.

Just outside Steeple Aston is **Rousham House and Gardens**. The house was built in 1635 and became a Royalist garrison during the Civil War. In more peaceful times the Dormer family, who owned it, invited such lovers of romantic landscapes as Alexander Pope, John Gay and Horace Walpole to enjoy the gardens, terraces and temples above the River Cherwell, designed by William Kent. His work remains intact and visitors are able to explore one of the few landscaped parks of the kind to have survived relatively unchanged.

The house has a fine collection of literary autographs and portraits as well as interesting interiors and furniture.

We hope you enjoy touring this less well-known part of Oxfordshire, with its surprising wealth of fine houses, but now we turn south-west towards Woodstock, where, in the next chapter, we explore one of the grandest of all the great aristocratic houses.

Minster Lovell Hall Ruins

74

CHAPTER FOUR

Oxford Cotswolds

Cotswold Wildlife Park, Nr Burford

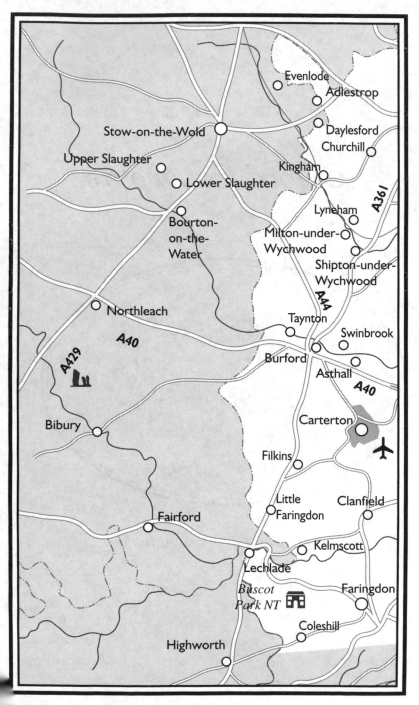

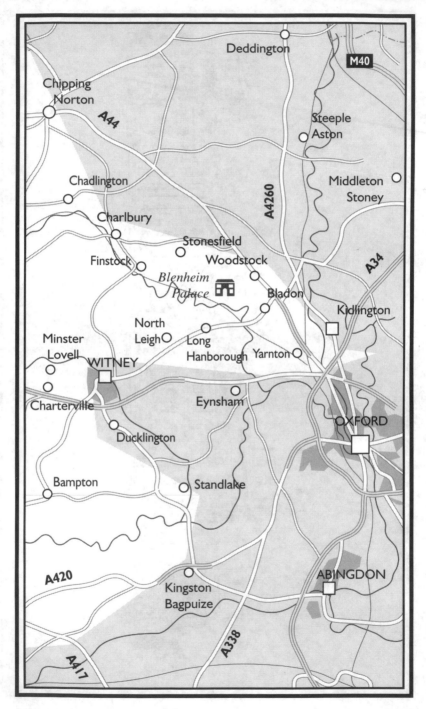

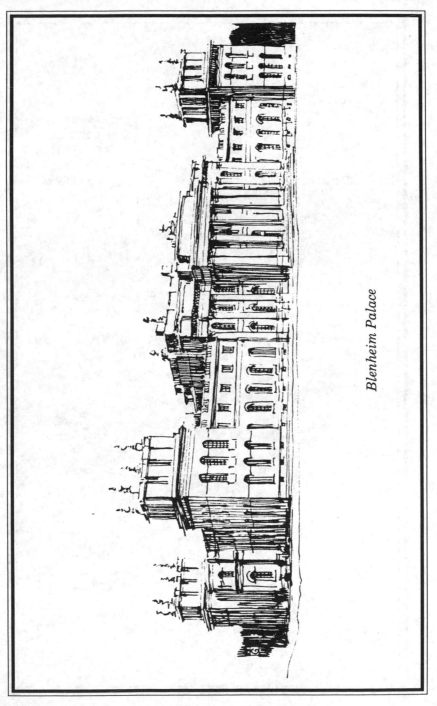

Blenheim Palace

CHAPTER FOUR

Oxford Cotswolds

WOODSTOCK

John Churchill (1650-1722), 1st Duke of Marlborough, was a brave soldier, skilful general and had, as we say nowadays, an eye on the main chance. And if he had lacked anything in this faculty it would have been more than made up for by his wife, Sarah. He was also, we are told, an even-tempered man and a loving husband and father, who was always concerned about the welfare of his troops. At the height of his power after the victory at Blenheim during the War of the Spanish Succession, he was received in London as a hero and Queen Anne proposed that he should be rewarded with a Palace. She gave him her manor at Woodstock as the site, but there the national gratitude seems to have run out of steam, for he paid for most of it himself in the end.

As his architect, Marlborough chose Sir John Vanbrugh whose life was even more colourful than that of his patron. He was at the same time both an architect (although at the time he was relatively unknown as such) and a playwright, and had the distinction of having been imprisoned in the Bastille.

The result of his work was the Continental-looking baroque **Blenheim Palace**, which we now see set in a very English park laid out later by Capability Brown. The new house did not meet with universal approval. It was ridiculed by Jonathan Swift and Alexander Pope; Duchess Sarah, who seems to have held the family purse strings, delayed paying Vanbrugh as long as possible. But recently its international importance has been recognised by inclusion in the UNESCO World Heritage List.

It is a magnificent Palace, both inside and out, and, after marvelling at the treasures and the more intimate souvenirs of Marlborough's descendant, Sir Winston Churchill, enjoy a refreshing walk through the formal gardens and park.

The Blenheim Orange apple got its name from here. It was first grown by George Kempster, a tailor from Old Woodstock. The exact date of the first apple is unknown. Kempster himself died in 1773 and the original tree blew down in 1853. A plaque in Old Woodstock marks its site. So famous did the spot become that it is said London-bound coaches and horses used to slow down so that passengers might gaze upon it.

Woodstock itself is a relaxed, unpretentious place giving no hint of the grandeur of its most famous building, which is approached through the main street. It has a much longer history than does Blenheim, however. It was formerly the centre of the glove making industry and was the site of one of the most splendid of the medieval royal Palaces, the scene of Henry II's courtship of 'the Fair Rosamond', and birthplace of the Black Prince. Elizabeth I was imprisoned there in 1554 by her sister, Mary Tudor. The old Palace was damaged during the Civil War, when it served as a Royalist garrison and the last remains were demolished in 1710.

The Church is interesting. The original medieval building was practically rebuilt in Victorian times, but the tower is classical, built in 1785.

John Vanbrugh was born in London in 1664 and is now most famous for his great contribution to British architecture giving us Castle Howard near York as well as Blenheim Palace. It is from this famous location and its connections that **Vanbrughs Coffee House** takes its name. Indeed it is believed that Vanbrugh stayed in this house whilst the Palace was being built.

Vanbrughs Coffee House, 16 Oxford Street, Woodstock Tel 01933 811253

Setting their own standards in healthy eating by participating in West Oxfordshire Environmental Health Department's Heartbeat Award, Vanbrughs Coffee House offers a Healthy Options Menu. Throughout the day a selection of imaginatively-prepared interesting dishes are served, anything from breakfast, coffee and pastries and light snacks to 'Woodstock Platters' with selections from the Deli counter, accompanied perhaps by a glass of wine. Lean ground Beef Burgers, sandwiches and cream teas are also on the menu. A tempting selection of concoctions from the ice cream parlour may prove to be too much, so be prepared to spoil yourself!

BLADON

Heading south from Woodstock along the A34 south and turning off onto the A4095 brings us to **Bladon** and the Churchyard where Sir Winston Churchill lies, together with other members of his family. The Churchyard, on the edge of the park, has become a place of modern pilgrimage. The village is on what must be one of the most evocatively-named of all English rivers, the Evenlode. We are now, of course, in the Cotswolds, that much loved part of England for which the phrase 'green and pleasant land' might have been coined.

NORTH LEIGH

Continue along the A4095, turning north-westwards up the delightful valley of the Evenlode in search of the **Roman Villa** at **North Leigh**. We last met the Romans around Bicester, and here they are again as we loop up to cross, once more, the line of Akeman Street as it runs south-west to meet the Fosse Way coming up from Bath towards the north.

The villa, one of several known to have existed in the vicinity, is at **East End** just outside the village of North Leigh itself. It was large, with over 60 rooms, two sets of baths, an under-floor heating system and mosaic pavements including one with attractive interlaced patterns. The site is known to have been occupied by Romans from the 1st Century AD, but the house, which is built around a courtyard, reached its present form in the 4th Century, when it was clearly the home of a prosperous farming family and their servants, able to 'export' their produce using the transport opportunities offered by Akeman Street.

Before leaving North Leigh, the Church is well worth a visit; it has a Saxon tower, and there is the small 15th Century Wilcote Chapel, built by Elizabeth Wilcote in memory of her two husbands and two sons, with intricate fan vaulting.

STONESFIELD

Further north is the village of **Stonesfield**. Having travelled through time from the Romans to a great leader of our own century, evidence of even older inhabitants has been found at Stonesfield. At a nearby quarry a geology student discovered the fossilised remains of the earliest known stegosaurus. These were fearsome looking dinosaurs, with lashing tails armed with spikes, who lived in the area some 160 million years ago. It seems hard to imagine them roaming through the peaceful landscape we see today.

The name of the village, incidentally, has nothing to do with quarries or the local stone, but is derived from Stunt's or Stunta's field - Stunt being a nickname from the Old English word for foolish!

FINSTOCK

To the east is the hamlet of **Finstock**. **The Plough Inn** at The Bottom can truly be described as a family-run inn for the family. Margaret, Sue, Keith and Nigel all pull together to make it happen at the Plough. Here you will find log fires ablaze and many stuffed animals and birds keeping a watchful eye from their assigned positions.

Built around 1772, The Plough Inn was first a farmer's cottage which later became a private dwelling and subsequently a pub called The Churchill in 1804; it was the first country inn to be owned by Halls Brewery. Copies of the original documents of the signing of the freehold are displayed on the walls of this lovely atmospheric pub.

There's a great welcome for everyone at this pub, babies, prams, pushchairs, dogs - all are welcome. The owners are great dog lovers and two champion canines are resident on the premises; many winning rosettes are displayed on the low beams. The inn is close to Wychwood Forest popular with walkers and cyclists; five walks have their starting point at the Plough. Many claims of ghost sightings are made by the villagers including Urchins, believed to be from Roman times, throwing stones in the village. A great place to make for with the reward of great hospitality, traditional home cooked food and some great ales.

The Plough Inn, The Bottom, Finstock Tel 01933 868333

Next we take the B4437 into **Charlbury**, a pleasant stone-built town, then the B4022 towards **Enstone** to visit **Ditchley Park**. The building of the house was begun about 1720 and was designed by James Gibbs in a restrained classical style. The interiors are splendid, having been designed by William Kent and Henry Flitcroft. Italian craftsmen worked on the stucco decorations of the great hall and the saloon, the first treated to give an impression of rich solemnity, the second with a rather more exuberant effect.

The house has associations with Sir Winston Churchill, who used it as a weekend headquarters during the 1939-45 War. Appropriately enough, given that Sir Winston had an American mother, Ditchley Park is now used as an Anglo-American conference centre.

CHIPPING NORTON

Leaving this fine house behind us, we take the road for **Chipping Norton** where a very pleasant surprise awaits. Chipping Norton is a lovely town, at the centre of the Evenlode valley's prosperous wool trade in medieval times, based on sheep which grazed the Cotswolds.

This wealth is reflected in the fine Church, where the Nave, built about 1485, is flooded with light from the clerestory and east window. The latter originally came from the Abbey of Bruern, a few miles to the south west, which was demolished in 1535 during the dissolution of the monasteries under Henry VIII.

The 'Chipping' part of the town's name comes from the Old English word for 'market' (the same word, incidentally, is the origin of the 'cheap' in Cheapside in London) and fittingly it has a fine market place. The surrounding streets more than repay a little wander, as there are many intriguing houses, including some attractive 17th Century almshouses.

CHURCHILL

Next we take the B4450 towards the village of **Churchill**. The 'father of British geology', William Smith (1769-1839) was born in this village. He began his professional life as a canal engineer, and went on to work out the method of telling the age of geological strata by the fossils found in them. In 1815 he published a geological map of England, the first of its kind. There is a memorial to him, an impressive monolith of local stone.

Less well served as far as memorials are concerned is James Langton, whose daughter erected a fountain in his memory here in 1870. This is, as the Buildings of England volume on Oxfordshire put it, 'memorably ugly'. However, the villagers may well have been grateful for it in the days before mains water and taps in every home.

Warren Hastings, who administered India on behalf of the East India Company from 1773 until 1784 was also born in this village. His is a vivid story, as colourful as India itself, full of intrigue, wars, corruption and allegations of corruption. In Hastings' own case such charges led to him being impeached before the House of Lords, and a trial which dragged on for seven years. Eventually he was personally vindicated and retired to be a country gentleman in Daylesford, not far from his birthplace. His house there had been his family home; buying it and living in it was for him the fulfilment of an ambition he had had since childhood.

At **Bledington** the village green is complete with brook and ducks - all known locally by name.

ADLESTROP

A nearby name on the map, **Adlestrop,** will be familiar to the lover of rural poetry, or anyone who ever thrilled to the romance of steam trains. Edward Thomas, who was to die at Arras in 1917, wrote a wonderful evocation of a rural station, and how the name was forever fixed in his memory 'because one afternoon, Of heat the express train drew up there, unwontedly. It was late June. No one left and no one came, On the bare platform. What I saw, was Adlestrop - only the name...' The station, alas, is gone, a victim of the branch line closures of the sixties.

Adlestrop has another literary association, as Jane Austen stayed in the Rectory in the summer of 1806. Her first novel was not published until 1811. Could she have been working on Sense and Sensibility or Pride and Prejudice at the time? Could her uncle possibly be a prototype for the Reverend Mr Collins?

After paying our respects to Edward Thomas and Jane Austen, we head back to the A463 before turning left to find **Chastleton House**. Here again we meet wealth derived from wool, because the estate was bought in 1602 by a wool merchant, who had a fine new house built there to reflect his status as a successful businessman. This is very much the building which we see now, a Jacobean manor house with a dramatic five-gabled front. The style suggests to many people that the house was designed by Robert Smythson, the most famous architect of his day, but there is no absolute proof of this.

Inside, the house has a wonderful collection of original panelling, furniture, tapestries and embroideries. The overall effect has led some to see it 'uninhibited by any considerations of insipid good taste'. Those with less austere standards should find it a feast for the eyes. Particularly impressive is the Long Gallery, which runs the entire length of the top floor at the back of the house. This has a wonderful barrel-vaulted ceiling plastered in intricate patterns of interlacing ribbons and flowers.

LONG COMPTON

Next we turn towards **Long Compton** in order to find, a little to the south, reminders of rather less urbane times, the prehistoric stone circle known as the **Rollright Stones**. These great knarled fists of stone stand on a ridge giving fine views of the surrounding countryside. They all have nicknames - the King's Men form a circle, the King Stone is to the north of the circle and a quarter of a mile to the west stand the Whispering

The Sundial Signpost, near Chipping Norton

Knights, which are in fact the remnants of a megalithic tomb which has lost its original covering mound of earth. Visitors soaking in the sense of the mysterious which these ancient stones seem to possess can only guess at their original purpose.

We now head south once again on minor roads, through **Kingham**, **Foscot** and **Fifield**.

What better way to spend a summer afternoon than watching a game of cricket on the village green. The Wychwoods nestle deeply into the beautiful Evenlode Valley where you can walk in the most glorious scenery.

MILTON-UNDER-WYCHWOOD

Our next stop is to be **Milton-Under-Wychwood**, which sits right in the middle of the square formed by Moreton-in-the-Marsh, Chipping Norton, Burford and Stow-in-the-Wold, but the easiest way to reach it is to take the A361 from Burford towards Chipping Norton. About a third of the way along the road you will come to **Shipton-under-Wychwood** where a signposted left turn will take you to Milton.

There are architectural styles of many different periods throughout Oxfordshire and Milton is no exception, having a school, teacher's house and Church designed by the prominent Victorian architect G E Street in 1853-4. The Church is a good example of Street's early Gothic style and has a lychgate. Together the buildings make an attractive group.

SHIPTON-UNDER-WYCHWOOD

Next we explore Milton's neighbour, **Shipton-Under-Wychwood**, which has a number of interesting buildings. The Church, which was begun about 1200, has a 14th Century porch with a relief of the Annunciation over the entrance showing the Virgin in elegant drapery.

Shipton Court was built about 1603. The front is elegant and well proportioned with five narrow gables but the overall lack of symmetry in the plan suggests that the house was based on an earlier one. The house was completely remodelled internally in a restoration carried out in the early years of this century. Among other buildings well worth a look is the **Shaven Crown Inn**, which dates from the 15th Century.

The suffix 'under-Wychwood' derives from the Wychwood, which was an ancient royal hunting forest, much larger than the remnant of woodland near Charlbury. The name has nothing to do with witches - 'wych' refers to the Hwicce, a Celtic tribe of whose territory the forest originally formed a part.

The forest was one of the alleged haunts of Matthew Arnold's 'scholar gipsy'. In the poem, published in 1853, Arnold tells the legend of the brilliant but poor Oxford scholar who, despairing of ever making his way in the world, went to live with the gypsies to learn from their way of life, and for long after could sometimes be seen 'leaning backward in a pensive dream, And fostering in thy lap a heap of flowers Pluck'd in shy fields and distant Wychwood bowers, And thine eyes resting on the moonlit stream ...'.

The distant Wychwood bowers are much less accessible now. The wood was for a long time completely closed to the public, but protracted negotiations have resulted in the opening of one footpath, leading into the forest just north of the village of **Leafield**, south east of Shipton-under -Wychwood.

We resume our journey by way of minor roads towards Burford, passing through the village where the great Victorian polymath, William Morris spent his summers, **Taynton**. The stone for Blenheim Palace, most of the Oxford Colleges, Windsor Castle and St Paul's Cathedral was taken from nearby quarries. The village itself is a charming huddle of stone-built thatched cottages grouped around an interesting Church which has a Perpendicular tower.

BURFORD

The honey-coloured Cotswold stone of **Burford** and its setting on the river Windrush (the name derived, apparently, from the prosaic 'white marsh') make it an unforgettable composition. When William Morris, revolted by the dirt and stench of Victorian London, wrote 'and dream of London, small and white and clean, the clear Thames bordered by its gardens green' it is quite easy to imagine Burford, or somewhere very similar, hovering at the back of his mind.

The wool of the Cotswolds, once again, brought Burford its medieval prosperity and today we can see the result in the houses of the wool merchants which still remain. By the beginning of the 15th Century it was already one of the leading wool markets, its wealthy heyday lasting until the early 16th. After that it declined, though it remained an important coaching centre with several large inns throughout the 18th Century.

After the main road to London and then the railway bypassed the town, it became a backwater until the tourist trade of this century revived its fortunes. What we enjoy so much rests on the fact of it having remained impervious to the progressive modernisation suffered by other towns.

Compton Mackenzie, who lived for a time in Burford before the 1914-1918 War, wrote about the town as 'Wychford' in his novel Guy and Pauline, which was published in 1915.

The Church is one of its great glories, the original Norman building having been added to over the centuries so that it gives the impression of having 'just growed'.

In 1649 it was the scene of the last act of a tragic aftermath of the Civil War. Troops from Cromwell's army who were representatives of the most democratic strand of thought in the Parliamentary army, known as Levellers, mutinied against what they saw as the drift towards the authoritarian rule they had been fighting to root out. While they were encamped in Burford, they were taken by surprise by Cromwell's forces. After a brief fight 340 prisoners were taken and placed under guard in the Church. The next day there was a court martial and three of the rebels were shot as an example to the rest, who were made to watch the execution.

Robert and Jayne Lewin invite you to explore the natural beauty of solid wood in their showroom at **Burford Woodcraft** in the High Street. Items are carefully chosen from the best the craftsmen create to offer a wide range, where the emphasis is on good design and quality of finish. Robert is one of the 50 talented British craftsmen whose work is displayed in the attractive showroom. By using a variety of techniques and finishes they hand-craft high quality furniture and products which complement the natural vitality of wood. If you are looking for original gift ideas, however modest or grand, there is much to delight and intrigue, not only the practical - furniture, lamps, clocks and bowls - but the creative - wonderful boxes to keep treasures safe. There are also carved birds, jewellery and one-off original pieces plus much much more including toys, mirrors and photoframes. Burford Woodcraft will welcome you with a friendly personal service.

Burford Woodcraft, 144 High Street, Burford Tel 01993 823479

Burford House is not difficult to find, being on the main street right in the heart of this picturesque place. The frontage of the hotel, whilst being quite beautiful itself, hides many delightful secrets. The oldest part of the hotel dates back to the 15th Century and there are many outstanding features, from original mullioned windows to stone fireplaces and low beamed ceilings. The house invites you to retire from the hustle and bustle to the peace and tranquillity to be found inside, in the cosy sitting rooms where a log fire burns in autumn and winter, and in the delightful flower-filled courtyard in the spring and summer. During the day, morning coffee and crumpets, light lunches and cream teas are served as well as aperitifs or something stronger should you desire.

Owned and run by Jane and Simon Henty who previously managed a Country House Hotel for the owners of the world famous Reids Hotel in Madeira, Burford House justifiably earns its AA 5Q Premier Select Award, the top rating for small hotels and inns. Furnished to the highest degree of tradition and comfort, the hotel offers seven individually styled bedrooms all en-suite and some with beautiful four poster beds and grand Victorian bathtubs. In each room will be found a traditional English Teddy Bear. The rooms are named after the local villages and hamlets.

One should appreciate that Burford House is also the home of the owners, reflected in the many personal touches to be seen around the hotel. Should you wish to move beyond the lovely town, which itself has a wealth of restaurants and antique shops, to explore the wonderful Cotswolds, this is the ideal centre from which to do this.

Burford House Hotel, 99 High Street, Burford Tel 01993 823151

Situated just 50 yards from Burford's High Street is the **Royal Oak**, a delightful 17th Century inn run by Gary and Sue Duffy. The property has a fascinating history stretching back to around 1615 when one Richard Meryweather owned the then new building that incorporates the present inn. Part of the structure was then an alehouse, and it has been serving ale on and off ever since.

The beamed bar is a pleasant place to enjoy the traditional hand-pulled Wadworth ales and admire the collection of over 400 mugs. The inn also serves good wholesome home made food at reasonable prices and to the rear there is a patio garden to enjoy in the summer months.

For those wishing to stay, there are two comfortable en-suite guest rooms which are centrally-heated and equipped with every convenience. The Royal Oak stands on Burford's one-way system and has its own car park, an important asset in this busy town.

The Royal Oak, Witney Street, Burford Tel 01933 823278

Near to the Golf Course, you will find the **Burford Lodge Hotel**, ideally situated for tourists and businessmen alike. The hotel exudes character and charm; it is built of local Cotswold stone and dates back to the early 19th Century. All of the rooms are en-suite and equipped to very high standards, with colour television, tea and coffee making facilities and direct-dial telephones. Satellite TV is available in the bar area.

The Burford Lodge Hotel, Oxford Road, Burford Tel 01993 823381

The hotel has a very good restaurant serving an excellent selection of dishes, all of which are home cooked and prepared using the very best local produce whenever possible. The Burford Lodge has a warm and friendly atmosphere which is enhanced by its intimate bar and log fires. This is one of the very best establishments of its type in the area and would make an ideal base for a family holiday, a short romantic break or a business stopover.

There are many places of interest to visit locally, pleasant walks along the river valley to neighbouring villages, fishing on the River Windrush and opportunities for horse riding; keen golfers are well served by the adjacent golf course.

This is a fine hotel, one to which you will undoubtedly want to return again and again. You will find it almost equidistant between Oxford (18 miles) and Cheltenham (21 miles) on the A40.

Just outside Burford is **The Cotswold Wild Life Park**. In its 120 acres of park and gardens rhinos, zebras, ostriches, tigers and leopards can all be seen in spacious enclosures. There are walled gardens with tropical birds and monkeys, a reptile house, an aquarium and a butterfly house. There are also picnic areas, an adventure playground and a narrow-gauge railway making it an ideal experience for children of all ages.

ASTHALL

Asthall is really no more than a hamlet, quite near Burford. It is of ancient origins and although it may be only small, it has a marvellous 12th Century Church with a unique medieval stone altar. The tower clock on the outside, was made locally and dates back to 1665.

The Jacobean **Manor House** which was built in 1620 has a most interesting recent history. In 1919, David Freeman-Mitford, Lord Redesdale, moved into the Manor together with his wife, son and six daughters who were later to become famous as the Mitford sisters, Nancy, Pamela, Diana, Unity, Jessica and Deborah. In some of her splendid books Nancy Mitford wrote about her family. Deborah Mitford is now the Duchess of Devonshire and Unity became notorious for her attachment to Hitler and Oswald Mosley.

A little tricky to find, Asthall is approached down a narrow country lane off the old A40 between Witney and Burford, just near the Witney by-pass roundabout.

SWINBROOK

Asthall is just south of the little village of **Swinbrook**, a collection of 17th and 18th Century farmhouses and some Victorian cottages built in Tudor style. A great mansion stood in the village, built about 1490 by the Fettiplace family, until 1805, when the last of the family died. No trace of it now remains but the little Church has a fascinating triple-decked monument to three of them, stiff 16th Century knights in armour with uncomfortable looking collars, all propped up on one elbow and seemingly about to draw their swords in this unlikely pose. A sight worth the detour before continuing on to Minster Lovell.

MINSTER LOVELL

Minster Lovell Hall was built about 1431-42 and was, in its day, one of the great aristocratic houses of Oxfordshire, the home of the Lovell family. It was arranged around three sides of a courtyard, which was enclosed on the river side by a wall. However, one of the family was a prominent Yorkist during the Wars of the Roses and after the defeat of Richard III at Bosworth Field, he lost his lands to the Crown.

The house was purchased by the Coke family in 1602, but around the middle of the 18th Century the house was dismantled by Thomas Coke, Earl of Leicester, and the ruins became lowly farm buildings. They were rescued from complete disintegration by the Ministry of Works in the 1930s and are now in the care of English Heritage. What is left of the house is extremely picturesque, and it is hard to imagine a better setting than here, beside the river Windrush.

Having seen the comparatively high-tech heating system of the North Leigh Roman Villa, it comes as something of a shock to realise that the Great Hall of this aristocratic house was heated by a fire on a stone hearth in the centre with ventilation provided by openings in the gables of the end walls. One fascinating feature which has survived is the medieval dovecot, complete with nesting boxes, which provided pigeons for the table in a way reminiscent of modern battery henhouses.

CHARTERVILLE

Making our way southwards we pass reminders of an idealistic social experiment at **Charterville**. All that is left to see are some small cottages with central gables and a towered school, remains of the Chartist Feargus O'Connor's attempt to establish families from the industrialised cities in smallholdings. This early experiment in self-sufficiency began in 1847 but it failed and the estate was sold in 1850.

We continue southwards through **Brize Norton**, home of the great RAF base, and on to **Filkins**, just off the A361. This tiny Cotswold village is now the home of a flourishing community of craft workers and artists, many of them working in restored 18th Century barns. Having been very much aware of the history of the wool industry in the area, it is particularly interesting to visit **Cotswold Woollen Weavers**, where the production process can be followed from fleece to finished cloth.

Located directly opposite St Peter's Church in picturesque **Filkins**, just north of Lechlade, **Cottage-by-the-Church** is a family home that has been welcoming guests for the past 350 years. This c1650 Grade II listed building was around during the reign of Charles I and was once three cottages and a farmhouse. Though tastefully converted into the modern dwelling that you see before you today, Cottage-by-the-Church still has many of its original features. This rural retreat gleans much of its traditional atmosphere from the heavily beamed ceilings, twisting staircases and inglenook fireplaces that add a distinct air of charm and history to this mellow sandstone building.

The guests' accommodation comprises two double en-suite bedrooms with patchwork quilts, tasteful furnishings and a complementary tea/coffee tray. Owned and very capably run by Jane, Cottage-by-the-Church provides a delicious full English breakfast every morning, whilst your evening meals can be enjoyed at either The Lamb Inn or The Five Alls Carvery Restaurant, which are both only five minutes' walk away. Surrounded by a stone-walled cottage garden, filled year round with shrubs and seasonal flowers, there is ample parking at the front of the house where you will find a small courtyard garden complete with its own freshwater well.

Cottage-by-the-Church, Filkins, Lechlade Tel/Fax 01367 860613

KELMSCOTT

From here we head on through **Little Faringdon** for **Kelmscott** or **Kelmscot** - opinions differ as to the spelling.

Nowadays William Morris is perhaps best known for his association with the Pre-Raphaelite artists and as a decorator, whose designs for wallpaper and curtain material are still available and popular. He was equally accomplished as a poet and writer, and as a printer. The books he designed and printed are now collectors' items, but his poetry and novels are less suited to modern tastes.

Still less well-known now are Morris' political opinions, formed from his horror of the poverty and ugliness of life for most people in Victorian England. In reaction he turned to the medieval chivalry, Norse heroes and gentler rural patterns of life in times past, and to the future, where he saw socialism as a cure for a world gone awry.

Manor House at Kelmscott was William Morris' country home from 1871 to 1896. It is built of a subtle grey stone, a gabled house near the Thames, dating from about 1570. Morris loved it dearly, and it is the scene of the end of his utopian novel 'News from Nowhere', in which he writes of a world where work has become a sought-after pleasure.

The house, which is open to visitors during the summer, has examples of Morris's work and memorabilia of Dante Gabriel Rosetti, who also stayed there. Rosetti is reputed to have found the village boring, so presumably the fact that he was in love with Morris' wife, Jane, drew him there. Morris himself is buried in the Churchyard, under a tombstone designed by his associate Philip Webb.

The Church itself is interesting, the oldest parts dating from the late 12th Century, and the village includes some fine farmhouses from around the end of the 17th and beginning of the18th Centuries.

Another attraction of a trip to Kelmscott is the chance to walk on the towpath beside the Thames using the excellent Thames Walk booklet written by David Sharp and published by the Ramblers' Association. The full walk would take you from Putney to the source of the Thames near Cricklade, but on this occasion just take the opportunity of walking down river to see **Radcot Bridge**. There has been a bridge at or near this site since Saxon times, but the present one is medieval, added to over the centuries. The stone comes from the quarries at Taynton. Upriver you can walk into the lovely Cotswold town of **Lechlade**.

BAMPTON

One of the nicest villages from which you can easily reach all the joys of the Cotswolds, is **Bampton,** perhaps best known for its Morris Dancers. It is full of history, close to the River Thames, some 12 miles west of Oxford and five miles south of Witney.

Edward the Confessor gave the estate at Bampton to his great friend and tutor, Leofric. It was a busy place then and he was one of the Royal Masons who were required to provide for the King and his household when they visited, but it was an expensive privilege.

The **Church**, along with those of Burford and Witney is among the largest in West Oxfordshire. The oldest parts of the building are probably Saxon. The Church we see now is mostly the result of remodelling carried out about 1270. At this time the spire was added and the aisle built.

However, a great deal of Norman work remains and it is interesting to spend some time 'spotting the styles'.

Other buildings well worth a look at are the **Public Library**, formerly the Grammar School, which was completed in 1653. There are a number of houses to be admired, including the stuccoed last Georgian **Manor House** and the **Deanery**, to the west of the Church, which is mostly 17th Century.

The remains of **Bampton Castle** are incorporated into **Ham Court**. **Weald House** was originally built in the 17th Century, but was extensively remodelled about 1730. There are many less grand houses in the centre, around which it is a delight to wander.

WITNEY

We now take the A4095 northwards to **Witney**. Wool was the economic base of life here, just as in so many of the places we have visited in this chapter, and the town is famous for its blankets which have been made here for centuries. The **Blanket Hall** in High Street has on it the arms of the Witney Company of Weavers. It was built for the weighing and measuring of blankets, in an age before rigid standardisation.

There is also a **Butter Cross** in Market Place, a steep roof on rustic-looking stone columns. It was probably built about 1600. Church Green has wide grass verges with pleasant houses set back from the road, and the Church at the south end, **St Mary's**, provides a dramatic focus.

Built in the 13th Century it is very spacious and the central tower and spire have been compared with Oxford Cathedral in their impact. Some elaborate chantry chapels were added in the 14th Century with a clerestory and a parapet with gargoyles around the whole Church in the 15th. Unfortunately the interior, having undergone restoration in the 19th Century, is rather a disappointment after the magnificent exterior.

STANDLAKE

Leaving Witney, we turn south on the A415 towards **Standlake**. Here the **Church** is well worth a visit. It has an unusual west tower, octagonal, with a small spire. The romantically-named **Gaunt House**, half a mile east of the village, was fortified and besieged during the Civil War. Most of what we see now, however, was built in about 1660.

Pause to look at the **New Bridge**, built at the point where the Thames meets the Windrush. Its six pointed arches make a fitting farewell to the current chapter, dominated by the Evenlode and the Windrush, and an introduction to the next, where the Thames will take over.

The Vale of the White Horse

Kingston House, near Kingston Bagpuize

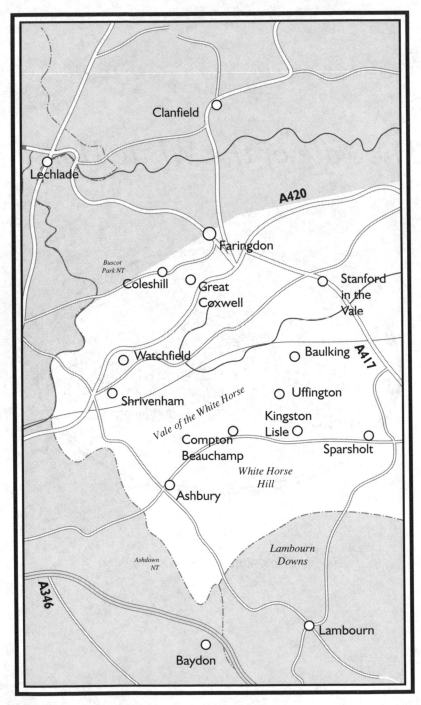

Clanfield

Lechlade

A420

Faringdon

*Buscot
Park NT*

Coleshill

Great
Coxwell

Stanford
in the
Vale

Watchfield

Baulking

A417

Shrivenham

Uffington

Vale of the White Horse

Kingston
Lisle

Compton
Beauchamp

Sparsholt

*White Horse
Hill*

Ashbury

*Ashdown
NT*

*Lambourn
Downs*

A346

Lambourn

Baydon

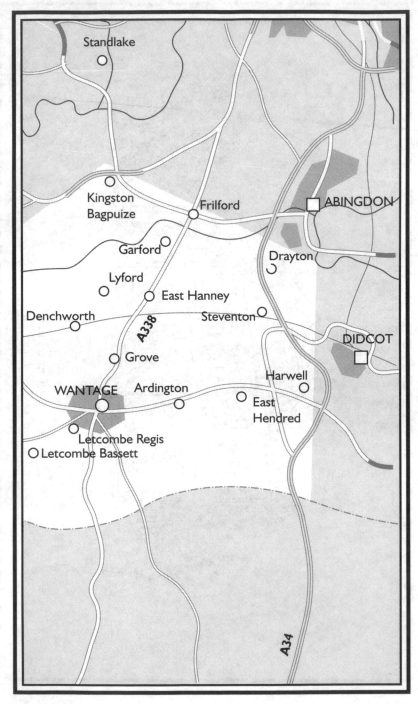

Standlake

Kingston
Bagpuize

Frilford

ABINGDON

Garford

Drayton

Lyford

East Hanney

Denchworth

Steventon

DIDCOT

A338

Grove

Harwell

WANTAGE

Ardington

East
Hendred

Letcombe Regis

Letcombe Bassett

A34

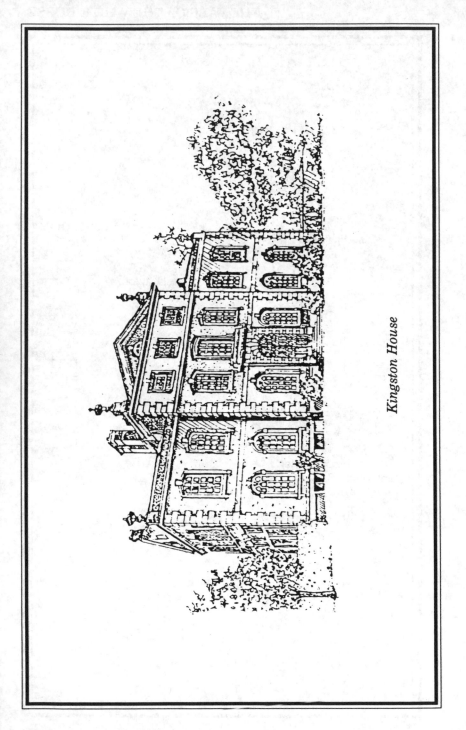

Kingston House

CHAPTER FIVE

The Vale of the White Horse

The Thames forms the northern boundary of this chapter and first we turn back towards its source to explore the southern side of the valley upriver from our crossing point in Chapter Four. Then we shall head southwards to the rising land of the Downs, classic chalk country with grassy, rolling hills and clumps of trees, often including the handsome, grey-barked beech. These Downs form part of the great ridge of chalk which runs across south and east England from Weymouth Bay to the Wash. Along the crest of it at this point runs the Ridgeway, the ancient track we shall meet more than once in this chapter.

Lower down, in the valleys of the little river Ock and the Thames, the land is more fertile and more intensively farmed.

KINGSTON BAGPUIZE

Our first destination for this chapter is **Kingston Bagpuize**. The name Tweedsmuir is usually associated with John Buchan and his famous novel 'The 39 Steps' but here live Lord and Lady Tweedsmuir at the beautiful Charles II Manor, **Kingston House**, a wonderful example of symmetry and fine architecture.

Lord and Lady Tweedsmuir or their friends act as your guides around the house, pointing out many things that you may otherwise miss but at the same time giving you breathing space to take in the magnificence of the cantilevered staircase, for example, or the handsome proportions of the panelled rooms. The furniture is particularly lovely and there are some fine pictures.

The house was built before 1670 and Sir Roger Pratt may have been the architect. You can see definite signs of the influence of Inigo Jones of whom Sir Roger was a disciple. Apart from the beauty of the house it has that special feeling only to be found in houses beloved by the family who live in them.

The gardens also are works of love. Miss Marlie Raphael lived here and for some 30 years she was the organiser of the Berkshire National Gardens Scheme. During that time she developed the present garden, and her niece, Lady Tweedsmuir, continues her work today.

The lawns fringed with fine trees, give way to a charming Woodland Garden with many unusual flowering shrubs and bulbs, and an herbaceous border. Seventeenth Century stable buildings surround a courtyard, while in another part of the garden you will discover an early Georgian gazebo built over an Elizabethan cock-pit.

A visit is an afternoon of enchantment. The opening times to the public are from April 1st until the 30th September on Sundays and Bank Holiday Mondays from 2.30pm-5.30pm.

GARFORD

Leaving that unusually named village, we take a minor road south across the river Ock and turn north and east to **Garford**. There is little to be seen here now but excavation has revealed that the village was inhabited in iron-age times. The earliest structures revealed by excavations were timber-built round huts with pits for storing grain. Towards the end of prehistory a shrine was built and a ploughshare, which had been deliberately buried beside one of the timber beams supporting the building, was found, as were a miniature bronze sword and shield, obviously offerings to the deity of the shrine.

With the coming of the Romans the site seems to have kept its religious significance, for a Romano-Celtic temple was built there at the end of the 1st Century AD. This was a sizable building for the time, a rectangle with sides 25ft long. About the same time a stone-built circular structure some 36ft in diameter was built just to the south of the temple. What was its use is unknown, but this was clearly an important centre of worship over a long period of time - the site seems to have been used for religious purposes well into the 5th Century.

FARINGDON

Faringdon is our next destination. The attractive name comes from the Old English for Fern Hill and it is a pleasant market town with an old market hall and some picturesque inns. The **Church** is in a very prominent situation at the top of the market place, a large cross-shaped building which has developed from a late Norman core. At one time it had a steeple, but this was destroyed during the Civil War. However, the ironwork on the main door has survived intact for 700 years and the Unton family are still commemorated by 16th Century memorials.

The beautiful 18th Century **Faringdon House**, to the west of the Church, was built by George III's poet laureate, Henry James Pye, some of whose family also have memorials in the Church.

Pye's main claim to fame seems to have been that he was universally ridiculed by the rest of the literary scene. He was also forced to sell the house after becoming an MP, partly due to election expenses. Political campaigning at the time was largely a question of how many voters the candidate could afford to bribe, so it was perhaps hardly surprising that he got into debt.

The house has other literary associations, one of them derived from a rather more chilling episode in the history of the family, which had lived in an earlier house on the same site. Legend has it that the headless ghost of Hampden Pye haunts the grounds. He was serving in the Navy as a midshipman when his stepmother, who wanted her own son to inherit, plotted with his captain to make sure he did not return alive. He was indeed killed in action at sea during which his head was blown off. This does not seem to have been a result of his step-mother's plot, but all the same he is said to have returned to haunt her.

This affecting story was told to Richard Harris Barham by Mary Anne Hughes, whom we shall meet again later in this chapter. Barham used it, under the name of 'The Legend of Hamilton Tighe' in one of his Ingoldsby Legends. These comic, irreverent, verses were published in book form in 1840 and were very popular.

Finally, in the 1930s, the house became the property of Lord Berners, remembered as a musician, author, painter and wit. Amongst his output were two ballet scores, one of which, The Wedding Bouquet, was based on a play by Gertrude Stein. He is said to have been the original for Lord Merlin in Nancy Mitford's novel 'The Pursuit of Love'. Perhaps life at the real Faringdon house in Lord Berners' day might have been something like her description of that at 'Merlinford':

'Modern music streamed perpetually from Merlinford, and he had built a small but exquisite playhouse in the garden, where his astonished neighbours were sometimes invited to attend such puzzlers as Cocteau plays, the opera 'Mahagonny', or the latest Dada extravagances from Paris. As Lord Merlin was a famous practical joker, it was sometimes difficult to know where the jokes ended and the culture began. I think he was not always perfectly certain himself.'

Perhaps most important, as far as present-day Faringdon is concerned, he built the folly on top of Faringdon Hill, across the road to the east, in 1935. The 140-ft high tower is made of brick, has an arcaded look-out room and culminates in a Gothic lantern tower. It was probably the last folly of any size to be built in Britain.

One definition of a folly is 'a costly but useless structure built to satisfy the whim of some eccentric' and they are perhaps out of tune with our pragmatic times. They were, however, commonly built to enhance a landscape by making a view more interesting. Perhaps that is something we should think about more often in our modern buildings. In Faringdon Lord Berners' folly can be seen as the last of a noble lineage.

GREAT COXWELL

Leaving Faringdon on the B4019, and turning off to the right brings us to **Great Coxwell**. The reason for our visit is its magnificent 13th Century **Tithe Barn**, originally built to serve the needs of the Cistercian abbey at Beaulieu in Hampshire.

The tithe was a tenth of the annual profits obtained from the occupation of land, whether from animals or from crops and was a tax designed to support the parish priest dating back to the 9th Century. As in the case of Great Coxwell, where the parish was provided with a priest by a monastery, the tithes went to that monastery and were stored and processed in barns which belonged to the Order. The Cistercians had between 2000 and 2900 such barns and this is the only survivor.

Its size is astonishing - 152ft long by 44ft wide by 48ft high at the ridge, but it was by no means the largest known to have existed. One was known to be 303ft long!

This was strictly a working building without decoration or aesthetic intentions, in which threshing the corn from the harvested sheaves and winnowing the chaff from the grain would have taken place, later being used for the storage of grain and straw. Nevertheless its mellow stone walls, tiled roof and perfect proportions make it as pleasing a building as many a great church. The posts which support the roof give the impression of a nave and aisles and William Morris, who trained as an architect, thought it 'as noble as a cathedral' and 'the finest piece of architecture in England'.

BUSCOT

Returning to the A417 Lechlade road take us to two National Trust properties at **Buscot**. **Buscot Old Parsonage** is a lovely house with a small garden on the banks of the Thames, built of Cotswold stone with a stone tiled roof in 1703.

Buscot Park is a much grander experience, a house with fine paintings and furniture built in 1780 and set in attractive gardens with a lake. This classical example of a late Georgian house contains the Faringdon Art Collection, which includes paintings by Rembrandt, Murillo and Reynolds.

One room of the house is decorated with a series of pictures painted by the pre-Raphaelite Edward Burne-Jones, an close friend of William Morris, whose house at Kelmscott can be seen across the river from Buscot. Burne-Jones was greatly drawn to subjects from myth and legend and the Buscot Park paintings, in the thick gilded frames he designed for them, tell the story of the Sleeping Beauty, or Briar Rose. They were painted in 1890.

Anyone particularly interested in Burne-Jones should also visit the Church, where a stained glass window showing the Good Shepherd was designed by him in 1891, when he was working with William Morris's firm Morris and Co. The Church itself is very nicely situated, by the river just outside the village.

Buscot is a National Trust village, and it's here you'll find **Buscot Village Shop and Tea Rooms**, just three minutes from the Thames path, weir and lock. The well-stocked shop has, amongst other things, an interesting range of dried flowers, paintings and costume jewellery. Owned by Gerald and Brenda for the past two years, it has become a popular stopping point for many visitors to the area. Brenda does most of the home cooking and her cakes, pastries, soup, sandwiches and baguettes are to be recommended. In the summer, cream teas are served *al fresco* in the garden, and home grown vegetables and plants are available for purchase. Suitable access is available for disabled visitors.

Buscot Village Shop and Tea Rooms, Buscot Tel 01367 252142

COLESHILL

From here we take the minor road south to **Coleshill**, where only mid-17th Century gate piers, some stables and a dovecote remain as a memorial to **Coleshill House**, built around 1650 but sadly burned down and demolished in the 1950s.

Next we join the B4000 and drive south into the Downland, heading towards **Ashdown House**, north of Lambourn. The house was built in the 17th Century and has a curiously tall, narrow look about it, with a roof arranged as a viewing platform and a cupola perched on the top. Indeed the views from it are very fine.

Inside the house seems to be arranged around the great staircase which rises from ground level to attic. It was built about 1665 by the first Earl of Craven, who devoted his life and much of his wealth to Elizabeth, daughter of King James I, who became Queen of Bohemia. The house was conceived as a sort of shrine to her. It is set amongst gardens and woodlands which offer inviting walks.

COMPTON BEAUCHAMP

We return now return north over the Downs in search of some of the most ancient of all England's ancient monuments, but on the way it is worth calling in at the pretty Church at Compton Beauchamp. It is dedicated to St Swithun, not a very common choice. Perhaps it is because St Swithun was Bishop at Winchester in the late 9th Century and was hence something of a local boy made good. Little else is known about him, and he is mainly remembered nowadays for the folklore tradition which says that if it rains on his day, 15th July, it will rain for the next 40 days. The interior of the Church is very attractive and was decorated with much white and gold in the 1930s.

UFFINGTON

In the nearby village of Uffington the literary imagination of Thomas Hughes, author of the classic Tom Brown's Schooldays, and grandson of Mary Anne Hughes, mentioned earlier in the Chapter, was fired, perhaps by the surroundings, perhaps by his grandmother's tales. The early chapters of his book deal with Tom Brown's childhood in the village, and the White Horse, Uffington Castle and the ancient Ridgeway track are described.

There is a memorial to him in the Church, where his grandfather was the vicar and in which he was baptised. It is an imposing building of the 13th Century except for the octagonal tower which was built in the 18th Century to replace a spire brought down in a storm.

This village is perhaps best known for the Uffington White Horse, where on the hillside a mysteriously abstract and very beautiful figure of a horse some 400ft long has been created by removing the turf to expose the gleaming white chalk beneath. It is a startling sight which can be seen from a wide area, and many a tantalising glimpse of it has been caught through the window of a train travelling through the valley below. Popular tradition links it with the victory of King Alfred over the Danes at the battle of Ashdown, which was fought somewhere on these Downs in 871, but modern scholarship now considers that it dates from about 100 BC.

If the White Horse is shrouded in mystery, it is in a place full of similarly mysterious remains. Above it is the Iron Age camp known as Uffington Castle, and to one side is a knoll known as Dragon's Hill where legend has it that St George killed the dragon.

The climb up to the top of the hill rewards you with some fine views over the surrounding countryside and following the ancient track which forms part of the modern Ridgeway long distance footpath brings you, just over a mile south-west, to **Wayland's Smithy**. This is a prehistoric burial place, and originally a long mound of earth would have covered a stone chamber. Now the stones, made from a variety of sandstone known as sarsen found in the valley below, are exposed and stand in a little wood, mysterious natural sculptures.

The Smithy was built about 2000 BC. Wayland the Smith was the smith of the gods, figuring in a number of bloodthirsty Teutonic and Norse myths, a cunning craftsman fashioning precious jewels or powerful swords according to the needs of the story. The local legend was that if you left your horse and a coin at the Smithy you would return to find the horse shod by Wayland. Sir Walter Scott made used of the story in his novel Kenilworth, published in 1821.

KINGSTON LISLE

Descending into the nearby village of **Kingston Lisle**, we have yet to finish with things prehistoric. A little south west of the **Church** (in which there are some interesting 14th Century paintings) is the **Blowing Stone**, a sarsen stone pierced with holes which, tradition tells, was blown on by King Alfred to summon his men to do battle with the Danes.

This really is countryside to fire the most unromantic of imaginations. It is here that we meet again Mary Anne Hughes, who probably lived in **Kingston Lisle House**. She was a great expert on the folklore of the area and it was she who told the story of the unfortunate little Pye midshipman to Richard Barham. She was also a friend of Sir Walter Scott, Charles Dickens and the Victorian writer of historical novels, Harrison Ainsworth. Ainsworth stayed with Mrs Hughes on many occasions and his novel 'Guy Fawkes', published in 1841, was dedicated to her. In another of his books, Old St Pauls, he describes some of the scenery of the area and the character of Mrs Compton is based on Mrs Hughes, whom we shall meet once more in this Chapter.

SPARSHOLT

Leaving Kingston Lisle we make a diversion to see the **Church of the Holy Cross** at **Sparsholt**, for it is a fine building set in a pretty village. Visitors will enjoy the wooden carvings of a knight and two ladies behind a wooden screen in the south transept. The Church has other interesting examples of woodcarving, some brasses and examples of old glass.

The village Inn is a wonderful 400-year-old Free House, **The Star**, much frequented by many top horse breeders, trainers and jockeys who live in and around the village. Visitors will receive a very warm welcome from hosts Allan and Marie Fowles, and be greeted by a fine traditional interior with wooden floor, beamed ceilings and feature stone fireplace with beam lintel. The 30-seater dining room serves plenty of home cooked food with an extensive menu that includes such culinary delights as Steak and Guinness Pie and the home-cured ham is a house speciality.

The accommodation comprises eight en-suite guest bedrooms situated in a fully renovated barn, part of the original building and located in a quiet annexe which offers plenty of private parking. You will find all the usual home comforts in your bedroom including colour TV, complimentary tea and coffee tray, disabled en-suite facilities and plenty of good quality furnishings and decor. If you enjoy horse riding then why not bring your horse along with you, for there are plenty of stabling facilities just around the corner from the Star. Outside there is a large rear garden which proves very popular with visitors in those long summer months. Discover this oasis yourself as it is situated just off the B4507 Wantage to Ashbury road.

The Star Inn, Watery Lane, Sparsholt, nr Wantage Tel 01253 751539

BAULKING

There are two more churches in the area worthy of our attention. At **Baulking** is a small, somewhat isolated building which has retained much of the appearance it would have had in the 17th and 18th Centuries, though its origins go back to the mid-13th Century. The chancel and nave are almost separated by a wall pierced by a door and windows, a most unusual feature.

STANFORD-IN-THE-VALE

At **Stanford in the Vale**, by contrast, there is a spacious Church with medieval ceilings. The churchyard has several attractive old headstones to look at, and would seem a good way to round off a day full of romantic and mysterious sights.

WANTAGE

We now travel into **Wantage**, the birthplace of Alfred the Great, who lived from 849-99, and there is a statue of him in the market place. He was King of the West Saxons and came to the throne at a time when the Danes had overrun most of England north of the Thames. His great victory at Ashdown, and eight other battles fought that year, gave only a temporary respite from their incursions and in 878 he was forced to flee to the Somerset marshes.

Eventually the tide turned and Alfred established a period of relative peace during which he was overlord of England. Although he lived in what we think of as the Dark Ages, he was an educated man who had visited Rome as a boy. He was an important influence in reviving learning and translated many documents himself as well as codifying the laws of his Kingdom.

Wantage has all the usual facilities for shopping and other needs, and there are some pleasant Georgian and Victorian houses, especially around the Market Place. The **Vale and Downland Museum Centre** is very interesting. It is in a house dating from the 16th and 17th Centuries in Church Street with modern extensions and a reconstructed barn. Its displays are dedicated to the geology, history and archaeology of Wantage and the Vale of the White Horse.

The Church, dating from the later 13th Century, is worth a visit. There is a rather touching monument to William Wilmot, who died in 1684, which depicts two figures with a baby between them. There are also some good monumental brasses, including one to Sir Ives Fitzwarin who died in 1414.

In Faringdon Road are the buildings of **St Mary's Convent**, built as the home of the Wantage Sisterhood, an Anglican Order, in the 19th Century. Three well-known Victorian architects were involved in designing buildings for it. G E Street undertook the earliest of them in 1855-6. He is best known for his building of the Law Courts in London. William Butterfield, architect of Keble College, Oxford, was responsible for the Noviciate building to the north and the Chapel, begun in 1887, is the work of John Pearson, architect of Truro Cathedral.

The town presents an ideal opportunity to explore more of the **Ridgeway**, just a mile and a half away, which we last visited above Uffington. The full length of the present day **Ridgeway Long Distance Footpath** is a Countryside Commission National Trail and is 85 miles long, starting at Overton Hill near Avebury in the west and ending at Ivinghoe Beacon near Tring. However, it is the western section of the Countryside Commission's route which we are exploring here, following the prehistoric track high over the downs. It is a path from which can be seen some stunning scenery and where traces of our most distant recognisable ancestors can be seen.

The Ridgeway was also one of the favourite haunts of Richard Jefferies (1848- 87), the son of a Wiltshire farmer and writer on nature who has recently attracted a new generation of readers, the result of our increasing awareness of the importance of the environment and our place in it. His powers of observation of the natural world are strikingly evident from his writings.

Jefferies' description of the Ridgeway catches something of the sense of being in a separate world, where time runs slower than down in the valley. 'A broad green track runs for many a long, long mile across the Downs, now following the ridges, now winding past at the foot of a grassy slope, then stretching away through cornfield and fallow. It is distinct from the wagon-tracks which cross it here and there, for these are local only ... Plough and harrow press hard on the ancient track, and yet dare not encroach upon it. With varying width, from twenty to fifty yards, it runs like a green ribbon...'

The Sparrow, South Street, Letcombe Regis Tel 01253 763228

110

Walking eastwards along the Ridgeway track gives you the opportunity to explore **Segsbury Camp**, sometimes known as **Letcombe Castle**. This is a massive iron age hill fort enclosing 26 acres of ground. It dominates the Vale over Wantage and must have been of prime strategic military importance. The low-lying Vale of the slow-moving waters of the river Ock making its way down to the Thames at Abingdon would have been very marshy then. The roads followed firm ground and to have command of them would be essential in dangerous times.

LETCOMBE REGIS

Immediately to the south of Wantage is **Letcombe Regis**. Located in South Street close to the village green is **The Sparrow**, a 300-year-old building which became a village pub some 150 years ago. It's a typical village pub with low ceilings, tiled floors, lots of brasses on display, dartboard and pool table. There is a woodburning stove to keep a cosy atmosphere on colder days.

The lounge bar has an eating area where children can also be served and offers a good selection of food. Daily specials are displayed on the blackboard and the well-kept real ales will add to your enjoyment. The Sparrow has three guest bedrooms which are in the converted stables so you may like to stop over and waken to the tranquillity of the village, enjoying a good pub breakfast before moving on.

LETCOMBE BASSETT

Just below Segsbury camp is the tiny village of **Letcombe Bassett** which has a notable place in literary history. It is called Cresscombe in 'Jude the Obscure', which Thomas Hardy wrote while staying there. Jonathan Swift spent the summer of 1714 at the Rectory and was visited by Alexander Pope.

GROVE

A short detour north of Wantage brings us to **Grove**, alongside the A338.

Although Ian and Jackie have only recently taken up management of **The Volunteer**, they are already well into the swim of things. The Volunteer presents a crisp white exterior with tub shrubs and window boxes set amongst well-established trees and provides a good car park and patio. Jackie collects pot pigs and things, so visitors have something to muse over - ask about Henry the missing pig!

The Volunteer, Station Road, Grove Tel 01253 769557

There's a nice friendly atmosphere and Real ales with a Guest monthly are served from the wooden bar. The air conditioning unit keeps the air clean and the temperature comfortable. Join in a game of Aunt Sally, which is a local game similar to skittles. The Volunteer has three guest bedrooms with en-suite facilities at very reasonable cost. The menu offers a selection of starters, grills, salads, snacks, sandwiches and children's choice. A roast is served every Sunday.

ARDINGTON

To the east of Wantage in **Ardington** village, just off the A417 is **Ardington House**, built in 1721 of grey brick with red brick facings, an attractive combination of colours. Inside, the house has an imposing staircase and a panelled dining room with a painted ceiling.

The **Church** is interesting, particularly to fans of Victorian ecclesiastical architecture. The tower and spire and a north chapel are Victorian, as is the stencilled decoration in the chancel. However, the Church has much earlier parts, starting with the north door, dating from the early 13th Century, which has a round arch decorated with mouldings and some dogtooth patterning.

Hendred Vineyard, Sheephouse Barn, Ludbridge, East Hendred Tel 01235 833277

EAST HENDRED

Hendred Vineyard covers roughly six acres and is on the sloping ground to the west of the village of **East Hendred**, one of the 'Spring Line' villages that sit just below the Downs in the Vale of the White Horse. The original Vineyard was planted in 1970 to produce white wine, and in 1976 the owners, Mr and Mrs Mackinnon, saw their first yield bottled. The 1995 vintage from the new Vineyard is a blend of two varieties, Seyval Blanc and Madeleine Angevine, that has produced a dry, crisp and aromatic wine. The grapes are harvested and immediately processed in the small winery attached to the vineyard so capturing the freshness that is so important to the quality of the wine. Weekends are the best time for visits and wine tasting. Open all year round 10am to 6pm, though it is advisable to phone first. Suitable for disabled visitors and children.

STEVENTON

A short distance north of East Hendred, adjoining the A4185 is **Steventon**. In the High Street will be found **The Fox Inn**. Painted in a sandy yellow finish, it is an old building from the 1800s at which time it was probably thatched. The Fox is open all day every day for food and drink. It has a very pleasant and cosy bar, a dining area and separate restaurant in which to enjoy good quality food. Larry, the present landlord keeps his real ales in top condition with a guest ale changing weekly.

At the time of writing The Fox has six en-suite bedrooms which are modern and brightly furnished with television and hospitality tray. However, a further 16 bedrooms are being built in 1997 when its facilities will be more like a Motel.

The Fox Inn, High Street, Steventon Tel 01235 821228

Arriving at **The North Star** public house in Steventon is truly an experience in turning back the clock! Jack Cox was born here 70 years ago and followed in the footsteps of his parents and grandparents who have owned the inn before him since 1842, giving 154 years of family ownership - something of a record, we think! Built in the mid-1400s it was probably first a coaching inn; the old Causeway which runs close by was built by the monks in the 12th Century.

The North Star, The Causeway, Steventon Tel 01253 831309

THE VALE OF THE WHITE HORSE

The North Star gained its present name from the first passenger train to run from London to Bristol and is a delightful cottage style building with an equally pleasant garden. This is indeed a step back into the past since there is no bar as such, drinks being served through a door behind which real ales are drawn directly from the barrels and bottles of beer and spirits find their home on the floor. The atmosphere is very cosy with very old oak beams and displays of horse brasses, rather like drinking in someone's house. Enjoy home-cooked ham, pork and cheese rolls at lunchtime and stroll in the garden soaking up the atmosphere of this wonderfully preserved historic pub. No doubt Jack has a tale or two to tell!

From here we set off to our next Chapter and the heart of Oxfordshire.

The Heart of Oxfordshire

Stanton Harcourt Manor

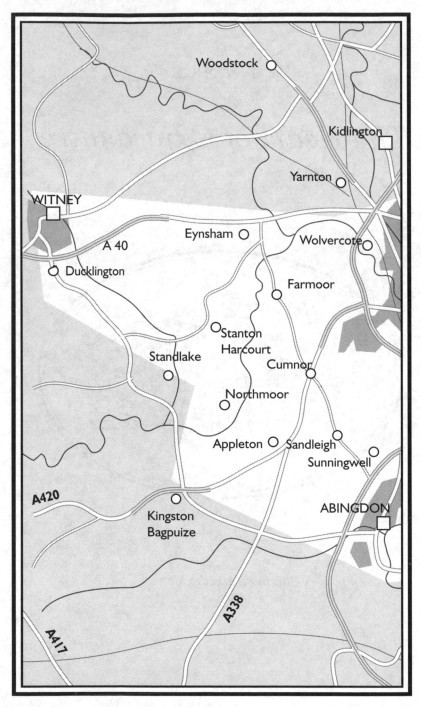

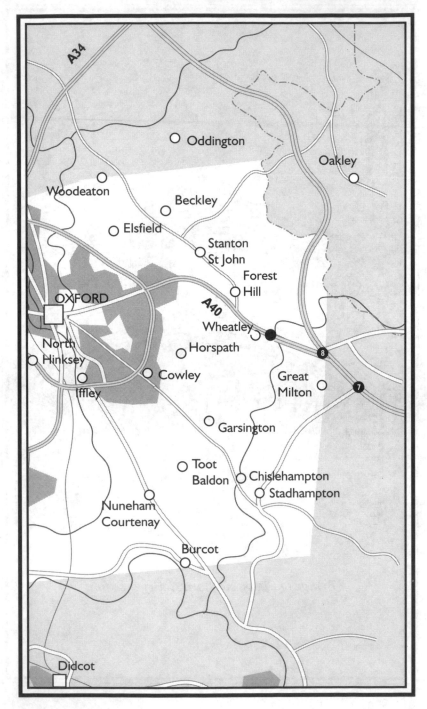

Bridge of Sighs, Hertford College, Oxford

The Heart of Oxfordshire

This chapter takes us on an exploration of Oxford and the area surrounding that much-described city. Edward Thomas thought that the countryside immediately around Oxford was transformed by its very presence.

'I know not how to describe the spirit which turns a few miles of peaceful southern country into something unique. But if I mention a wood or a stream, let the reader paint in, as it were, something sweet and shadowy in the distance, with his imagination or recollection; let it be as some subtle perfume in a pot pourri which makes it different from all others.'

The subtle perfume is of course, the distant vision of the city itself - the 'dreaming spires' which are mentioned by everyone when talking of Oxford. But how many who use the words know their origin? In fact they come from a poem by Matthew Arnold, 'And that sweet City with her dreaming spires, She needs not June for beauty's heightening.' Indeed she does not, one of the few places capable of being beautiful even on a grey day in November.

ABINGDON

Our travels for this chapter begin in **Abingdon**, an attractive town with a pleasing name if a bit puzzling. It first appears as Abbandune in 968 when King Edgar granted a charter to an Abbey there. Abbandune means 'the hill of Aebba', the 'dune' deriving from the Old English word for 'hill'. Yet Abingdon, then as now, was not on a hill, but on flat land by the Thames.

The town owes its origin to that Monastery, which was founded in 675, growing up around a market held immediately in front of the Abbey gateway. And it is this gateway which is the most impressive remaining monument to what was once a thriving religious community. It was built in the late 15th Century, though of the three arches we see now the southern one is a 19th Century reconstruction. Above the middle arch is a niche which originally held a statue of the Virgin Mary.

Built on to the gateway is the **Church of St Nicholas**, which retains some Norman features although there is a lot of later work. Not much is left of the **Abbey** considering its original extent, but some of the secular buildings have survived and can be visited. The **Long Gallery**, partly built of stone and partly timber-framed, dates from about 1500, while the **Checker Hall** is a 13th Century stone building with an unusual chimney.

Apart from the remnants of the abbey, Abingdon has many interesting buildings. The **County Hall** in the Market Place impressed even Sir Nickolaus Pevsner who commented 'Of the free-standing town halls of England with open ground floors this is the grandest.' It was built from 1678-82 and makes for a very harmonious whole, with its warm brown stone and hipped roof topped off with balustrade and cupola. It was built to house the local market (at street level), while upstairs was the court. Inside there is now a museum devoted to local history and archaeology, well worth a visit.

The **Church of St Helen**, whose steeple dominates the view southwards along the street, dates largely from the 15th and 16th Centuries, when Abingdon grew rich from the wool trade and remodelled the existing church to create something more spacious. The main glory of the building is the ceiling of the Lady Chapel, which was painted with figures of prophets and kings at the very end of the 14th Century.

The churchyard, entered through an Elizabethan arch is most interesting. It contains a curious small brick building, the blowing chamber for the church organ. There are also three sets of almshouses. In the centre is **Christ's Hospital**, originally built in 1446, though the cloister walk and porch are much later. On the right are **Twitty's Almshouses** of 1707 and to the left **Brick Alley Almshouses** built in 1718. It is a charming scene, and as Pevsner comments 'no other churchyard anywhere has anything like it.'

Abingdon is a place which amply repays time spent simply wandering about the streets, soaking up the atmosphere. There are many attractive houses to be seen, particularly **Stratton House**, in Bath Street, built in red brick about 1722 featuring a handsome doorway with doric pilasters.

The view of the town from the bridge should not be missed. The bridge itself dates from 1416, though it was extensively rebuilt in 1927. The town has plenty of open space, too.

Abingdon was the birthplace of Dorothy Miller Richardson, whose novels, written between 1915 and 1938, pioneer the 'stream of consciousness' method.

Another literary association is with John Ruskin, who lodged at the **Crown and Thistle Inn** - try to look in on its quaint courtyard - on Bridge Street. He lived there in 1871 after having been appointed Slade Professor of Art at Oxford, before moving into rooms at Corpus Christi College. Ruskin was an interesting character, little read nowadays, but immensely influential and controversial in his time.

As an art critic he was an early champion of the Pre-Raphaelite painters with whom Burne-Jones, whose paintings we saw at Buscot Park, and Morris, whose house we saw in Kelmscott, were associated. Ruskin has some similarities with Morris, in that the squalor in which the poor of his time were living revolted him so much that he too was led into seeing far-reaching social change as the only remedy. But while Morris was a revolutionary, Ruskin was more of a philanthropist, spending much of his large inherited fortune on schemes to help the working people. His enthusiasm for the Pre-Raphaelites seems to have survived the fact that his wife left him to marry (after her marriage to Ruskin had been annulled) Sir John Everett Millais, another member of the group.

In more recent times Abingdon has been home to the MG car factory, which turned out thousands of open topped sports cars and sporting saloons until its demise in the early 1980s.

The public house which occupies the corner of Thomas Street and Bridge Street is known as the **Broad Face**, and with such a name it was inevitable that various fanciful stories concerning its origin should have arisen in the past, but the actual derivation of the name seems unknown. The records show that the pub was leased from the Borough by John Francis Spenlove in 1840 and described as being newly erected. However, a previous building was occupied by various brewers' tenants and in 1734 was named as the Broad Face on a polling list.

Recent new tenants to the Broad Face, John and Denise have settled in and offer a nice selection of meals and snacks including toasted baguettes, salads, ploughmans, seafood platter, home made curry and steaks with daily specials and vegetarian selections. Sunday roast lunch is proving especially popular. Real ales with an occasional guest ale are supplied by Morland. There are good facilities for disabled customers.

The Broad Face, Bridge Street, Abingdon Tel 01235 524516

123

SUNNINGWELL

Leaving Abingdon we take the B4017 and make a stop at **Sunningwell**. Roger Bacon, the medieval philosopher and scientist who invented the magnifying glass, is believed to have used the tower of the Church as an observatory for his studies in astronomy after his return to Oxford from Paris in about 1250. He was a Franciscan monk and his scholarship caused problems due to the prejudices of his time. The head of his Order had him imprisoned in 1277 for 'suspected novelties' and he was only released just before his death in 1292.

The Church itself is an interesting one, with a unique seven-sided porch known as the Jewel Porch after John Jewel, who was rector at the time of its construction about 1551. He went on to become Bishop of Salisbury. Apart from the porch the Church, which is dedicated to St Leonard, is mostly perpendicular in style. It has an extremely interesting east window designed by J P Seddon, who restored the church in 1877. Seddon was a friend of William Morris and the Pre-Raphaelites and his window is clearly influenced by their aesthetic ideas.

From Sunningwell, head south-west towards the A420. Set back just a little way from the A420 is the village of Fyfield with its Manor, Church, green, and historic **White Hart Inn**. Built in the 15th Century as a Chantry House in the reign of Henry VI, it has a long and interesting history. When extensive repairs were carried out in 1963, the 15th Century arch-braced roof was uncovered and the interior was rearranged in such a way as to preserve all the other surviving features of the original building.

The White Hart, Fyfield Tel 01865 390585

A fine, wide-ranging menu to suit all tastes is offered, which seasonally includes venison, pheasant, partridge, pigeon and hare as well as a good selection of vegetarian meals and a reasonably-priced wine list. The

124

cellar restaurant gallery overlooks the restored hall with its mounted stags' heads and tapestry - the atmosphere is added to by candlelit tables and log fires. Open seven days a week with food served every lunchtime and evening. Not to be missed!

APPLETON

A short distance north, again along the A420 brings you to **Appleton**.

For a good lunchtime or evening meal, or just refreshment **The Thatched Tavern** (which has never been thatched) in the village is well worth a visit. This 16th Century building was converted to a pub some 200 years ago after being handed over by the Lord of the Manor for the benefit of the local thatchers. There is a full menu offering a good selection of grills, poultry and vegetarian dishes with daily specials served in the dining area, whilst lighter meals and snacks such as 'Thatchers lunch', jacket potatoes, scampi and sandwiches are served in the bar. The Sunday roast looks good and changes every week. Small parties can be catered for. Breakspears real ales are permanently available. Children are welcome and dogs on a lead.

The Thatched Tavern, Appleton Tel 01865 864814

CUMNOR

Further north, we pass through the village of **Cumnor**, which has an intriguing place in the byways of English history. In this village is the site of **Cumnor Place**, where in September 1560 the body of Amy Robsart was found at the foot of a staircase. She had been the wife of Robert Dudley, Earl of Leicester and favourite of Queen Elizabeth I. The house belonged at the time to one Anthony Forster and he is widely suspected of having arranged her death at the behest of her husband.

The house is gone, but the Church is worth investigating. It has a statue of 'good Queen Bess' (considered by some to have been party to the plot to do away with her favourite's wife), memorials to Amy and the ornate tomb of Anthony Forster. We also cross once again the footsteps of Matthew Arnold's scholar gipsy wandering on Cumnor Hill 'in days when wits were fresh and clear, And life ran gaily as the sparkling Thames'.

NORTH HINKSEY
North Hinksey has a reminder of rather more prosaic aspects of life in the past. Nowadays we take it for granted that we can turn on a tap in our kitchen or bathroom and water will flow out, forgetting when such a thing would have been an impossible dream. Here at North Hinksey there is a roofed reservoir built early in the 17th Century to collect and store water for Oxford's first water mains which was piped to a conduit in the city.

EYNSHAM
From Hinksey, rather than keeping to the busy main roads, a detour along the quiet B4044 will bring you to **Eynsham**, once the site of an important Benedictine Abbey, founded about 1005. Little now remains as it was demolished after the Reformation and much of the stone sold. The centre of Eynsham is quite attractive with stone cottages grouped around the Market Square, and for anyone tempted to try a boating holiday on the Thames this would be an excellent place to start. The Thames Hire Cruiser Association based here have 350 boats to choose from.

The name of the town immortalises a long-vanished farmer called Egon. The name was spelt Egonesham in a document of 571, which means either Egon's homestead or Egon's water meadow - being situated near both the Thames and the Evenlode the latter seems highly likely.

SOUTH LEIGH
To the south-west of the town along the minor roads is the village of **South Leigh**. Close to the 12th Century **Church**, world-famous for being where Wesley delivered his first sermon and for its glorious wall murals. Dylan Thomas moved to this peaceful and picturesque village of South Leigh and began writing 'Under Milk Wood',

Just two miles off the main A40, South Leigh is 3 miles from Witney, 9 miles from Oxford. You'll love it.

STANTON HARCOURT

A little further to the south on the B4449 is **Stanton Harcourt** and the famous **Manor House**. It could be reasonably argued that to have to open your own home to the general public to soften the demands of death duties, is a hard option. However the old maxim that the seed of adversity produces greater benefit has to apply at the Manor House, where the same family have lived for 850 years.

It was the death of William Edward, 2nd Viscount Harcourt in 1979 which led to this wonderful place being opened to the public. We should point out at this moment that the title is the second creation because as you will read further on, there were earlier Viscount Harcourts but the title died out. Lord Harcourt's daughter, The Hon. Mrs Gascoigne lives here now with her husband and family, opening the house and the gardens regularly, but it is wise to ring and confirm the opening times before visiting because they vary. The telephone number is 01865 881928.

From the moment you walk through the door you are aware of its great beauty and the wealth of history that has made it such a fine place. Yet not for one moment are you allowed to forget that this is a family home. You may well find the grandchildren's toys about or books left open on tables.

The Manor of Stanton came to the Harcourt family as the dowry of Isabel de Camville on her marriage in the 12th Century to Robert de Harcourt, who died in 1202. She was the daughter of Richard de Camville and Millicent, cousin of Queen Adeliza, second wife of Henry I. The Queen gave the Lordship of Stanton to Isabel as a wedding gift, and the Manor has been known as Stanton Harcourt from the time of that marriage.

The original house, one of the earliest unfortified Manor Houses in England, was built over the period 1380 to 1470 and comprised three sides of a square. The western side contained servants' quarters and offices, including the Great Kitchen with its conical roof, which is still standing. The north side, which contained the Hall and Great and Little Parlours and the Chapel, has disappeared except for the north east corner known as 'Pope's Tower'. The eastern side containing the family bedrooms has now entirely disappeared. The present rose garden is on the site of the Inner Courtyard and the croquet lawn on that of the Outer Courtyard, reached through the Porter's Lodge which forms the centre of the entrance front of the present house. The arch of the original gateway may still be seen from the village street.

The house was the home of the Harcourt family until the death, in 1688, of Sir Philip Harcourt, when it was left as a jointure to his widow, Elizabeth, his second wife, daughter and heiress of John Lee of Ankerwyke.

Shortly after the death of Sir Philip, she returned to her family home, sold all the furniture and other contents of Stanton Harcourt and allowed the house to fall into a state of complete disrepair. Her stepson, the first Viscount Harcourt and Lord Chancellor to Queen Anne built himself a house three miles away at Cokethorpe and in order to save expense he had the more ruinous parts of Stanton Harcourt pulled down, using much of the stone for his new house, Nuneham. Since that time the gatehouse at Stanton Harcourt has been used at various times as a Dower House until, on the sale of Nuneham in 1948, it became again the family home.

Pope's Tower acquired its name when the tower was lent to Alexander Pope in the years 1717 and 1718 as a place in which to work on his translation of Homer's Iliad. Pope recorded this by writing on one of the windows: 'In the year 1718, I, Alexander Pope, finished here the fifth volume of Homer'.

The ground floor consists of the domestic **Chapel** of the original Manor House. The chancel which dates from 1470 has a fan vaulted stone roof and is divided from the body of the Chapel by an archway over which, facing the altar, you can just see the outline of what was once an opening through which members of the family were able to join in Mass from the Assembly Room over the nave which was only ever used for retainers. There is a lot to see here such as the fine red velvet armchair which was the throne of the Hon. Edward Harcourt who was Archbishop of York between 1807-47.

The nave of the Chapel has a wooden ceiling which was once painted with a blue background, having gilded stars in the middle of each panel with red and gold mouldings.

At the west end of the **Assembly Room** the window originally formed the entrance from the gallery of the Great Parlour. The room over the Chancel of the Chapel, which is oak panelled, was the priest's living room, and above that a simple room was his bedroom. Above that again is a room with panelling of the period of Charles II which Pope used as a study.

The **Great Kitchen** is the oldest surviving medieval kitchen in the country. The exact date of the foundations are not known but they are undoubtedly the earliest part of the original house and almost certainly date from about 1380. The building is square and the roof octagonal. There is no chimney, the smoke from both the open fireplace, the remains of which can still be seen, and the ovens, collected in the cone of the roof and went out when the wooden louvres were opened, according to the direction of the wind. The Kitchen is unique in England. There is something similar to it at Glastonbury in the Abbot's Kitchen but that one

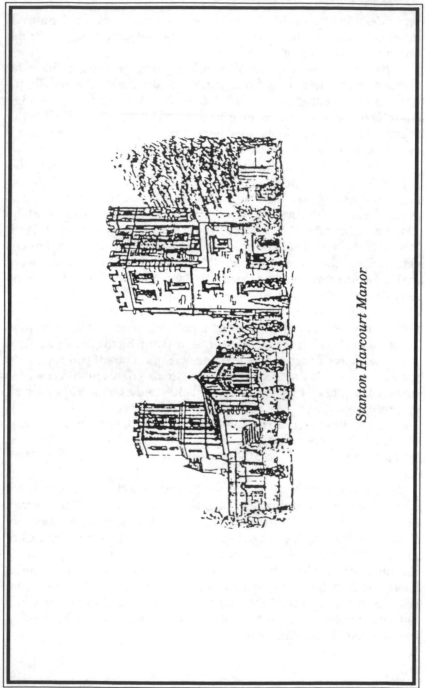

Stanton Harcourt Manor

is considerably later and has four chimneys, one in each corner. The former servants' quarters of the house adjoining the Great Kitchen now form the farmhouse of the Manor Farm.

The present residence consists of four parts: the entrance hall, the central block on the garden front which includes the library, the dining room and two bedrooms over, added to the back of the Porter's Lodge about 1860; the west wing with offices and bedrooms formed out of the original stable block, and the west wing consisting of the drawing room and garden hall with a bedroom over, added in 1953.

Having soaked in all this history a walk in the garden is a fitting end to your visit. The garden as it now exists has been entirely developed since 1948 and consists of two contrasting areas, the formal garden within the area of the original buildings and the wild garden around the manorial fishponds. The largest of the ponds, known as Church Pool, was, until the late 18th Century, joined to the churchyard by a flight of steps and was the source of fish for the whole of the Manor. These were bred in the surrounding stew-ponds, the largest of which is known as the Lady Pool, and the fish, on reaching a certain size, were transferred to the Church Pool where they were available to be caught by the villagers, an early predecessor to today's fish farms, although then the fish was free!

Stanton Harcourt is a working enterprise run by the family so there is almost always someone around to answer questions; if you happen to be there on a Sunday or a Bank Holiday Monday they will direct you to the excellent Cream teas served by the ladies of the Church to which all the profit goes.

Before visiting check to make sure of the open days as they can vary, but seem to be every other Thursday and Sunday and all Bank Holidays, between Easter and the end of September. The time is always from 2pm-6pm.

The village, with its thatched cottages, makes a charming setting for the house and the **Church of St Michael** is well worth a look. The Norman Church built about 1150 was enlarged in the 13th Century, but there are plenty of remaining Norman details. It also has a Harcourt Chapel of about 1470, a perpendicular style addition. There are memorials to the Harcourt family over some 500 years as well as a fine wood chancel screen and some fragments of the shrine of St Edburg saved from Bicester Priory at the time of the Reformation. To the north of the Church is a cottage in which the founders of Methodism, John and Charles Wesley, stayed when visiting the vicar.

YARNTON

Turning back north to travel through Eynsham once again towards Kidlington, we come to the village of **Yarnton**, just outside Kidlington, which has an interesting **Church**. The original Church was Norman, but it was almost completely rebuilt in the 13th Century and enlarged in the 17th by Sir Thomas Spencer, of Yarnton Manor, starting with the chapel in 1611. It is perpendicular in style and still has its original timber roof carved with pendants where the beams intersect. Inside are some grand monuments and fine examples of wooden screens, that to the Spencer Chapel being particularly lavish, with the strapwork motifs so characteristic of Jacobean decoration. There are also interesting examples of medieval glass and alabaster carvings. Sir Thomas' other extension to the church was the porch, built in 1616.

KIDLINGTON

Just north of Yarnton is **Kidlington**, the home of the Thames Valley Police Headquarters. Simon and Sharon Jackson offer a friendly welcome at the **Britannia Inn**, a very old building which no-one is quite certain which year it dates back to! A large beer garden features an Aunt Sally pitch - a traditional Oxfordshire game which involves throwing wooden sticks at a doll! Food is available from 11am through to 7pm. Live entertainment is featured at weekends. The Britannia is a 'let's get down to it' traditional fun, no frills, type of pub where you can enjoy a good pint and friendly banter. Dogs are welcome and you can smoke where you like!

The Britannia, Church Street, Kidlington Tel 01865 372038

On the north side of Oxford, just off the ring road is the pleasant village of Marston.

Situated within a mile-and-a-half of Oxford's bustling city centre yet having the atmosphere of a secluded country pub, the **Victoria Arms** at Old Marston is a hidden place which is well worth making the effort to find. This celebrated pub and eating place stands at a former ferry crossing point on the River Cherwell; indeed, it was originally known as the Ferry and can still be accessed by river. For the brave and experienced, punts can be hired at the Cherwell boat house for the 30-minute river journey to the pub, although be warned - punting is not as easy as it looks! For those preferring to arrive by car, the Victoria Arms can be reached from the Marston Ferry Link Road; after turning north into the centre of Old Marston village, it can be found at the end of Mill Lane on a beautiful tree-lined site beside the river.

The pub, and much of the surrounding land, was purchased by the Oxford Preservation Trust in 1959, who subsequently leased it to Wadworth & Co of Devizes. Today it is managed by Angela and Peter Blight who, along with their friendly and enthusiastic team of staff, provide a warm welcome, fine traditional ales and some of the best food in the district. The bar meals menu contains such superb dishes as beef and stout casserole, and home made chilli topped with tortilla chips and melted cheese, and includes one of the best vegetarian selections to be found at any pub in Oxford. There is also a special choice for children and an imaginative range of light meals and snacks, including filled jacket potatoes, ploughman's lunches and delicious sandwiches made with ciabatta bread. In addition, there is a separate evening menu containing a selection of more elaborate meals, including steaks, grills, fish, stir fry and pasta dishes, plus an excellent choice of vegetarian items, such as vegetable balti and creamy leek and tarragon crepes.

Victoria Arms, Mill Lane, Old Marston, Oxford   Tel: 01865 241382
Fax: 01865 201958 E-mail:
Victoria.Arms@Wadworth.Prestel.Co.UK.

Angela and Peter also organise a range of special events throughout the year, including medieval banquets, murder mystery evenings and outdoor barbecues; they are also happy to cater for private dinner parties and corporate functions. The Victoria Arms is open throughout the day during summer, with food being available between 12 noon - 2pm, and 6pm - 9pm. Like many well-known landmarks in the Oxford area, it has featured in the popular television series, *Inspector Morse*.

Still on the north side, take a short drive or bus ride from Oxford city centre to **The Somerset** pub on Marston Road - well worth a visit. If you are looking for a quiet drink, make for the lounge with its book-lined walls, where books on various subjects may be selected for a quiet read to unwind, or for a relaxing drink and a chat. In complete contrast, the lively bar is fitted out with pool table, jukebox and dartboard. Traditional pub games are also provided and occasionally there are live music, quiz nights and discos. The bar gives access to the garden and children's play area where the traditional Oxfordshire game of Aunt Sally can be played. Daily bar snacks are available (except Mondays) between 12.00 - 2.00pm.

The Somerset, 241 Marston Road, Oxford   Tel: 01865 243687

OXFORD

Having travelled in a half circle around the western side of Oxford, we now turn south to the city itself.

There is so much to see and do in **Oxford**, and so much has been written about it that it is difficult to know where to start. The city will take up at least one very busy day just to get a taste of it, and so local accommodation should be a priority.

Architecturally the city is of course a treasure house. Edward Thomas, in his book called simply 'Oxford' wrote in 1903:

'Only the recent architects who have endeavoured to work in harmony with the place have failed. I am no lover of Georgian architecture and am often blind to the power of Wren; but in Oxford I have no such incapacities; and I believe that here architecture should be judged, not as Norman or classical but as Oxford architecture. The library at Christ Church, or any other work of the eighteenth century, seems to me as divine a thing, though as yet it lacks the complete unction of antiquity, as Mob Quad at Merton or Magdalen Tower. To pass from the Norman work of St Peter's in the East to the Palladianism of Peckwater quadrangle, is but to descend from one to another of the same honourable race. If certain extremely new edifices wear out a thousand years they will probably be worthy of reverence at the end of that time, and be in harmony with Merton chapel and Balliol hall at once.'

That which Thomas probably found too rawly new - it might have been, for example, the high-Victorian **Keble College** - will now have mellowed by age. It remains to be seen whether more recent additions will do the same. The best place from which to get an overall view is from the top of **Carfax Tower**, which was the west tower and is now all that remains of the 14th Century Church of St Martin. There is also an informative display on the first floor and a well-stocked souvenir stall.

Looking down from Carfax Tower, from where, one wonders, did that other famous quotation about Oxford - that it is the home of lost causes - originate? With none other than the originator of the 'dreaming spires' Matthew Arnold, who wrote in 1865 about Oxford as the 'home of lost causes, and forsaken beliefs, and unpopular names, and impossible loyalties'. He also speaks of the city 'whispering from her towers the last enchantments of the Middle Age', a phrase which fits very well the courtyards and streets.

Oxford, of course, is not just a collection of fine architecture but a living city. In the centre, however, it is the famous **University** which seems to dominate.

All the old Colleges have their own special interest, but you should be sure not to miss **St Edmund Hall**, part of which is the only surviving medieval academic hall. It also has a Norman crypt and a 17th Century dining hall. Many greatly enjoy the charm of the quadrangle, especially the north range with its mullioned windows and sundial, contrasting vividly with the classical library and chapel entrance which adjoins it.

If you would like to find out rather more about the university a 'magical history tour' is available at the innovative **Oxford Story** museum on Broad Street. Here you sit down in a scholar's desk and are transported through time to discover its 800-year history through its characters, sounds and, not least, its smells.

If you become fascinated by the past of this delightful place you will also want to visit the **Museum of Oxford**, where there are permanent

Sundial and Perpetual Calendar,
Corpus Christi College, Oxford

displays showing the archaeology and history of the city from the earliest times to the present. This is housed at St Aldate's, in the centre of the town.

The **Ashmolean Museum** cannot be missed. It is the oldest museum in the country, having first opened in 1683, although the present building dates back 'only' to 1845. There are archaeological collections from Britain, Europe, the Mediterranean, Egypt and the Middle East, a very fine coin and medal collection as well as Italian, Dutch, Flemish, French and English old masters as well as more modern paintings and prints. There are also collections of far eastern art, ceramics and lacquer work, Islamic pottery and Chinese bronzes.

One museum which would captivate many who are not particularly interested in art is the **Museum of the History of Science**, which has the largest collection of astrolabes in the world and is housed in the original Ashmolean building in Broad Street.

You should not miss **Curioxity** (yes, it really is spelt like that) in the Old Fire Station in George Street, near the Bus Station. This is a new 'hands-on' science gallery where adults and children can explore the world of science and technology and have fun at the same time.

That still leaves **Oxford University Museum**, housed in a splendid high Victorian-Gothic building on Parks Road. Here you can see the remains of the dodo, extinct since about 1680, as well as fossilised dinosaur remains and much else.

Another section of the same museum, where you can listen to recordings of musical instruments from all over the world on display there, is to be found at the **Balfour Building**, 60 Banbury Road.

Anyone with a particular interest in music should not miss the **Bate Collection of Historical Instruments** in St Aldate's. Those captivated by old masters must make time (and energy) to visit the **Christ Church Picture Gallery**, which has paintings by Tintoretto, Van Dyck and Carracci, as well as drawings by Leonardo, Michaelangelo and most of the major Italian masters from the 15th to the 18th Centuries.

If you are in Oxford on a Sunday afternoon in summer you will have the opportunity to see the **Rotunda Museum of Antique Dolls' Houses** and their contents. The exhibits date from 1700 to 1900. As you see, there are museums to suit most people's tastes.

A wondrous collection of antique prints, maps and books can be found in several specialist shops, the sort of places where you can spend hours just browsing, digging into the piles of stock - sometimes still priced in shillings rather than decimal money.

Attas Brasseria, 9a Avenue One, Covered Market, High Street, Oxford Tel 01865 203900

Tucked away from the bustling crowds on the corner of Oxford's covered market, **Attas Brasseria** has been owned and personally run by Peter Leathley and Atta Mustafa for just over a year. This attractive eating house has a large plaque in the entry stairwell telling visitors of the great riot that once took place on this very spot on 29th May 1715 when much local property was attacked and destroyed. You will find the atmosphere much more tranquil these days, with mellow jazz music playing in the background with hanging greenery and pink panelled interior giving the brasseria a feeling of light and space.

Atta and Peter have an ever-changing menu which specialises in traditional French cuisine in the evenings and deliciously varied business lunches in the daytime. You will find the clientele just as diverse, ranging from students just out for a quick snack and a drink to professionals meeting to enjoy a working lunch, so whatever your requirements, Attas Brasseria will cater for them all.

For the green fingered there are the **Botanic Gardens**, down by the river at the end of High Street. The gardens were founded in 1621 when plants were the only source of medicines. Recently we have seen a revival of herbal remedies as well as a return to the fashion for herbal teas and the use of herbs for pot pourri to perfume our homes. Whether you are interested in plants for their uses or just like exploring gardens you will enjoy this one, which is home to some 8000 species of plant from all over the world.

Down on the river, at **Folly Bridge**, you can hire a punt or, if you have more time to devote to the fascination of the Thames, which changes its name to the more poetic Isis in Oxford, you can take a trip on one of the passenger boats which go to Abingdon, Reading, Henley, Marlow, Maidenhead, Windsor, Runnymede and Staines. There are also day or evening trips with a bar, food and music available.

The Head of the River, Folly Bridge, St Aldates, Oxford Tel 01865 721600 Fax 01865 726158

The Head of the River at Folly Bridge dates back to the 1820s when it was used as a warehouse. The Head of the River came into the ownership of Fuller, Smith and Turner in August 1994 since when the building has undergone extensive refurbishment which complements the warehouse's original architecture.

The en-suite guest rooms which overlook the Thames have cottage-style pine furniture and amenities including television, hospitality tray and hair dryer. The patio by the waterside has easy access for wheelchairs. The new kitchen serves the bar area and outside patio and the use of fresh foods provides a wide selection of culinary delights - there are also vegetarian dishes, a children's menu, desserts and various teas and coffees. To accompany your meal, choose from many fine wines and Fuller's award-winning ales. After a satisfying meal you can rent a punt or boat on the river or take a stroll into Oxford centre.

The city has paid host to a bewildering number of literary figures. For instance, John Buchan, whose house we saw at Kingston Bagpuize, was at **Brasenose College** from 1897-9 and won the Stanhope Prize for an essay on Walter Raleigh. W H Auden was an undergraduate at **Christ Church** from 1925-8. C S Lewis, who wrote religious and scholarly works as well as his well-known Narnia series of books for children was a fellow

Tom Tower and Memorial Gardens, Oxford

at **Magdalen College** from 1924-54. Rose Macauley, Dorothy L Sayers, Vera Brittain and Winifred Holtby were all at **Somerville College**. Somerville is also, of course, where Mrs Thatcher, former Prime Minister, studied as an undergraduate. J R R Tolkien, creator of Middle Earth, was a fellow of **Merton College** and Merton Professor of English from 1945-59

The Victoria, 90 Walton Street, Oxford   Tel 01865 554047

The Victoria is a typical suburban pub used extensively by Oxford University students creating a great ambience for those enjoying lively company. The ceiling of the lounge bar has a copy taken from the painting in the Cistine Chapel in Rome and is quite a tourist attraction. Val and Kevin are great hosts and serve a good variety of food at very reasonable prices. The menu changes regularly and there is something to suit all tastes. Those more concerned with the type of liquid refreshment on offer will find themselves well satisfied with the selection of ales, wines and spirits on offer. This being a busy venue, Kevin keeps his cellar in good order. There is a nice garden to sit out in during the summer months and although on a busy route it is a quiet area. For those wishing to get a flavour of student life or re-visit old haunts and re-live *a certain past*, this pub should suit admirably.

There are two literary figures whose footsteps are particularly worth tracking.

The first is Lewis Carroll, author of Alice's Adventures in Wonderland and Through the Looking Glass. His real name was Charles Lutwidge Dodgson and he was an undergraduate at Christ Church from 1851-55, staying on as a lecturer in mathematics. He was a very shy man with a stammer, who yet seems to have had a talent for relating to children. His great children's classics had their origin in a punting expedition he took on the river with Alice Liddell, daughter of the Dean of his College and it is very pleasant to think of the timid don for once at ease, spinning fantasies for an enraptured little girl.

Our other literary pilgrimage takes us to **Balliol College**, where the poet Gerard Manley Hopkins was an undergraduate in the 1860s and wrote of Oxford as a 'towery city and branchy between towers; Cuckoo-echoing, bell-swarmd, lark-charmd, rook-racked, river-rounded'. He was later a curate at the **Church of St Aloysius** at the south end of Woodstock Road.

It was during that period of his life that Hopkins wrote the wonderful poem 'Binsey Poplars' mourning the felling of some favourite trees. As you walk along the towpath to this small Thames-side village you can think of Hopkins, another painfully shy man, mourning the loss 'All felled, felled, are all felled; Of a fresh and following folded ran, Not spared, not one'.

Binsey is a pleasant oasis with a Church approached along an avenue of chestnut trees. In the churchyard there is a well dedicated to St Margaret and connected with the legend of St Frideswide, patron saint of Oxford. This shadowy saint is thought to have died about 735 and to have been the daughter of a Mercian prince. She fled to Oxford to avoid being forced to marry, founded a Nunnery there and became its Abbess. The well in this quiet churchyard was for some time a place of pilgrimage for people seeking her intercession.

In and around the city of Oxford there are many good places to stay in order to give yourself time to explore the area thoroughly.

At **Hinksey Hill Top,** just off the A34 is the delightful **Westwood Country Hotel** run by Tony and Mary Parker for 18 years. This award-winning, 3-Crown establishment is an hotel with the added attraction of a nature reserve. The reserve, which is also run by Tony and Mary, was opened by David Bellamy in 1990 and has since been the recipient of a Special Conservation Award and was the 1996 winner of the Environmental and Conservation Award. Guests are free to explore and Mary will provide you with plenty of information to help you appreciate the sights, sounds and work that goes on there. The food at Westwood Country Hotel is quite excellent with Tony and Mary often catering for weddings and conferences. You will find full facilities for wheelchair users and children are always welcome.

Westwood Country Hotel, Hinksey Hill Top, Oxford Tel 01865 735408

The Trout at **Lower Wolvercote** is a true representation of a fine English pub, and although reliable sources date the present building as 17th Century, it is thought that its roots may well date back to the 12th or 13th Century. Certainly the inn has seen a great deal of historic activity over the years. More recently The Trout has gained wider repute as the favourite haunt of Inspector Morse, resulting in an occasional television appearance.

The Trout, 195 Godstow Road, Lower Wolvercote Tel 01865 554485

Retaining much of its original charm, The Trout has been totally refurbished and a fine kitchen caters for a varied selection of meals at sensible prices. To give a flavour of the menu, the Savoury Bacon and

Cheddar Melt would make a good start, followed by Beef and Ale Pie, Hunters Chicken or Seafood Salad perhaps, with a Caramel Apple Granny or School Pud to finish. Host Colin Swallow is undoubtedly responsible for greatly enhancing The Trout's already formidable reputation and although large, the pub has a cosy atmosphere and friendly ambience. The gardens run down to the river and are a wonderful place to relax in the summer time. A really super place!

IFFLEY

On reaching the now suburban **Iffley** our goal is the magnificent Norman **Church of St Mary**. Built about 1170-1180 it has lavish decoration in the style typical of the late 12th Century. The deeply recessed doors and windows are enriched by geometric patterns with some naturalistic details which anticipate the Gothic style later to supersede the Norman.

Do make the opportunity to visit this, one of the best preserved village churches of its age in England. The west front was carefully restored in the last century and now the round-headed door, the circular window above it and three rounded-headed windows above that stand out in patterned glory in the light, creamy stone.

The village has other interesting buildings, including a barn which has had fragments of medieval carvings built into it.

NUNEHAM COURTNEY

From Iffley we briefly take the A423 south to **Nuneham Courtenay**. The village is an interesting example of an 'estate village', built in the 18th Century when many aristocrats wished to lay out a magnificent park uncluttered by the hovels of the local village. Unlike some great landowners, Simon, first Earl Harcourt, 1714-1777, built a replacement village for his tenants and the cottages he built then still face each other in matched pairs on either side of the main road.

It has been argued that this is the origin of Oliver Goldsmith's poem The Deserted Village, as an example of a practice which he thought cruel and leading to the ruin of the peasantry. There is a tradition that he witnessed the clearing of Nuneham Courtenay in 1761, although the poem did not appear until 1770. It seems rather ironic that the removal of a village should have inspired his criticisms, as so many villagers elsewhere were treated in a much more cavalier fashion than here - but it was the general practice which shocked Goldsmith.

The second Earl entertained many literary figures in the park and gardens which took the place of the former village. One of them may have been Jean-Jacques Rousseau, who is said to have planted many foreign wild flowers in the park. The diarist Fanny Burney visited the house in 1786 with King George III and Queen Charlotte and records that she got lost in it. It was at the time being remodelled, together with the garden, to fit in more closely with the fashion of the time, that everything should be made to look as natural as possible - all done in a very artistic manner, with classical urns placed here and there, rather in the fashion of the classical landscapes of the French painter Claude. For example, a classical-style Temple of Flora was built, and has survived later changes to the garden. The park now forms the **Arboretum** of the University of Oxford, with many rare trees, and is open to the public. Its 55 acres of woods, meadows, walks and ponds are a perfect setting for an afternoon stroll.

Returning north to the Oxford ring road, we come to **Cowley**, the suburb of Oxford in which another William Morris, very different from the one we have met several times on our travels so far, founded his factory for producing motor cars on the production line system. We will cross his footsteps again too, before very long.

ELSFIELD

Following the ring road anti-clockwise brings us round past Headington in the east and then Marston from where a short diversion leads to our next destination, **Elsfield**, which is a place of literary pilgrimage on two counts. John Buchan, who was at Oxford University and whose house at Kingston Bagpuize we visited in Chapter 5, lived in Elsfield at the Manor House from 1919 to 1935, when he was appointed Governor General of Canada. He wrote several of his novels during that time and 'Midwinter', published in 1923, opens on nearby Otmoor. His grave is in the churchyard of the little aisleless **Church of St Thomas of Canterbury**, the oldest parts of which are 12th Century, although it has been much remodelled since.

R D Blackmore, whose most famous novel is perhaps 'Lorna Doone', also lived in the village as a child, at the vicarage. He set one of his books, Cripps the Carrier, published in 1876, in the area, Cripps' cottage being on the road from nearby **Beckley** which also has literary associations.

Beckley Park is said to be the model for the house in Aldous Huxley's Crome Yellow, published in 1921. The site of the house has a long history. It once belonged to King Alfred, and after the Norman conquest a castle was built there, with three rectangular moats, the remains of which can still be seen. The present house dates to 1540, and was probably a hunting lodge. It is built of attractive plum-coloured bricks with black bricks forming patterns of the type known as diapering. Evelyn Waugh also lived in the village, at the **Abingdon Arms**, and wrote much of his book on Dante Gabriel Rossetti there in 1928.

We leave Beckley to skirt Otmoor and pass through **Stanton St John**, where the grandfather of John Milton lived, and **Forest Hill**, where he met his wife. It is a somewhat romantic story. Milton visited the village in 1643, possibly to collect money owed by Richard Powell. A month later he returned to London as the husband of Richard Powell's 17-year-old daughter. The story is told in Robert Graves' novel 'Wife to Mr Milton' in which many local scenes are featured.

Here we leave the city of learning and its nearby delights to cross into our next chapter.

CHAPTER SEVEN

Thame, Thames and Chilterns

Milton Manor

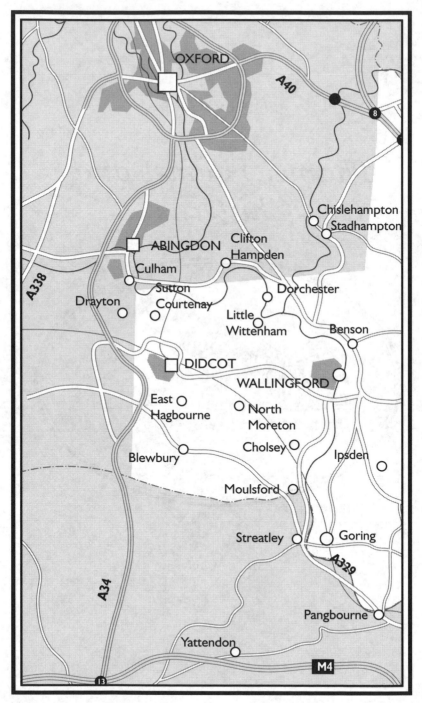

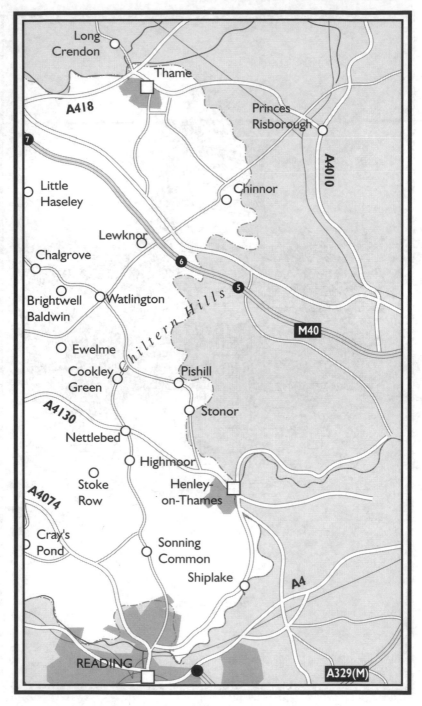

Wheatley Lock-up

Thame, Thames and Chilterns

Just off the A40 at **Wheatley** we cross the boundary into a chapter in which we explore the valleys of the rivers Thame and Thames as they make their way through southern Oxfordshire, and become acquainted with the gentle delights of the south-eastern Chilterns.

GARSINGTON

We turn south to follow the valley of the Thame, which meets its near namesake, the Thames, at Dorchester. Our first stop is at **Garsington**, where the **Manor House** has an indelible place in literary history as the home, from 1915 to 1927, of Lady Ottiline Morrell. She and her husband Philip were unflaggingly hospitable to a whole generation of writers, artists and intellectuals including Katherine Mansfield, Lytton Strachey, Clive Bell, Siegfried Sassoon, D H Lawrence, T S Eliot, Rupert Brooke, Bertrand Russell and Aldous Huxley. Huxley based an account of a country house party in his novel 'Crome Yellow' on his experiences at Garsington, thereby causing a rift with his hostess. She found his description all too apt, and felt betrayed. Huxley insisted that he had not meant any harm, but she remained hurt and they were estranged for some time.

Lady Ottiline was not very lucky in the artists on whom she lavished her attention and hospitality. D H Lawrence also quarrelled with her after drawing a less than flattering, but clearly recognisable, portrait of life at her house in 'Women in Love':

'The talk went on like a rattle of small artillery, always slightly sententious, with a sententiousness that was only emphasised by the continual crackling of a witticism, the continual spatter of a verbal jest, designed to give a tone of flippancy to a stream of conversation that was all critical and general, a canal of conversation rather than a stream.'

The house itself is attractive, 16th Century in origin though remodelled in the 17th, built from stone with mullioned windows and dormer windows under gables projecting from the attics.

Garsington's other claim to literary fame is that Rider Haggard was sent to the school run by the Rev H J Graham at the rectory in 1866, when he was ten. The present house is later, built in 1872, but across the road from the Church is a 16th Century gateway from the house he would have known. While there the boy became friendly with a local farmer named Quartermain whom Haggard must have remembered with affection as he used the name for his hero many years later in his novel 'King Solomon's Mines'.

The village Church is nicely situated, with pleasant views south to the Chilterns.

CHISLEHAMPTON

Still heading south, we take the B480 to **Chislehampton**, where **St Katherine's** is a well-preserved example of an 18th Century Parish Church. It is not the work of a great architect, but a local builder's interpretation of the Georgian style. The internal fittings, have remained unusually intact, complete with box pews and a gallery at the west end. The only major exception is a Jacobean pulpit, but luckily it is being well looked after by the Redundant Churches Fund and has recently been restored.

CLIFTON HAMPDEN

From Chislehampton we take the B4015 to **Clifton Hampden**, where we meet the Thames once again and where the characters in Jerome K Jerome's 'Three Men in a Boat' stayed just as the author had done himself, at the Barley Mow Inn. As the narrator says, 'Round Clifton Hampden, itself a wonderfully pretty village, old-fashioned, peaceful and dainty with flowers, the river scenery is rich and beautiful.'

The village **Church** has a dramatic position, perched on a cliff overlooking the river and approached up flights of steps. Built into its north wall is a 12th Century relief of a boar hunt which may have come from the original building, but the Church was practically rebuilt in the last century under the supervision of the Victorian architect G G Scott.

LONG WITTENHAM

We cross Clifton Hampden bridge, also rebuilt by Scott in 1864, to make our way to **Long Wittenham** to see a particularly charming and unusual museum - the **Pendon Museum of Miniature Landscape and Transport**. Here some extremely skilful modellers - and if you are lucky you may be able to see them at work - have created a miniature country landscape of the 1930s, complete with a rural railway line of the kind lost in the 1960s.

The village was also the home of Robert Gibbings, whose topographical books were illustrated with his own woodcuts. Through them, and through the Golden Cockerel Press which he ran, he did much to revive the art of woodcutting and wood engraving. He was a great traveller and has the distinction of being the first artist to use diving equipment so that he could make underwater drawings. Two of his books deal with the Thames by which he chose to spend his life, 'Sweet Thames run Softly', published in 1940, and 'Till I End My Song', published in 1957, the year before his death. He is buried in the churchyard.

CULHAM

At the nearby village of **Culham**, north of the river, there are a couple of interesting houses. The west wing of the **Manor House** was originally a grange, or barn, belonging to the Abbots of Abingdon and is probably 15th Century. The garden side was remodelled in the 17th Century. **Culham House** is early Georgian, though extended about 1800.

A modern bridge has been built to cope with present-day traffic, but its predecessor, built 1416-22 by the Abingdon Guild of the Holy Trinity, can be seen to the south.

SUTTON COURTENAY

Across the river from Culham is the delightful village of **Sutton Courtenay**. The Church, **All Saints**, is well worth a visit with something to show from all the periods of its long history, starting with a Norman tower through to modern wall paintings. It has fine examples of stone carving and woodwork.

In the churchyard is buried Herbert Asquith, Liberal Prime Minister for eight years from 1908. After taking his first class Degree in Classics at Balliol College Oxford, he became a barrister, and entered Parliament in 1886. His term of office was marked by the beginnings of the welfare state, with the introduction of old age pensions, the last, violent, stages of the agitation for votes for women with the suffragettes and the beginnings of a war which was to bring a level of carnage to Europe unknown in previous conflicts. One of the victims was his own eldest son, Raymond, killed in action in 1916. Asquith is also supposed to be the original of the man 'with a face like a Roman bust' who chases young girls across the lawn in 'Crome Yellow', which gives a rather different picture of his character from that in the official biographies. His second wife, Margot, was a brilliant figure on the social scene of the time.

In the same churchyard is the simple headstone which marks the grave of Eric Blair, who wrote under the name of George Orwell, very much a political writer though not a practising politician. He fought with the Republicans during the Spanish Civil War and was wounded in action. He always considered himself a democratic socialist but his hatred of totalitarianism in all its forms was directed later on exclusively against communism in 'Animal Farm' and 'Nineteen Eighty Four'. Other novels, such as 'Coming up for Air' published in 1939, are full of perceptive insight into the lives of ordinary people.

MILTON

Our next stop is **Milton**, to visit the delightful **Manor House**. This is an elegant, graceful house, standing in a setting of fine trees, green lawns and a serpentine lake. It has been open to the public since 1952, some six years after it was given to Marjorie Mockler nee Barrett, and her husband Surgeon Captain E.J. Mockler, Royal Navy, and their four children.

Marjorie Mockler was once a Barrett and it was her ancestor Bryant Barrett who bought the house in 1764. He was 'lace man' to the Prince of Wales, afterwards George III. He was a devout Catholic and a strong if somewhat secret supporter of Bonnie Prince Charlie.

When Bryant Barrett acquired the house from the Misses Calton whose family had owned Milton Manor since 1548, he had to work hard to restore the neglect of years. He employed an army of workmen, only two of them local men. Their task was to build two Georgian wings, extend the house with a great new kitchen, plus a bakery, laundry and brewery. The latter was a must in the eyes of Bryant Barrett who was very keen on his grape wine.

The gardens were also very important to him and he kept detailed notes of the planting of bushes and trees around the house and grounds.

The work that was carried out has made it the fine house it is today together with the loving care and attention to the structure and interior by Captain and Mrs Mockler which enable Milton to be appreciated as one of the important lesser houses of the English Restoration and mid-Georgian periods.

Wherever you go in this house you will find something to interest you. There is a remarkable Monks' Settle of the 16th Century in the Hall which is believed to have belonged to the Abbots of Abingdon. In the Drawing Room which is one of the most charming rooms in the house, is found the superb carved ceiling consisting of Oak and Bay leaves. There is a pianola by Steck which was especially made for Princess Beatrice, the youngest daughter of Queen Victoria.

A lovely carved mantelpiece, by Richard Lawrence and perfectly proportioned alcoves make the Dining Room special. The Strawberry Hill Gothick Library, where Richard Lawrence, a London carver, worked with Stephen Wright, the architect, is spectacular.

Lawrence and Wright were also responsible for the Chapel which is Roman Catholic. Outstanding are the 13th and 14th Century stained glass windows which came from Steventon Church. Bryant Barrett paid £7 for them - a considerable sum of money at that time.

Although the Chapel is still in use, only direct descendants of the Barretts can be married in it. Within the last few years both the younger son and younger daughter of the present owners have been married here.

Five hundred years after the last Roman Legion had abandoned Britain to the Barbarians, King Edwy of Wessex granted a large tract of land at Milton to a certain Alfwin and that is where the story of Milton Manor began.

DIDCOT

From Milton we take the road to **Didcot** where a fascination with the history of railways, particularly steam trains, can be indulged at **Didcot Railway Centre**. Once a busy engine shed, the Centre recreates the golden age of the Great Western Railway with a collection of GWR rolling stock housed in a GWR engine shed. They have 20 steam locomotives, a diesel railcar and have reconstructed a typical GWR station. They have 'steaming days' on summer Sundays, when engines operate and rides are available.

Otherwise there is not a great deal in Didcot to attract the tourist, though the facilities of a town can be very useful when travelling largely from village to village, with limited shops and similar practical facilities.

Sir Nicholas Pevsner describes the **Church of All Saints**, in a part of Didcot 'which has managed to remain villagey', as being in the Decorated style 'but much pulled about'. It does, however, have a very fine tomb effigy of a mitred Abbot, thought to be Ralph de Dudecot, who died in 1293 or 94. This old form of the name shows that it originally meant Dudda's cottage, or shelter, which sounds very rural for the most urban place our journey has seen for some time.

EAST HAGBOURNE

Our next destination is **East Hagbourne**, which has three distinct areas of architecture, the oldest and most attractive being the predominantly 17th Century 'Main Road' which runs a quarter of a mile between two ancient crosses. This part of the village remains untouched by time and provides a wealth of interest for artists and students alike.

The timbered and whitewashed houses, thatched cottages, magnificent Norman church and beautiful private gardens are all part of an annual battle to win the 'Best Kept village' award. Their biggest rivals are neighbouring Dorchester for whom they have no neighbourly feelings of goodwill as the time for the competition comes round.

In addition to the scenic delights, the village also boasts an interesting history. In 1644, the Royalists were defeated at Newbury and Charles I, fleeing to Oxford, was pursued by Cromwell who quartered 6,000 horsemen in Main Road. The Puritan troops registered their disapproval of the Established Church by smashing the two village crosses and sharpening their swords on the remains. The stump of one cross still remains alongside the war memorial at 'Lower Cross'.

The 'Upper Cross' has subsequently been rebuilt and is famous if only because 'Dr Who' was tied to it during the filming of an episode. A mock up of the **Fleur de Lys Inn** was also constructed for filming, and frequently plays host to pilgrims from the Dr Who Society who fervently visit scenes of the Doctor's adventures.

The origins of The Fleur de Lys are steeped in history. It was originally an ale house owned by the Church, as was all the surrounding area. It first became a Freehouse, owned by a Mr Dupont, shortly after 1346. This gentleman was a yeoman who accompanied the army of Edward III to the Battle of Crecy, where he captured a French knight and held him to ransom, buying the freehold of the pub with the proceeds upon his return to England. The French connection is doubtless reflected in the name of the pub. It was not until after World War II that The Fleur de Lys lost its freehouse status.

In 1659 a massive fire consumed much of East Hagbourne and such was the extent of the conflagration that Charles II personally appealed to his subjects to come to the aid of the inhabitants. Five years later, fate decreed that Hagbourne should reciprocate when the City of London was consumed by the Great Fire. Local legend has it that many old ships' beams were used in the rapid reconstruction of Hagbourne which accounts for the convoluted shapes evident in some of the houses.

BLEWBURY

We now journey into the foothills of the Berkshire Downs to the pretty, and prettily named, village of **Blewbury**. The scenery is lovely and the village is full of attractive timber-framed houses. The Church is flooded with light, a spacious and dignified building. Kenneth Grahame, best known for his classic 'The Wind in the Willows' lived in the village from 1910 to 1924 and described it as 'the heart of King Alfred's country'. The Tudor brick house in which he lived is still there, but the fields around it have disappeared under new housing.

Nottingham Fee, a no-through-road off the main A417 Wantage/
Reading road in Blewbury which meanders down to the mid-17th
Century Inn, is a tiny road, its unusual name coming from the de
Nottingham family who owned the Manor House in the 13th Century.

WALLINGFORD
From there we make our way on minor roads to **Wallingford**, where
William the Conqueror crossed the Thames in 1066 on his way to take
London. The use of this ford is clearly very ancient, for the name means
'the ford of Wealh's people' and was mentioned in a chronicle of 821.
Fortifications which date back to Saxon times are clearly visible on the
east side of the town and Wallingford was such an important centre in the
12th Century that it had 10 or 11 churches and a small Benedictine Priory.
However, its prosperity seems to have declined somewhat by the 15th
Century, with only four Churches left, of which three remain today.

The **Castle** was in the north-east quarter of the town and there is now
little to be seen, but the site has been nicely laid out as a garden, just the
place for a picnic on a bench or a quiet walk amongst the embankments.

In the streets there are a number of handsome Georgian houses. In the
Market Place is a **Town Hall** built in 1670 with the traditional open ground
floor for the market, with the upper floors supported on sturdy columns.
There is a **Museum of Local History** in the High Street.

The river is no longer crossed by ford, but on a bridge which has no
less than seventeen arches. Its earliest parts date from the 13th Century.

SHILLINGFORD
We now take the A329 towards Dorchester and find ourselves in the
village of **Shillingford** where the Irish poet W B Yeats - also a friend of
Lady Ottiline Morrell - lived with his wife and child in the summer of
1921 while Civil War raged in Ireland. It was there that he began writing
a series of poems which he described as 'a lamentation over lost peace
and hope'.

DORCHESTER
Dorchester - 'Dor' from a Celtic word for 'good looking', 'chester'
from a Roman camp by the Thames - is one of the early shrines of
Christianity in Britain. The town became a centre of missionary activity
when, in 635, King Cynegils of Wessex gave it to St Birinus. Known as the
'Apostle of the West Saxons', Birinus was consecrated in Genoa, landed
in Wessex in 634 and converted and baptised the King in the following
year.

The **Abbey Church of St Peter and St Paul** is all that remains of the Augustinian Abbey which was built on the site of the original Saxon Church in 1170. Its chief glory is the 14th Century Choir and the huge 'Jesse' window, showing the family tree of Jesus, which has retained its original glass. The story, along with the history of settlement in the area going back to neolithic times is told in the **Abbey Museum** which is housed in a former Grammar Schoolroom, built in 1652.

There are a number of pleasant houses in the village, which amply repay a stroll through the streets. As Jerome K Jerome comments in 'Three Men in a Boat', 'it is very old and it was very strong and great once. Now it sits aside from the stirring world, and nods and dreams.'

In the 18th Century the High Street would have been a busy thoroughfare but it has now been by-passed which has had the effect of turning the street into a peaceful backwater.

THAME

And so on to the town and river of **Thame**. Only 39 miles from London's Heathrow Airport and within easy reach of Oxford the delightful market town has made its mark. A little time spent in discovering an English country town is always delightful and the rewards are rich for those visiting this particular area.

There are many fascinating places to visit and one of them is **The Spread Eagle**, one of England's most well-known coaching inns. Set amid such beautiful countryside this famous inn has quite a history. The Spread Eagle was a favourite with the farmers and in 1922 was taken over by John Fothergill. Fothergill made little attempt to befriend the farmers and continued running the inn in the traditional manner. He made several attempts to build trade one way or the other but was not very successful, and in the end he almost deliberately began to discourage most of the clientele he had.

Gradually a new kind of customer began to replace the old. Fothergill's many society friends passed the word around and people came from London. Word soon reached the ears of the Dons and wealthy undergraduates of Oxford.

However, John Fothergill did not entirely approve of this sector of society and this led to him making an unfortunate mistake. One day he received a letter from Queen's College Oxford requesting that he prepare a special dinner for two. Assuming that the letter had been sent by a rich undergraduate, and always keen to teach people a lesson he winkled their oysters, substituted chicken for pheasant and stuffed cucumbers instead of aubergines. When the diners arrived they just happened to be the most eminent gourmets in the entire university, Mr T W Allen, a fellow of Queens College, and Dr Cowley, the Curator of the Bodleian.

One consolation was that Fothergill was able to serve them with the best wines!

Fothergill did not begrudge his distinguished customers the very best and he states in his innkeeper's diary that 'when I took this shop, I thought round for all the things I found best wherever I'd been and sent for them.'

John Fothergill sold the Spread Eagle in 1931 after having lost a sizable amount of money. Today it is still one of the most superb places in this area and well worth a visit.

Thame first became a market town in the 13th Century, and its importance as a commercial centre resulted in the wide main street we see today. It is lined with old inns and houses, some of which go back to the 15th Century, with some pleasant Georgian brick frontages.

The imposing **Church** was built in the 13th Century. The aisles were widened in the 14th Century and the tower heightened in the 15th, resulting in a large but somewhat bleak building. The monument to Lord Williams of Thame, who died in 1559, and his wife Elizabeth is in the centre of the chancel and has some very fine carving.

To the west of the Church is the **Prebendal House**. A prebend was an income granted to a priest by a Cathedral or Collegiate Church. This one was established about 1140 by Lincoln Cathedral and a special house for the holders of the office is first mentioned in 1234. What remains seems to have grown up piecemeal over the centuries, but the earlier parts are 13th Century. The chapel is a particularly fine example of the Early English style, built about 1250.

The Yeats family moved to Thame and stayed at **42 High Street**, a house which they reported to have a haunting scent of roses, even when no roses were blooming.

The town also had a famous **Grammar School**, housed in a Tudor building in Church Lane. The schoolmaster's house faces the road and over the doorway are the arms of Lord Williams, who founded the school in 1558.

John Hampden, one of the Parliamentary leaders during the Civil War, was at school here and also died at Thame. He was an MP from 1621 and sat in Parliament whenever it had not been dissolved by the King. He denied the right of the King to raise taxes without the sanction of Parliament and in 1636 refused to pay the 'ship tax' the King was demanding. As a result he was successfully prosecuted with the result that he became a popular leader in the country. When the Civil War broke out he raised a regiment of infantry for the Parliamentary Army and fought with great bravery at Edgehill and Reading. However, he was wounded at the battle of Chalgrove Field in June 1643 and carried to Thame, where he died some days later in an inn which used to stand on the High Street.

A little to the south of the town is **Thame Park**, a house built on the site of a Cistercian Abbey founded in 1138. The present house incorporates some of the former monastic buildings to which has been added a gracious Georgian house. As Pevsner comments, 'The two main facades are a delightful contrast: on the west Georgian uniformity and restraint, on the south the comfortable sprawling Late Gothic range with crenellated turrets and mullioned windows.'

To the west of the town, close to the M40, are the famous gardens of **Waterperry House**. These are a must for anyone even slightly interested in gardens. Set in 83 acres of Oxfordshire countryside, there are magnificent herbaceous, shrub and heather borders, alpine gardens, rock gardens and a newly laid out formal garden. The nurseries and greenhouses are a treasure house for keen gardeners. The gardens are host each summer to Art in Action, bringing together many of the world's finest craftsmen.

The **Church**, which is Saxon in origin, has some good 14th and 15th Century stained glass, Georgian box pews and some memorial brasses. The house is not open to the public, as it is an educational establishment, but is a fine classical building of 1713.

To the south of Waterperry is the **Rycote Chapel**, set among trees. There also used to be a mansion there which has long since vanished. The private chapel was built in 1449 and still survives with some of the original seating. However, its great glory is the 17th Century fittings. These include two magnificent domed and canopied pews. One may have been used by Queen Elizabeth I, who is known to have stayed at the house, and the other was installed for Charles I.

We now take the A40 to turn off south on a minor road to **Chalgrove**, a village with thatched cottages and an obelisk commemorating the battle at which John Hampden was mortally wounded.

EWELME

We now make our way to **Ewelme** just off the B4009. It is a village in a pretty situation and in the centre is a magnificent group of buildings, Church, Almshouses and school, all of the 15th Century. They were the gift of Alice Chaucer, granddaughter of the poet Geoffrey, and her husband William de la Pole, Duke of Suffolk. There is a wonderfully elegant alabaster carving of Alice in the church. She wears simple drapery apart from a delicate coronet, her head sheltered under an elaborately carved canopy. Under this effigy is another rather macabre carving of a shrivelled cadaver.

The **Almshouses** were founded in 1437, intended to house 13 poor men and were provided with two chaplains to care for them. It is one of the earliest examples of almshouses built around a quadrangle like an Oxford College. They also show one of the earliest examples of the use of brick in Oxfordshire. The **School** was founded in the same year and is also of brick. In the schoolmaster's house lived one of the Almshouse chaplains, who moonlighted as a teacher in the school. The house was extensively altered in Georgian times.

Geoffrey Chaucer, according to tradition, visited his granddaughter here. Jerome K Jerome, whom we have previously mentioned lived here at the foot of the Chilterns. He moved to an old farmhouse on a hill to the south-east of the village after the financial success which 'Three Men in a Boat' brought him, attended the Church and is buried in the churchyard.

Ewelme is also well known for its watercress beds in the river.

From Ewelme our journey meanders south using the spider's web of minor roads to arrive at the foot of the Chilterns. Along here runs the **Icknield Way**. This ancient track once ran from the Wash to the south coast. It is prehistoric in origin and the Romans recycled parts of it in their road system. Because of its name, it is tempting to assume a link to the Iceni tribe who had their capital near the Way's east coast end in Norfolk, but this seems to be unfounded. Edward Thomas, whom we have met in Adlestrop and Oxford, was sufficiently drawn to this mysterious trackway to write a book about it. Now part of it is included in the Countryside Commission's Ridgeway Long Distance Footpath, even though the classic Ridgeway is the one with which we became acquainted in the dramatic hills above Uffington and the White Horse. However, this Chiltern section has much charm.

NUFFIELD

Nuffield must be the most inappropriately named village in England for those who remember Nuffield Motors.

The name is no accident. We have come across two gentlemen called William Morris on our journey through Oxfordshire. One, the Victorian craftsman, had a lovely house beside the Thames at Kelmscott. The other, William Richard Morris, 1st Viscount Nuffield, began his brilliant business career by making bicycles and later moved on to cars. By 1910 he was already producing the prototypes of his famous Morris Oxford and became the first British manufacturer to develop the mass production methods which made cars cheap enough for ordinary people to aspire to, rather than status symbols for the wealthy. His car manufacturing plant at Cowley has already been mentioned. He amassed great wealth in the process and gave lavish donations to charities and Oxford University. He also endowed the famous Nuffield Foundation for social, scientific and medical research.

Lord Nuffield took his title from this little Chiltern village and is buried in the churchyard, his grave marked by a simple grey stone with handsome lettering. The Church, which has some Norman features, hospitably offers fresh water and shelter from rain to walkers on the Ridgeway.

Lord and Lady Nuffield's home from 1933-63 was **Nuffield Place**, in the next village, the somewhat uncomfortably named **Nettlebed**. The house was built in 1914 but was enlarged for the new occupants in 1933 and is a rare survival of a complete upper middle class home of the 1930s, complete with the furniture which Lord and Lady Nuffield chose for it. Some of it is antique but much of the rest was specially made, and there are some very fine clocks, rugs and tapestries. Several of the rooms are decorated in 1930s style. The garden is lovely, laid out just after the 1914-18 War with mature trees and a rockery.

IPSDEN

For a complete change of mood we make our way south on minor roads to **Ipsden** and the delightful **Wellplace Bird Farm**, home not just to birds but to lots of animals, including lambs, goats, monkeys, donkeys, otters, ponies and llamas, as well as, of course, a collection of brightly coloured tropical birds.

After a highly enjoyable interlude among these exotic inhabitants of the Oxfordshire countryside, we continue south to the A4074.

MAPLEDURHAM

Turning off on a little 'no through road' brings us to **Mapledurham**. At the end is a small community mostly consisting of Mapledurham House, the Watermill and the Church, in a picturesque setting by the Thames.

A beautiful Elizabethan mansion standing on the Oxfordshire bank of the Thames, **Mapledurham House** has all the ingredients for an enjoyable day out. This imposing brick-built country house lies four miles northwest of Reading and is signposted from the A4074 Caversham to Oxford road. Constructed on the site of an earlier manor house by the Blount family in the 1580s, it has continued to be the home of their descendants ever since.

The house has literary connections with, amongst others, Alexander Pope, who was a frequent caller in the 1700s. Present-day visitors can tour the house and view its magnificent plaster ceilings, great oak staircases and superb collection of portraits and period furniture.

Another attraction of the estate is the old riverside **Watermill**, a handsome late 15th Century building which stands on the site of an earlier structure mentioned in the Domesday Book. The mill remained in operation until 1947 and was the longest surviving working watermill on the Thames. In recent years it has been restored to its former glory so that today visitors can see the traditional machinery in action grinding wholemeal flour, samples of which can be purchased at the mill shop.
162

The beautifully-landscaped grounds offer some ideal picnic spots, most notably along the Thames riverbank and on Mill Island. The grounds also contain some spectacular plants and trees, including magnolias, cedars and Judas trees, as well as a solitary *gingko*, or maidenhair tree, the only pre-Ice Age species to survive. Cream teas are served in the 14th Century Old Manor and can be enjoyed at tables on the lawns sloping down to the river, or inside the stable block.

A particularly attractive way to visit Mapledurham is to take a river trip from Caversham Bridge for a 45-minute cruise along the Thames. Outbound trips depart at 2pm and return at 5pm, allowing over two hours to visit the estate.

There are also a number of well-appointed self-catering holiday cottages available for short-term lets on the estate farm or in Mapledurham village. These lovely period buildings sleep between five and ten people, and are all extensively restored and modernised. Contact the Estate Office for further details. The Mapledurham Estate is open on Saturdays, Sundays and Bank Holiday Mondays between Easter and the end of September.

Mapledurham House, Mapledurham Tel 01734 723350 Fax 01734 724016

The **Church** is well worth a visit, particularly for the tower, which was restored in 1863 by William Butterfield. This Victorian architect was something of a poet in the use of patterns in multicoloured brickwork but here he used, for his refacing of the tower, a bold chequered pattern in flint and brick. The village also has some Almshouses dated 1613.

We skirt Reading to explore the host of lovely villages that cluster around the town of Henley-on-Thames.

Just to the north is **Greys Court**, a house which has grown over the centuries. It dates mainly from the 16th Century but stands in the

Mapledurham House

courtyard of its 13th Century predecessor opposite a 14th Century tower. It was added to in the 18th Century and inside there are some fine furniture and decorations from this period.

There is a whole series of gardens, one of which is a rose garden dedicated to the old fashioned varieties which always seem to have more perfume. In the spring the wisterias are a mass of purple blooms. Don't miss the wheelhouse, where once a donkey, who must have had a very dull life, worked a treadmill to draw up water from the well. A relatively new feature is a brick maze laid out in 1982.

Another fine house to visit near Henley is **Fawley Court**, a great architectural contrast with Greys Court, which brings together the work of four key figures in English architecture. It was designed by Sir Christopher Wren and was built in 1684 in cheerful red brick with white details. Inside can be found decorations by Grinling Gibbons whose wood carvings of natural subjects, usually great masses of fruit, flowers and leaves, were much in demand. Later decorations are by James Wyatt, and the park was laid out by Capability Brown. The building contains a museum and library dedicated to Polish history, a collection of documents on the Polish kings and objects related to the Polish army.

Next we make our final call of this chapter, and take our farewell of Oxfordshire, at **Stonor Park**, five miles to the north. The setting would be magnificent even without the house, tucked away in a Chiltern valley apparently 'clyminge on an hille' as it was described in the 16th Century. There was a house on this site before the Conquest, but the present building has been built over the centuries from about 1190. It has been the home of the Stonor family for over 800 years.

It was also a house where Catholicism was practised throughout the period when attendance at Church of England services was required by law and Catholicism was regarded as tantamount to treason. In Stonor Park's medieval Chapel Mass has continued to be celebrated to this day.

In 1581 it provided a sanctuary for St Edmund Campion, first of the English Jesuit martyrs, but later the same year he was captured, tortured and hanged. He was beatified in 1886 and canonized in 1970. There is an exhibition devoted to his life and work at the house.

In spite of these rather sad associations, Stonor is a cheerful and peaceful place. The house is a family home and has a fine collection of family portraits, as well as furniture, paintings, drawings, tapestries sculptures and bronzes from Britain, Europe and America.

We now turn east and head into Buckinghamshire.

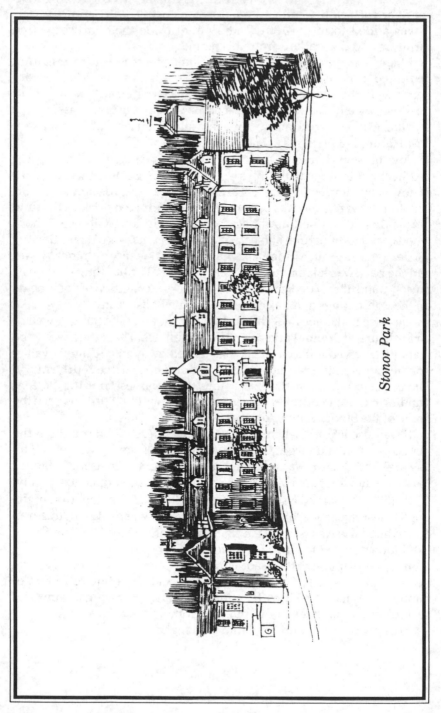

Stonor Park

CHAPTER EIGHT

Vale of Aylesbury and Wycombe Chilterns

The Suspension Bridge at Marlow

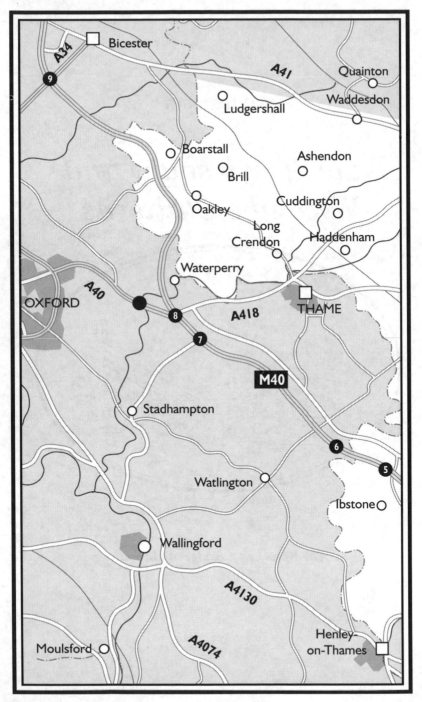

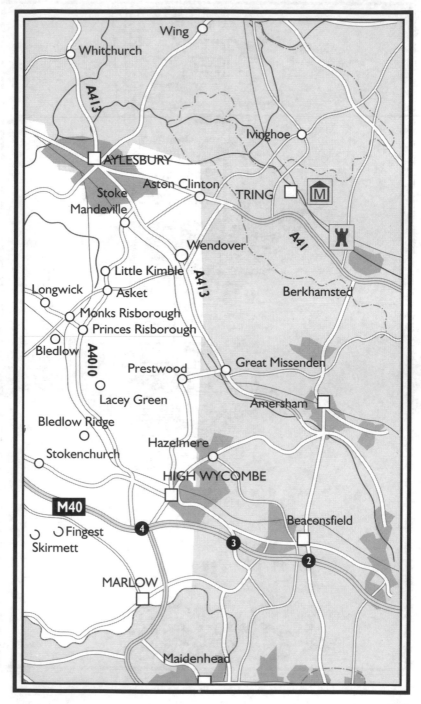

Waddesdon Manor

Vale of Aylesbury and Wycombe Chilterns

From Stonor House we cross into Buckinghamshire. There is no perceptible change in the landscape to mark the boundary - our way simply penetrates a little deeper into the Chilterns, whose gentle slopes are still clothed with the beech woodland which fed the furniture industry centred on High Wycombe, about which we will learn more later. But first we will turn north and after a while descend to the plain, agricultural land drained by the innumerable streams and little rivers which run down to meet the Thame.

FINGEST

Our first stop is the village of **Fingest**, a tiny place with attractive houses grouped round a **Church** with a massive tower which looks as though it must have been intended for a much grander building. Both tower and nave are Norman, and the former is topped by an unusual double roof which was added later, possible in the 17th Century. The chancel is 13th Century.

IBSTONE

We continue on to **Ibstone** where parts of the film 'Chitty, Chitty, Bang, Bang' were filmed at a windmill just a mile down the lane from the inn.

This part of the country is also home to the last red kites in England and on the edge of the Wormsley Valley you can see some wild fallow deer or the smaller muntjac deer. Around the whole of the area there are clearly-marked walks provided by the Chiltern Society.

STOKENCHURCH

Gibbons Farm and Rare Breeds Centre is based on a traditional working farm, boasting a farmhouse built in 1760, owned and managed by Sue and John McKelvey. Set in 84 acres, their farm offers visitors exploring this area of outstanding natural beauty, plenty of excellent facilities. Those feeling in need of some refreshment will be interested in the delightful tearoom, which provides a good selection of hot and cold snacks.

Gibbons Farm, Big More Lane, Horsleys Green, Stokenchurch Tel 01494 482385

The Rare Breeds Centre has a terrific assortment of traditional and rare farm animals, from pigs and chickens to the more unusual Manx Loghton Sheep. Should you wish to prolong your stay among the rolling Chiltern countryside, there is bed and breakfast accommodation available in a nearby comfortable barn conversion. All of the six rooms have full en-suite facilities and there is also a licensed camping and caravan site, which is open all year and provides perfect facilities for walkers who are travelling along the Ridgeway long distance footpath. Visit this excellent working farm and you can be sure of a warm welcome and an educational experience.

BLEDLOW

From **Chinnor** then up towards **Bledlow** our journey takes us, to see **Bledlow Cross** about a mile south-west of the village. At some time a great white cross has been cut into the turf of the hillside, exposing the gleaming white chalk below in the same way as at the White Horse above Uffington. It is 75ft across altogether and can be seen for miles. Why it was made is something of a mystery, even more so as it has a twin just a few miles away. Some say it is an Anglo-Saxon waymark on the **Icknield Way**, the great prehistoric track from the south coast through East Anglia to the Wash which passes along the foot of these hills. Seventeenth Century, say others.

We continue into the village and find, almost equally dramatically sited, the **Church of the Holy Trinity**, a flint church perched below the Chiltern escarpment, which has the remains of some 13th Century wall paintings.

172

LACEY GREEN

We continue north on minor roads through the hills, crossing the A4010 to take another minor road to the village of **Lacey Green** where there is a **Smock Mill**. Buckinghamshire rather specialises in windmills and we will meet others on our travels. The earliest type of windmill is the post mill, where the body of the mill, which carries the sails and all the machinery necessary for grinding the grain into flour, is mounted on an upright post, usually of oak, which can turn through 360 degrees and thus always face the wind.

Smock mills, like the one at Lacey Green, are more technologically advanced. Only the cap carrying the sails rotates and this means that the body of the mill, housing the milling machinery, can be much bigger and stronger. Tower mills are similar in principle, but whereas a smock mill is covered with weatherboarding above a brick base, tower mills were built as a single tower, usually of brick, right up to the cap which rotates as in the case of a smock mill. The Lacey Green example was first built around 1650, but was moved to this site from Chesham in 1821.

The poet Rupert Brooke used to spend weekends in this village with his friends at a local public house, charmingly named the **Pink and Lily**. Son of a master at Rugby School and a student at the University of Cambridge, he began writing poetry as a boy. In the years just before the 1914-18 War he travelled widely. When the war began he took part in the unsuccessful defence of Antwerp and died in 1915 on his way to the attempted landings at the Dardanelles in Turkey. His war poetry shows all the boyish enthusiasm of the early patriotic phase of the war, in vivid contrast to the bitter disillusion which marked the later work of his contemporaries. His early death and good looks have made him the very model of the doomed young poet.

Nearby is **Speen Farm**, a home of rest for horses which is open to visitors. The farm is run by a charitable organisation established in 1886 to care for horses, ponies and donkeys which have finished their working lives. Perhaps the most famous former resident was Sefton, the cavalry horse so horribly injured in the Hyde Park bomb blast.

We now come down the Chiltern escarpment into two Risboroughs, Princes and Monks. 'Princes' is named after the Black Prince, Edward the eldest son of Edward III, who held the land and a palace there. One of his predecessors as Lord of the Manor was King Harold, last of the Saxon Kings, who died at Hastings in 1066. 'Monks' refers to a Monastery sited somewhat to the north, which belonged to monks from Canterbury until the Order were disbanded and their property seized by Henry VIII. Just to complete the picture, 'Risborough' means 'hill where brushwood grows'. But they are not just pretty names and are well worth a stop.

The associations of the area are not just historic, they are even older, for the **Icknield Way** here continues its way along the foot of the Chilterns, sometimes part of the road system, but also used by the Ridgeway Long Distance Footpath.

PRINCES RISBOROUGH

Princes Risborough has many attractive little streets with 17th and 18th Century cottages, particularly around the market square, where stands the **Market House**, built in 1824, supported on oak pillars. The space underneath provides shelter for the market stalls and the Town Council still meets in the room above.

The Church is a handsome 13th Century building in stone and flint, though the spire, which dominates the town, is a modern addition. Nearby is the **Manor House**, dating from about 1670 and built of red brick. It is an early example of this style of house, which became much more common around 1700.

MONKS RISBOROUGH

The **Church** at **Monks Risborough** is also interesting. It is dedicated to St Dunstan, possibly chosen here because he was Archbishop of Canterbury from 960, Canterbury being the Mother House of the Monastery around which the settlement clustered. Like its neighbour at Princes Risborough it is built of stone and flint but its rather squat tower gives it a more massive appearance. The windows, in the Perpendicular style, are very fine.

Near the Church some old thatched cottages have survived modern development and just beyond is a dovecot, probably 16th Century, which has recently been restored. The birds got in through the lantern-like wooden arrangement on the roof to use the nesting boxes inside.

Also part of the parish are the pretty hamlets of **Askett**, with some pleasing old houses, and **Whiteleaf**, which lies on the route of the Icknield Way. Just above it another towering cross, like that at Bledlow, has been cut into the turf on the hillside, exposing the chalk. The cross is 80ft long, 72ft across, and its triangular 'plinth' has a base measuring 340ft.

Tucked away in the hills near **Kimble**, a little to the north-east, is **Chequers**, the 16th Century brick mansion which is the country residence of Britain's Prime Ministers. The **Church**, just beside the estate, has a series of early 14th Century wall paintings and it is interesting to speculate whether, over the years, Prime Ministers might have had their minds concentrated by one of them, now somewhat fragmentary, depicting the Last Judgement.

The Chiltern Hills are lovely and our journey returns to them soon but now we turn northwards across the plain drained by the river Thame, on the way down to its namesake town.

LONG CRENDON

Our first destination is **Long Crendon**, a picturesque village of 16th and 17th Century cottages on the B4011. It has a large **Church** with a tall Perpendicular-style tower and a number of other attractive buildings, such as the late 17th Century **Manor House** near the church and **Long Crendon Manor**, the core of which is 15th Century and which has a Gatehouse of the same age.

The **Court House** is a timber framed building which was probably built as a place for storing wool in the early years of the 15th Century. However, in medieval times it came to be used as a court and continued as such until the last century. It has an impressive Tudor chimney and the timber roof is original, though the windows and doors have been changed over the years.

BOARSTALL

To the west is the picturesque village of **Worminghall** from where we take the minor road north for our next destination, **Boarstall**, where a **Conservation Centre** is run by the National Trust and the Berkshire, Buckinghamshire and Oxfordshire Naturalists' Trust. A curious feature is a duck decoy, built in the 18th Century to catch ducks for eating. Nowadays we are interested in wildlife for its own sake, as the existence of the conservation centre shows. But, as in the case of the dovecot we saw in Monks Risborough, our ancestors' interest in birds concentrated on their use for the table.

Three miles away is **Boarstall Tower**, a Gatehouse which is the last remnant of a fortified mansion which received its 'licence to crenellate' in 1312. The house was demolished around 1750, but the Gatehouse still keeps guard and although it was somewhat altered in the 17th Century it retains its cross-shaped arrow slits.

BRILL

There is a handsome weatherboarded postmill at nearby **Brill**, built in the 1680s. Brill is a good place to build a windmill. The village is perched on a 700ft hill which gives wonderful views over the flatter land all around. Grouped around its village green are some lovely houses, mostly Georgian but including a handsome Elizabethan **Manor House** in warm red brick.

WOTTON UNDERWOOD

Buckinghamshire is full of fine houses and this part of the journey provides a feast of them. We thread our way north-eastwards to **Wotton Underwood**, where **Wotton House** stands in lovely parkland laid out from 1757-60 under the direction of the great landscape gardener

'Capability' Brown. Built between 1704 and 1714, it is said to be practically identical to the original Buckingham Palace in London.

A little to the south is **Dorton House** in the village of **Dorton**, a large Jacobean mansion in red brick built in 1626 around three sides of a courtyard.

We continue south east to the pretty village of **Nether Winchenden**, through which the River Thame flows on its way down from near Aylesbury, and where there is a **Manor House**, originally medieval but to which substantial additions were made in Tudor times, including some nice ornamental brick chimneys. The 18th Century saw further alterations, this time in the 'Strawberry Hill Gothick' style. It was the home of the last British Governor of New Jersey and Massachusetts, Sir Francis Bernard.

The **Church** is interesting too. It has escaped the tidying-up tendencies of Victorian restorers, so still has its hatchments, box pews and gallery containing the organ, giving us a glimpse of a village Church typical of the Georgian period.

WADDESDON

We have saved the most magnificent of the country houses in this area until last, making our way north to the A41 for **Waddesdon Manor**. It is a remarkable sight, a 19th Century version of a French Renaissance chateau set down in rolling English countryside, built for Baron Ferdinand de Rothschild between 1874 and 1889. Baron Ferdinand came from the Austrian branch of the great banking family, but lived in Britain from the age of 21. In 1874 he bought the Waddesdon and Winchenden Estates from the Duke of Marlborough and set about building his country house.

It was an immense operation and a steam railway was specially constructed to move materials, but in the end what had been a bare hill top was topped by a magnificent building, which borrows elements from several different French chateaux in the 'mix and match' 19th Century manner, surrounded by formal gardens and mature trees. The French influence extended even to the carthorses used on the site - powerful Percheron mares imported from Normandy.

The building aims for a 16th Century effect, but inside the rooms are decorated in 18th Century style - French, of course, with furniture and objets d'art of the highest quality. At the time all this luxury brought out, as might be expected, much jealousy and snobbery about the goings-on of the 'nouveaux riches'. Mary Gladstone, daughter of the Prime Minister, commented in 1885 that the pictures were 'too beautiful' but 'there is not a book in the house save 20 improper French novels.'

QUAINTON

Our next destination, by way of a complete change, is the **Buckinghamshire Railway Centre** at Quainton Road station just north of the A41. This is a must for all railway buffs and a very pleasant outing for almost everyone. The Quainton Railway Society have restored a rural station and amassed a collection of historic steam engines, wagons, carriages and all the other paraphernalia characteristic of the steam age - porters' trolleys, milk churns and those wonderfully nostalgic enamel advertisement panels. Experts will find the collection of engines very comprehensive - there are steam and diesel from the mainline to those which worked on London's underground railways, in factories and coal mines. In fact it has one of the largest collection of industrial locomotives in the country. An interesting programme of special events runs at weekends, catering for all sorts of transport enthusiasts, from bicycles to classic cars.

The village of **Quainton**, a little to the north, is also worth a visit. It has some pleasant Georgian houses and a row of Almshouses near the village green. These were built in 1687. The Church has a fine collection of 17th and 18th Century monuments and on the north side of the village is a tower windmill about 100ft tall dating from 1830.

AYLESBURY

From Quainton it is a short drive into **Aylesbury**. The town was comprehensively redeveloped in the 1970s and lost some of its character in the process, but in exchange it gives the traveller the opportunity to use a modern shopping centre.

Temple Street has survived relatively intact and Church Street also has some pleasant buildings. The **Church** itself retains some early English style features, but it was extensively restored in the 19th Century by George Gilbert Scott, one of the most famous of the Victorian church restorers. Its best features are the 15th Century Lady Chapel and the beautifully carved late 12th Century font. Sir Nicholas Pevsner called it 'a beautiful, restrained and civilised piece'. There is also a **County Museum** with displays on local history.

Just to the south is the village of **Stoke Mandeville**, which has become famous for its hospital specialising in the treatment of spinal injuries and burns.

HAZLEMERE

We now make our way towards High Wycombe but before reaching the town we turn off to visit **Hughenden Manor** near Hazlemere, home of the great Victorian Prime Minister Benjamin Disraeli, Earl of Beaconsfield, from 1847 to 1881. Disraeli was also a novelist, son of a

Buckinghamshire Railway Centre, Quainton

writer and literary critic called Isaac D'Israeli, who lived for a time in the village of Bradenham on the other side of High Wycombe.

Disraeli's literary career is now almost entirely remembered only in connection with the idea of 'one nation Toryism' which he explored in three of his novels. Briefly, he rejects the idea that there are inevitably 'two nations', the rich and the poor, and sought, in fictional form, to impress upon the rich their duty to care for the poor, thereby creating one nation. In this way he allied himself with, and gained a leading position among, the group of radical Tories known as the Young Englanders.

Disraeli bought Hughenden shortly after the publication of the third of his novels dealing with this theme, 'Tancred'. He did so because it was felt that a leading conservative politician ought to have a 'stately home' of his own. But Disraeli was not a wealthy man. The solution was for his supporters to lend him the money so that he could have this essential characteristic of a gentleman.

What we see now is a remodelled 18th Century house, which has been refaced with bricks of several colours, giving it a somewhat hybrid but not unpleasing effect. Pevsner, however, disliked it and called it 'excruciating, everything sharp, angular and aggressive', so the visitor wil have to make up their own mind. The interior decoration is a good example of the Victorian Gothic style and there is an interesting collection of memorabilia of Disraeli's life, including much of his furniture and his library.

Disraeli enjoyed being there. He wrote, 'When I come down to Hughenden I pass the first week in sauntering about my park and examining all the trees, and then I saunter in the library and survey the books'. He is buried in the nearby churchyard, where there is a monument to him given by Queen Victoria. The Queen and he were great friends, and she is said to have much preferred him to the other great statesman of her time, William Gladstone.

HIGH WYCOMBE

We now continue on to **High Wycombe** and its environs. This is the largest town in Buckinghamshire, traditionally known for the manufacture of chairs, particularly the famous Windsor design. It is still a centre of furniture manufacture and two factories, G Plan and Ercol, welcome visitors. It is a town with a pleasant centre, a wide High Street and a **Market House** which was designed by Robert Adam.

There is also a **Guildhall** which is the scene, each year, of a traditional ceremony showing a healthily sceptical attitude to politicians on the part of our ancestors. Each year the mayor and councillors are publicly weighed - to see if they have become fat at the expense of the citizens.

All Saints Church, in the centre of the town, is a fine large building dating from the 11th Century and enlarged in the 13th. In the north chapel is a large and very classical memorial by Peter Scheemakers to the Earl of Shelburne, erected in 1754.

Wycombe Local History and Chair Museum is housed in an interesting building. The original 18th Century house was extended in the 19th Century, when the front was given its attractive flint facade, and added to again at the beginning of our own century. In the grounds is a medieval 'motte' - an artificial mound usually built as a base for a castle - which may, in this case, have been little more than a wooden tower.

The displays give an excellent idea of the work and crafts of local people over the years. There is, of course, an excellent collection of chairs and other furniture of the type which would have found a cherished place in the homes of ordinary people, rather than in the halls of the great like Waddesdon and Hughenden. Other crafts are well represented, such as the lace for which Buckinghamshire was once famous, rushwork, papermaking and, of course, agriculture.

To the east is our next destination, **West Wycombe Park**. The House itself is a beautiful Palladian style mansion. It was originally built in the early 18th Century but was boldly remodelled around the mid-century for Sir Francis Dashwood. The park around the House was landscaped by Thomas Cook, a pupil of Capability Brown, and Humphry Repton, very much a classical landscape with temples, an artificial lake shaped like a swan and statues. Inside is a good collection of tapestries, furniture and paintings, and the frescoes and painted ceilings are particularly good examples.

Hewn out of the nearby hillside are **West Wycombe Caves**, created, possibly from some existing caverns, by Sir Francis Dashwood as part of a programme of public works. After a series of failed harvests had created great poverty and distress in the countryside nearby he employed labourers to excavate chalk from the hill to be used to surface a new road between West Wycombe and High Wycombe. In so doing he created an underground world where winding passages lead to small chambers, some with artificial stalactites and stalagmites.

There was a racier side to Sir Francis' character than is suggested by this example of a 'one nation' approach before its time. He was an interesting character, a great traveller and dabbler in the arts, an MP and quite a successful politician. But he is now most remembered as the creator of the Hell Fire Club, better known to the members as the Brotherhood of St Francis or Dashwood's Apostles. They were a group of rakes who met a couple of times a year; the tales that are told of their activities are highly coloured and based on very little evidence. No doubt they included large amounts of alcohol and the company of women they would not have acknowledged elsewhere. Tradition has it that meetings were held in these caverns, though the Brotherhood usually met, from about 1750 to 1774, at Medmenham Abbey.

The **Church** is another marvel. It is sited in the remnants of an iron age fort and was originally built in the 13th Century. It is in an isolated spot simply because it was originally the church of the village of **Haveringdon** which has since disappeared. Sir Francis made the tower higher and placed on top a golden ball inside which six people can sit. He also entertained his friends there - he had a taste for hospitality in strange settings, obviously - one guest reporting that he had been regaled with 'divine milk punch and jolly songs very unfit for the profane ears of the world below.'

The interior of the Church was also remodelled by Dashwood to look like the 18th Century notion of 'a very superb Egyptian Hall'. It must be one of the more surprising treatments ever given to an English village Church.

Once more on the track of Sir Francis, we head off south on minor roads to **Medmenham Abbey**. The house was built on the site of a Cistercian Abbey founded in the 13th Century, of which only fragments remain. As it stands now it is partly late 16th Century, partly 18th Century Gothic but most of it dates from 1898. The 18th Century 'Gothick' part dates from the time when it was leased by Dashwood, and was used by his group of friends as the main location of the meetings of 'the mad monks of Medmenham'. The brotherhood is said to have had as its motto 'do whatever you like'. And, apparently, they did just that!

MARLOW

Finally we make our way to **Marlow** and to the Thames once again, where Jerome K Jerome, of whom we have already made the acquaintance further upstream, wrote his masterpiece 'Three Men in a Boat' at the Two Brewers pub in St Peter Street. He obviously enjoyed being there, for he wrote,

'Marlow is one of the pleasantest river centres I know of. It is a bustling, lively little town; not very picturesque on the whole, it is true, but there are many quaint nooks and corners to be found in it, nevertheless - standing arches in the shattered bridge of Time, over which our fancy travels back to the days when Marlow Manor owned Saxon Algar for its lord, ere conquering William seized it to give it to Queen Matilda, ere it passed to the Earls of Warwick.....'

In fact, it seems to be a good place for writing, for Mary Shelley, wife of the poet, finished writing her novel 'Frankenstein' after the newly-married couple moved there in 1817. Thomas Love Peacock, a novelist and poet nowadays almost completely forgotten outside examination syllabi, lived in West Street while writing one of his works, 'Nightmare Abbey', published in 1818. We may owe the idea of the 'country house novel' to him, for he often used the idea of a group of oddly assorted people brought together in a house in the country as a framework for

Hughenden Manor

amusing conversation and absurd incidents. He was a friend of the Shelleys and they may have moved to Marlow to be near him.

The architectural feature by which the town is best known is its suspension bridge, finished in 1836 and designed by the same architect responsible for the famous bridge which connects Buda and Pest, the two halves of the Hungarian capital. Nearby is the **Parish Church** which was built in 1835. Other interesting buildings are the **Old Parsonage**, part of a 14th Century house, **Marlow Place**, built in 1720 with, as Pevsner puts it, 'the oddest details on its facade', and **Remnantz**, in West Street, a curiously named house of the early 18th Century.

Marlow is probably best known for its annual Regatta, held in June, but all year round there is activity on the river, with pleasure boats giving rides as well as canoes and rowing boats for hire.

For a refreshing drink or a tasty homecooked meal, visitors to Marlow would be well advised to call in at **The Royal Oak,** situated one mile from the centre of Marlow in a wonderful and picturesque area for walkers and ramblers. There's a warm and welcoming atmosphere for everyone and as well as being patronised by local trade, The Royal Oak is popular with the many visitors touring this area throughout the year. Refurbished in traditional country kitchen style you'll find plenty of character here.

*The Royal Oak, Chalk Pit Lane, Bovingdon Green, Marlow Tel
01628 483875*

The pleasant dining area provides a cosy and comfortable setting in which to enjoy your meal; choose from a menu which offers a good and varied selection to suit all tastes. Sunday lunch is particularly popular. The pub is open all day and has a very good selection of wines, malts and cask ales. The large garden and lawn area is ideal for families who are welcomed all year round. With extensive parking, good food and space to move about, The Royal Oak is an easy place to call in, relax and enjoy refreshment.

From Marlow we turn briefly away from the Thames and head eastwards, out of this chapter and into the next.

Metroland and North Chilterns

Cliveden

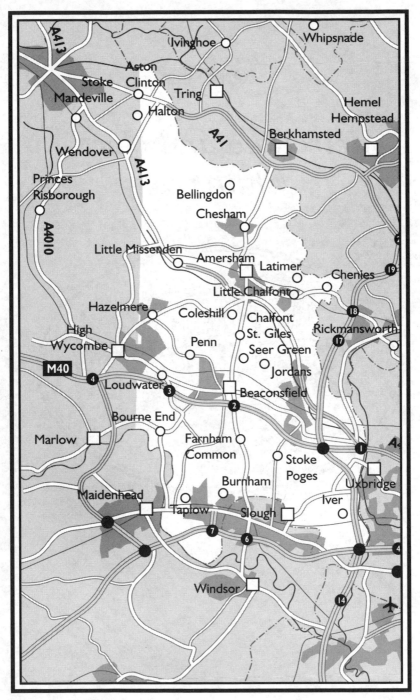

Metroland and North Chilterns

With Chapter Nine we approach Outer London, and touch the western outcrops of 'Metroland' - where new housing followed the Metropolitan Railway, ancestor of the 'Met' line of the London Underground. The phrase was invented by the Railway itself, to publicise its sideline in housebuilding near its own stations.

But it was John Betjeman who made the phrase live beyond the generally short life of the advertising slogan, looking with an affectionate eye on the dreams of the people who lived in the new houses as well as mourning the loss of countryside which their building brought about. The trains which take the commuters to work have also, of course, taken generations of Londoners to walk and picnic in the woods and hills of the Chilterns.

The Chilterns we will explore in this chapter are the mysterious **'Chiltern Hundreds'** for the stewardship of which Members of Parliament apply when they wish to resign. The practice grew up because although an MP technically has no right to abandon his seat he cannot be both an MP and hold 'an office of profit under the crown'. Originally the stewards of the Chiltern Hundreds guarded travellers against bandits who infested these hills, now so pleasantly civilised. For this service the stewards were paid and although both the job and the pay are now nominal, the conditions necessary for resignation are fulfilled.

Our first destination is the country house of **Cliveden**, near **Taplow**, once the home of Lady Nancy Astor, the first woman to take her seat as an MP. Women first gained the right to vote and stand as Parliamentary candidates in 1918. When, in 1919, Nancy Astor's husband became a Viscount and moved from the Commons to the Lords, she stood as candidate for his Plymouth seat and was elected. In Parliament she was mostly concerned with social questions.

Cliveden became a glittering centre of the social and political scene and the 'Cliveden set' was associated, in the 1930s, with the school of thought which favoured the appeasement of Mussolini and Hitler.

The house was built in the middle of the 19th Century, to quite a restrained design in the Italian renaissance style by Sir Charles Barry.

Cliveden

However, the site 200ft above a bend in the Thames makes up for any lack of drama.

Most of the house is not open to the public, but the grounds are. These are very fine, with temples, statues and fountains set in formal gardens, including rose and water gardens and a magnificent parterre. Parterres, formal arrangements of beds of flowers in intricate geometrical patterns on a completely flat area, belong, as the name suggests, pre-eminently to the French school of landscape gardening and are particularly associated with the work of Andre Le Notre, gardener to Louis IV. All depends on human skill in disposing nature in an orderly and ornamental way, the complete opposite of the Capability Brown school which aimed to beautify a natural landscape by using art to conceal art.

TAPLOW

After leaving Cliveden, with its gardens and political associations, we head south to **Taplow** itself. The **Church** has a brass monument to Nichole de Aumberdene of about 1350, a bearded figure only 12 inches high in the head of a Cross. It has the distinction of being the oldest brass commemorating a civilian. The figures on the monument to Richard Manfield who died in 1455 are very skilfully carved.

The name Taplow is derived from Taeppa's mound, the Old English for mound being 'hlaw'. (Just as we have found that 'downs' can be 'ups' in English place names, so 'lows' can mean 'highs'.)

The remains of Taeppa's mound, a Saxon burial mound on high ground above the Thames were opened by archaeologists in 1883 and revealed treasures second only to those found in the Sutton Hoo ship burial, including the arms of the buried hero, together with more peaceful utensils such as bowls, drinking horns, glass beakers and a gold buckle of very fine workmanship. They are now in the British Museum. But of Taeppa himself and, if the mound is indeed his grave, why he should have been buried in such princely state, nothing is known.

To the south of Taplow can be found **Wickenden Vineyards**. Vine growing is not a very common feature of our agricultural scene, but some of the wines produced in English vineyards are well considered by connoisseurs. Wickenden was established in 1976 and now has four acres under 5000 vines.

BURNHAM

Our next call is at **Burnham**, which has grown a little since it was named 'homestead by a stream', though it retains a rural air, before continuing southwards to **Dorney Court**. This lovely pink brick and timbered house was built about 1440 and has substantially kept its original appearance, a many-gabled Tudor house with tall brick chimneys. Inside is a feast of furniture, oak from the 15th and 16th Centuries and examples of lacquered furniture from the 17th. In addition there are 400 years of family portraits.

The house, which has been in the ownership of the same family since 1542, has associations with Barbara Lady Castlemaine, for many years the mistress of Charles II, who married into the family about 1659. She was beautiful and, according to Count Grammont's memoirs of the court, 'a woman lively and discerning'. She was also extremely elegant. Pepys admitted, in his diary for 21st May 1662, ogling the washing in her garden; 'saw the finest smocks and linen petticoats of my Lady Castlemaine's, with rich lace at the bottom, that ever I saw; and did me good to look at them.' She also managed to scandalise the unshockable Restoration court with her other liaisons, particularly one involving a tight-rope walker!

The **Church** is mainly 14th Century and built of stone and flint, but with an early Tudor brick tower and a brick porch dated 1661. The mixture gives it a cheerful look which complements the nearby house very nicely.

Just to the north are **Burnham Beeches**, which have long been a place of rest and recreation for Londoners. How the area has survived to our day as open space is an early example of a successful effort to save a stretch of well-loved landscape for the general public. In 1879 it was put up for sale by public auction. There were fears that the trees would be cut down and the land developed as London expanded. One of the earliest pieces of legislation by which countryside could be protected from development allowed the City of London Corporation to purchase open land in order to preserve it for public access. The problem in the case of Burnham Beeches was that it was included in a lot with some arable land, which, under the legislation, the City Corporation could not buy. However an MP called Sir Henry Peek bought the whole lot and sold the Burnham Beeches part to the Corporation. It was then dedicated to be kept as an 'open space for ever' for the recreation and enjoyment of the public.

From Burnham Beeches we cross to **Farnham Common**, following in the footsteps of George Orwell's couple, Rosemary and Gordon, in his novel 'Keep the Aspidistra Flying', published in 1936. They travelled to Farnham Common 'in an absurd chocolate coloured bus with no top' and 'exclaimed at the loveliness of everything. The dew, the stillness, the satiny stems of the birches, the softness of the turf under your feet!.' And then 'All around them the beech-trees soared, curiously phallic with their smooth skin-like bark and their flutings at the base. Nothing grew at their

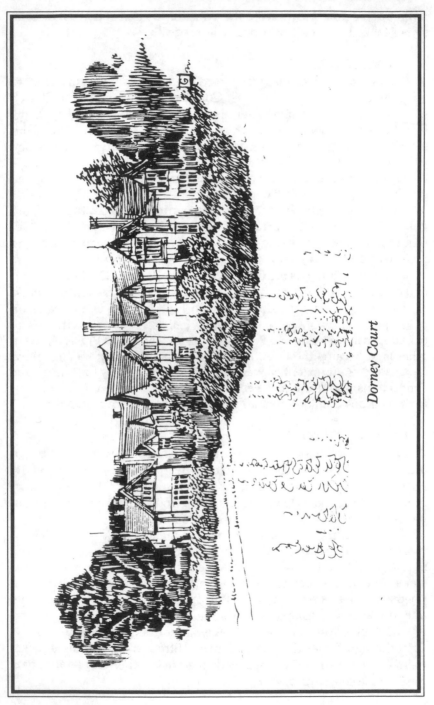

Dorney Court

roots, but the dried leaves were strewn so thickly that in the distance the slopes looked like folds of copper-coloured silk.'

STOKE POGES

It is to **Stoke Poges** that we go next. Thomas Gray was inspired to write his famous 'Elegy Written in a Country Churchyard' by the Church here, which he often visited after his mother came to live in the village. He is buried with her in the churchyard, among those in whose 'short and simple annals of the poor' he saw heroism and nobility: 'Some village Hampden, that, with dauntless breast, The little tyrant of his fields withstood, Some mute inglorious Milton here may rest, Some Cromwell guiltless of his country's blood.'

The **Church** itself is very handsome, particularly from the east end, where the three gables of the 16th Century Hastings chapel, the 13th Century chancel and, above them, the Norman nave form a charming picture huddled against the foursquare tower with its pyramidal roof.

East of the Church is the **Gray Monument**, designed by James Wyatt and erected in 1799. Gray's mother stayed with her sister at **Stoke Park**, a large late-Georgian mansion, originally built for John Penn, grandson of William Penn, who, persecuted for his beliefs, left Britain with a party of Quakers in 1682 to found Pennsylvania and the city of Philadelphia in what later became the USA. He later returned to work for his fellow Quakers. To some extent he was personally protected by his aristocratic connections, and through his efforts in 1686 all persons imprisoned for their religious opinions, including 1200 Quakers, were released.

BEACONSFIELD

Our next destination is **Beaconsfield**, where there are a number of interesting old houses around the old town, mainly Georgian in mellow red brick though the **Old Rectory** dates back to about 1500. The new town is now, as Sir Nicholas Pevsner puts it, 'Metroland, shopping terraces of between the wars and well-to-do suburban housing.'

The poet Edmund Waller, who was born in the village of **Coleshill** three miles to the north, lived here in Beaconsfield. After getting involved in a Royalist plot in 1643 he was banished from Parliament and spent some time in exile before returning to Beaconsfield to concentrate on poetry. He took care to write poems in praise of Cromwell and the King, once the latter was restored to the throne. Perhaps he had himself in mind when he wrote 'The soul's dark cottage, batter'd and decay'd, Lets in new light through chinks that time has made; Stronger by weakness, wiser men become, As they draw near to their eternal home.' He has an ornate tomb in the churchyard.

Another literary association is with G K Chesterton, who wrote his 'Father Brown' crime stories while living in the town. Edmund Burke, the statesman and political philosopher, bought an imposing Palladian house called **Gregories** just outside Beaconsfield in 1768 which enabled him, as he wrote, to 'cast a little root in this country'. It also meant that he was financially embarrassed for years afterwards. He is also buried in the churchyard.

Beaconsfield is also the setting for the charming model country of **Bekonscot**. Time has stood still for over 60 years in this miniature wonderland of make-believe, which portrays rural England in the 1930s, and is the oldest Model Village in the world.

It all began in the late 1920s, when a London accountant, Roland Callingham, built models in his garden in Beaconsfield. He then bought the field opposite, built more intricate models and a friend from Ascot added a miniature railway, creating the name 'Bekonscot'. When the village was opened, people started throwing coins into a bucket for charity, and even today, under the management of the Church Army, all surplus profits, so far totalling more than one million pounds, go to charity.

As you meander through six little villages, each with their miniature population going about their daily routine, the paths take you past knee-high houses, churches, schools and lush lawns. The local hunt gives chase near a cricket match, while animals at the zoo look on. Aeroplanes are waiting to take off from the airfield, and a tram shuttles backwards and forwards on the promenade. An elevated walkway gives a different dimension to the village, and Adams Park, the home of Wycombe Wanderers, is also reproduced, depicting an exciting home match.

The gardens are a delight, and in order to preserve the proportions, many conifers are replaced yearly by smaller ones, as keeping a sense of scale in the garden is crucial to its success.

The 'village' covers one and a half acres and although the bustling town of Beaconsfield has grown around 'the oldest Model Village in the World' since the 1930s, the little patch of nostalgia which is Bekonscot still manages to maintain its serenity.

WOOBURN GREEN

A little to the south the small village of **Wooburn Green** is well worth visiting.

The Queen and Albert stands on the east side of The Green in the village. Its traditional style large bay windows, colourful signs and hanging baskets create an inviting appearance. Valerie Noble has been the owner of this old coaching inn for the past 18 years and enjoys a good clientele. It's a 'chatty' pub where visitors and locals gather to exchange and discuss the latest news.

This old inn was rebuilt in the 1700s and tie rails for the horses are evidence of its coaching history. Inside the pub is a traditional inglenook fireplace, wood panelling and displays of brasses and other decoration line the walls.

Specialities include three real ales with a rotating guest. Good pub fayre is generally available and Valerie's own Honey Roast Ham is a particular favourite. Enjoy the award-winning garden with its Pergola, rock-rimmed pond, Petanque pitch, lawned seating area and patio.

The Queen and Albert, 24 The Green, Wooburn Green Tel 01628 520610

The Red Cow, 14 The Green, Wooburn Green Tel 01628 531344

Also in Wooburn Green, **The Red Cow** is a lovely old village pub and eating place which provides a warm welcome to visitors and locals alike. Originally a cottage dating from the 14th Century, it was extended in the 16th Century and later became a coaching inn on the Oxford to London route. The building is reputed to have been haunted ever since a coachman's cape was found hanging in an upstairs room and disintegrated on touch. At one time cattle were regularly sold and slaughtered on the nearby green, an occurrence which is thought to have given the pub its name.

Today the atmosphere at the Red Cow is relaxed and welcoming, with half-panelled walls, exposed timber beams and an open log fire in winter. The bar serves a selection of ales from the oldest independent brewery in the country, Morland, along with a wide variety of cocktails personally mixed by landlord Chris Ashton.

Chris also provides an excellent range of English pub fare, all home made from fresh locally-supplied produce. The menu includes a selection of sandwiches, steaks and game dishes, along with a traditional roast lunch on Sundays. The Red Cow also has an attractive patio to the rear, rising to a beer garden which looks out across rolling fields to a tree-lined horizon.

SEER GREEN

Just to the north of Beaconsfield is **Seer Green. The Three Horseshoes** is an impressive country pub and eating place which stands behind the Church in Seer Green. Built in 1800, this handsome old inn offers a warm welcome, fine traditional ales and exceptional home-cooked food. The regular menu is enhanced with a selection of appealing fish dishes and daily specials, such as duck breast in orange and Cointreau.

Three Horseshoes, 22 Orchard Road, Seer Green Tel 01494 677522

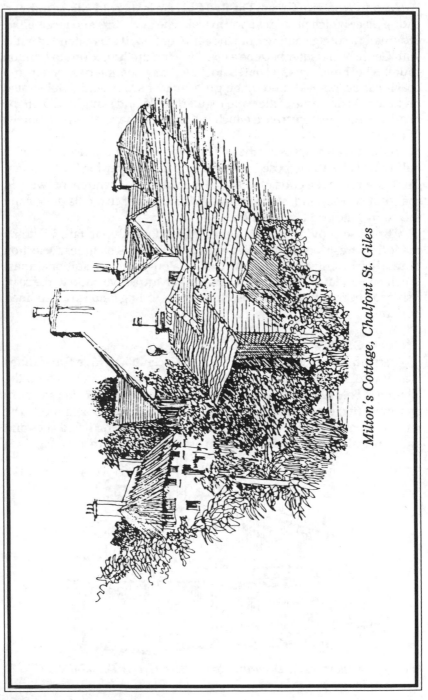

Milton's Cottage, Chalfont St. Giles

Patrons can choose between the relaxed atmosphere of the lounge bar with its beamed ceilings and deep curtained windows, and the lively public bar with its range of popular pub games. Proprietors Viv and Grant Woffinden also organise regular themed evenings with dishes from around the world and live music to match. Children are welcome and there is an attractive beer garden to the rear with its own safe play area.

PENN

Also to the north of Beaconsfield is the village of **Penn**, said to be the ancestral home of William Penn, the Quaker and American pioneer with whose grandson we became acquainted in Stoke Poges. The village **Church** has a very fine roof, constructed on the tie-beam principal, with carved tracery between the beams. Inside there is a 15th Century wall painting of the Last Judgement and an 18th Century pulpit decorated with marquetry work. There are a number of interesting monuments, including some brasses to the Penn family. The village has some pleasant houses and is well worth the short detour.

Just north west of Penn beyond Tylers Green, the place to go for superb freshly-baked bread, cakes and confectionery is the **Progress Bakery** in **Hazlemere**. Well worth making the effort to find, it is situated opposite Holy Trinity Church and adjacent to The Crown public house on the A404 Amersham road, a short distance to the east of its junction with the B474. A handsome detached shop which has been a bakery for over 100 years, for many decades it was run by the Banham family who made their deliveries by horse and cart before becoming the proud owners of the first motorised delivery van in the village.

Progress Bakery, 273 Amersham Road, Hazlemere Tel: 01494 530149

197

Today, the bakery is owned and personally run by Angela and Richard Crapp, charming people with over 20 years' experience in baking. Famous locally for their crusty well-fired loaves, a wide range of traditional and continental-style bread is baked in the time-honoured manner on the oven sole. On entering the shop, customers are met by the wonderful aroma of freshly-baked bread which is also sold to wholesale customers throughout the district, a testimony to its fine quality. In addition, a mouthwatering selection of cakes is produced by the Spanish confectioner, including celebration cakes, doughnuts and naughty-but-nice cream cakes.

As well as being an accomplished baker, Richard is a model flying enthusiast who takes his large quarter-scale aeroplane all over the world. It is also worth visiting the Progress Bakery in Little Chalfont: run by Angela and Richard's daughter, it incorporates a pleasant coffee shop.

JORDANS

After our exploration of Beaconsfield and its surroundings we head eastwards with a pause at **Jordans**, once more following the footsteps of William Penn.

The village of Jordans is interesting from an architectural point of view, having its origin in a 'garden suburb' type development begun in 1919. The red-brick houses are in what Sir Nicholas Pevsner calls a 'comfortable simplified Tudor' style.

Possibly the most famous of all Quaker Meeting Houses, where Penn and other members of his family are buried, is here. It is also one of the earliest, built in 1688, a simple red-brick building among beechwoods.

Nearby is **Old Jordans Mayflower Barn** which is believed, though without much supporting evidence, to contain beams salvaged from the original Mayflower ship which took the Pilgrim Fathers to New England.

CHALFONT ST GILES

A fascinating time is guaranteed at **The Chiltern Open Air Museum** at nearby **Chalfont St. Giles**, which rescues buildings of historic or architectural importance from across the Chilterns region and re-erects them on its 45-acre site of beautiful natural meadow and woodland.

Offers of buildings come from many sources and the Museum will only accept one if it is to be demolished, always preferring to see a building remain where it was originally built. Once a decision to move a building has been made, it is surveyed in great detail, then slowly and painstakingly dismantled and stored at the Museum until time and funds allow for re-erection.

Once restored, the Museum likes to use them to display artefacts and implements appropriate to their history and use. This has led to the Museum becoming a renowned educational centre with themed visits for school parties linked to the National Curriculum.

Over 30 buildings are now on display, including an Iron Age House and cast iron Edwardian Conveniences. There is a complete Victorian farmyard, with appropriate livestock including a Shire horse, Aylesbury ducks, chickens, geese, turkeys, Jersey cattle, Oxford Down sheep and goats. Other buildings include a blacksmith's forge, a toll house, 18th Century thatched cottages, a 1940s prefab and a Victorian Vicarage room.

Three acres of fields are farmed in a medieval method, organically growing historic crop varieties including woad, from which indigo dye is extracted and used in dyeing demonstrations.

In a 19th Century barn rescued from Skippings Farm in Chalfont St. Peter is the **Hawk and Owl Trust's National Education and Exhibition Centre**. The Trust is dedicated to conserving wild birds of prey in their natural habitats through practical research, creative conservation and imaginative education.

The Museum holds lots of special events throughout the year to bring the buildings to life including Music and Dance through the Ages, Victorian Christmas, Harvest Celebration and an annual Open Air Theatre. But even if you visit on a quiet day there is plenty to see and enjoy.

Not content with such an attraction Chalfont St Giles is a pretty village with several interesting houses, including **Milton's Cottage**, where the blind poet John Milton wrote 'Paradise Lost' and began work on its sequel, 'Paradise Regained'. He moved to this cottage, found for him by a former pupil, another Quaker named Thomas Ellwood, in 1665 to escape the plague which was raging in London. He returned to London in 1666, but this is the only one of his homes to have survived. The 16th Century timber-framed building has been preserved as it was at the time Milton lived there, complete with a cottage garden. There is a display of rare books, including first editions of Paradise Lost and Paradise Regained as well as other items of interest on Milton, the area and some old maps.

LITTLE CHALFONT

From Chalfont St Giles we make our way upstream along the valley of the prettily named River Misbourne to **Little Chalfont**. Another Chalfont in this area, further down river, is called **Chalfont St Peter**. 'Chalfont' means 'the spring where the calves come to drink' and must point to a long history of raising cattle in these gentle, well-watered hills and valleys. At Little Chalfont we cross over into the valley of the River Chess to visit the Manor House at **Chenies**.

Chenies Manor was built in the 15th and 16th Centuries and was the original home of the Earls (later Dukes) of Bedford before they moved over the county boundary to Woburn. Among the distinguished visitors who are reputed to have slept here are Henry VIII and Elizabeth I. Inside the house are contemporary tapestries, furniture and a collection of antique dolls, as well as plenty of material for the imagination in the form of hiding places and secret passages. Below the house is a medieval undercroft and well, and the house includes a fortified tower, relic of insecure days when an aristocratic household might need a strong refuge at any time.

It is a very attractive house to look at from outside, with its stepped gables and elaborately-patterned high brick chimneys. There is every incentive to explore it from outside as well as in, because the gardens are full of interest, among the delights being a Tudor-style sunken garden and a 'physick garden' with a great variety of herbs used both for medicinal purposes and for culinary purposes in the kitchen. There is also a maze and a Victorian-style kitchen garden with unusual fruit and vegetables.

The nearby **Church** should not be omitted. It is 15th Century, though much restored in the 19th. The hammerbeam roof, for example, is Victorian. The great glory of the Church is the magnificent series of monuments to generations of Bedfords which are of a quality to interest those not normally greatly taken with such things.

LATIMER
We now follow the valley of the Chess north-west towards Chesham, but pause in **Latimer**, a picturesque place with a waterfall by the bridge. There was a Roman villa nearby and tiles from it turn up in the oddest places, such as the paths on the village green.

CHESHAM
Chesham is a pleasant town among wooded hills with a number of interesting houses of the 18th and 19th Centuries and a large **Church** with a wall painting of St Christopher wading through the water. Its growth from a sleepy market town has been due to the 'Metroland' factor. It is one of the termini of the Metropolitan Line of the London Underground system. The Metropolitan Railway Company began by operating the first urban underground railway in the world from 1863, running trains

from Paddington to Farringdon Street in central London. However, the company was never content with being only an urban or even, later, suburban railway and pushed its main line ambitions through a policy of acquiring other lines to link into its system as well as building its own. At its high point the Metropolitan operated trains as far into Buckinghamshire as Quainton Road, where we visited the Buckinghamshire Railway Centre, and Aylesbury. The Metropolitan Railway began its services here at Chalfont in 1889.

AMERSHAM

We turn south now, to **Amersham**, the other Buckinghamshire terminus of the Metropolitan Line. The Metropolitan Railway used to continue to Aylesbury, though London Underground trains now end here. Amersham is the sort of unassuming place which well repays a wander round its streets, an attractive old town with a number of interesting buildings including lots of 18th Century houses and some Almshouses established by Sir William Drake in 1657. The red brick and stone **Town Hall** was built a little later in 1682.

The Church dates mostly from the 14th and 15th Centuries and has some 17th Century stained glass. It also has a very fine collection of monuments, many of them to the Drake family, including one to Elizabeth Drake, an elegant example in 1757 of the work of Sir Henry Cheere.

Between Amersham and Little Missenden is **Shardeloes**, built in the 1750s by another William Drake, this time the local MP. It was altered and completed by Robert Adam, his first notable work. Adam has been described as 'the greatest British architect of the later 18th Century' and 'equally if not more brilliant' as a decorator and furniture designer. Together with his brother James, Adams presided over a change in taste in British architecture from the rather formal Palladian to a freer and more romantic approach to classical themes.

Just outside Amersham, **The Plough** at **Hyde Heath** is a delightful inn which stands overlooking the cricket green in the centre of the village. The only survivor of Hyde Heath's four pubs, it was converted to an alehouse from a row of farm workers' cottages over 150 years ago. Inside the atmosphere is warm and welcoming, with half-panelled walls, brick fireplaces, brass ornaments and an antique clock ticking reassuringly on the mantelpiece.

The Plough, The Common, Hyde Heath Tel 01494 783163

Lee and Neil Phillips serve fine traditional ales and excellent pub food, with local lamb a speciality. Children are very welcome, both inside and in the attractive courtyard garden to the side. In winter, customers can sit beside an open fire enjoying one of Neil's celebrated mulled wines.

LITTLE MISSENDEN
In the lee of the Chiltern Hills, lying amid rolling meadows is the extremely attractive village of **Little Missenden**, skirted to the rear by the River Misbourne with an abundance of ducks and geese congregating under the little wooden bridge.

GREAT MISSENDEN
We continue our journey to **Great Missenden**, which has an attractive flint and stone Church and **Missenden Abbey,** an 18th Century Gothic house, known to many nowadays through its popular Adult Education courses and summer schools. The Abbey which gave the house its name was originally a community of Arroasian canons, founded in 1133, and the present house occupies the site of the cloisters.

While here, look out for the **Old Court House**, to the rear of The George. There are only two Court Houses in the Chiltern Hundreds - one at Long Crendon, and the other here at Great Missenden which dates from the early 1400s.

The George Inn, 94 High Street, Great Missenden Tel 01494 862084

On the main street in Great Missenden you will come across **The George Inn,** where the hosts Guy and Sally will make you feel very welcome. The building has a 500-year history and has always had strong links with the nearby Abbey. The pub is cosy and very olde worlde, featuring timbered walls, moulded beams and small alcoves. There is a fine range of beers, all hand pulled, and in winter mulled wine is served. The six bedrooms are also of character, in particular the Queen's Arch Honeymoon Suite. All are individually furnished with full facilities.

The food is mostly home-cooked and the menu is expansive. If you have a hearty appetite then try the Gargantuan Sunday Lunch - a half shoulder of lamb and one other roast always available.

WENDOVER

Our next pause is at **Wendover,** a pleasant town set in lovely countryside. Edmund Burke, whom we met in Beaconsfield, was MP for the town, elected in 1765. Elections at the time were anything but democratic and usually involved large amounts of alcohol for the few voters, so is it perhaps not surprising that Burke wrote to a friend, 'Yesterday I was elected for Wendover, got very drunk, and this day have an heavy cold.'

The main street has half-timbered, thatched and mellow brick houses, mostly of the Georgian period. The Church is 14th Century. Inside is an appealing brass monument to William Bradschawe, who died in 1537, and his wife. It shows the two of them kneeling, their nine children kneeling below, and below them the names of their 23 grandchildren.

Wendover is a good place to plan a walk from, as **Wendover Woods** have several delightful forest walks among the trees. The town is also on a branch of the Grand Union Canal, running down to meet the main Canal near Tring. This section, together with one to Buckingham, was authorised by an Act of Parliament in 1794, and was completed two years later. Although there was some commercial traffic it was mostly intended to feed water into the main canal, but in fact it leaked and actually drained water from the main channel.

ASTON CLINTON

The canal can still be followed on foot, down through Halton to skirt **Aston Clinton** where, from 1925 to 1927, Evelyn Waugh was a schoolmaster beginning work on his novel 'Decline and Fall'.

A 19th Century Lodge House, once part of the de Rothschild Estate, **West Lodge Hotel** has been transformed into a place of beauty. The atmosphere created by proprietors Irene and Jeffrey Burlinson is pleasant and relaxed, the welcome they give is warm and sincere. Each of their seven en-suite rooms is individually furnished with the best facilities. The elegance of the Victorian era is reflected in the restaurant which offers fine cuisine themed with Montgolfier Hot Air Ballooning. There are also the facilities of an indoor swimming pool and jacuzzi.

West Lodge Hotel, London Road, Aston Clinton Tel 01296 630362
Fax 01296 630331

METROLAND AND NORTH CHILTERNS

The West Lodge offers the very best in accommodation all year round. Beautiful gardens feature quiet seating areas, an aquatic garden and parklands. Add a touch of excitement and originality to your stay by booking a flight on The West Lodge's own hot air balloon, a fantastic way to see the countryside. Discover the West Lodge Hotel on the A41 at Aston Clinton.

It is from Aston Clinton that we slip out of this chapter, heading into north Buckinghamshire.

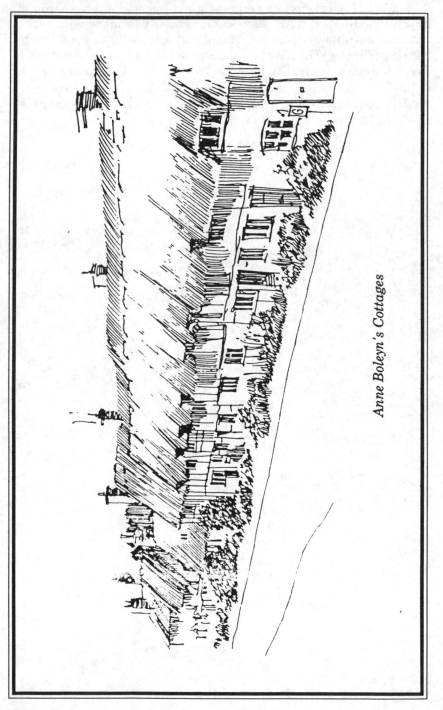

Anne Boleyn's Cottages

CHAPTER TEN

The Great Ouse

Winslow Hall

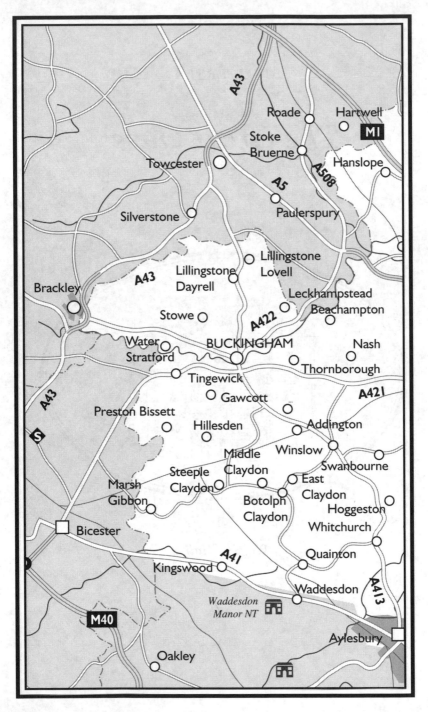

208

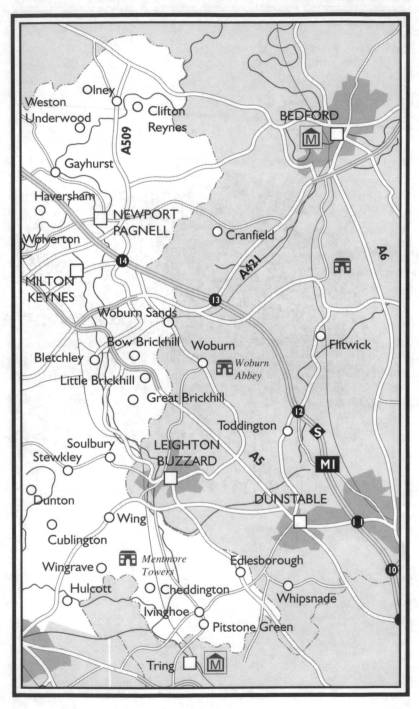

Stowe Gardens

CHAPTER TEN

The Great Ouse

Coming down from the Chilterns we enter the rolling plain of north Buckinghamshire. Until now our journey has been dominated by the Thames and the rivers which run down to it. Here we have a change of direction and the rain which falls on the green fields through which we now travel is drained by the Great Ouse making its way eventually via the Wash into the North Sea.

In this borderland at the foot of the Chilterns we are still in Rothschild country. Our first pause in this new chapter is the village of **Wingrave**. Hannah, daughter of Mayer Rothschild, for whom the magnificent house at Mentmore which we will see later in this chapter was built, had several cottages and a school built in the village after she married Lord Rosebery in 1878.

Across the A418 from Wingrave in **Cublington** there is a mound which is a legacy to the landscape from a vanished Norman castle. An 18th Century stable block recalls a lost Manor House. In places like this, off the normal tourist track, we are often reminded that all the English countryside is like a palimpsest, a manuscript on which different stories are written one on top of the other.

Just a short distance away, **Dunton** has a Church with a Norman nave which retains the box-pews and gallery which the Victorian church restorer loved to sweep away in the name of architectural purity. **Hoggeston**'s Church has an unusual weather-boarded bell turret of the 16th Century and the Manor House is Jacobean.

Mursley village has the distinction of having a Royal Charter which means the villagers can hold markets and close off the village to the outside world if they choose.

Swanbourne is an attractive place with several old cottages and an Elizabethan Manor House. To the south of the village are the grounds of **Swanbourne House**. An earlier house on this site was the home of Elizabeth Wynne, one of the contributors to the collection of letters and diaries known as the Wynne Diaries. Elizabeth Wynne and her sisters spent their early lives on the continent and the Diaries are a fascinating glimpse of life at the time. Elizabeth married Captain Thomas Fremantle, later an Admiral, who was a friend of Lord Nelson. The marriage took place at the house of Lady Hamilton at Naples in 1797.

These villages, interesting though they are in their own right, are also the overture to two fine historic houses, **Winslow Hall** in the village of **Winslow**, and **Claydon House** in nearby **Middle Claydon**.

WINSLOW

This is a pleasing country town with 18th and 19th Century houses, shops and inns grouped round the market square. The **Church** is 14th Century and has some late 15th Century wall paintings, one of which shows the murder of Thomas a Becket. There is also a touchingly simple Baptist chapel dated 1695 with 18th Century furnishings.

Winslow Hall was built between 1698 and 1702, almost certainly to designs by Christopher Wren, and has retained most of its original features. Sir Nicholas Pevsner describes it as 'Very stately, very restrained, and very urban.' The house is not open to the public very frequently, but for those who have the opportunity to go inside there are collections of 18th Century furniture, mostly English, and Chinese art, particularly from the Tang period, as well as some fine pictures, clocks and carpets to see. The gardens are very beautiful and contain some rarities which will interest keen gardeners.

There are four Claydons, East, Steeple, Botolph and Middle, all worth a visit.

East Claydon has attractive cottages and a Church practically rebuilt to designs by the Victorian church restorer George Gilbert Scott.

Steeple Claydon has a library housed in a building, originally a school, built in 1656.

At **Botolph Claydon** there is an 18th Century house built as a Dower House - a house for the widow after her son and his wife take over the 'great house' - for the Verneys, the aristocratic family which lived at Claydon House. One of the family, Sir Edmund, died at the battle of Edgehill in 1642, where he was standard bearer to the King.

Claydon House at **Middle Claydon** was itself built in the middle of the 18th Century and from outside looks a very restrained example of the classical style. The House contains a number of state rooms with magnificent carved wood and plaster decoration. The ceilings and walls are alive with delicately-carved flowers, fruits, animals and birds; the delightfully named Luke Lightfoot did the woodwork. The plasterwork was probably the responsibility of Joseph Rose, who had a more restrained imagination and worked for the Adams brothers. Particularly delightful is the Chinese room, reflecting the fashion for decorative things Chinese characteristic of the mid-18th Century.

The sister of Florence Nightingale married into the Verney family and the pioneer of modern hospital care spent long periods at the house, especially in her old age. Her bedroom and a museum of her life and experiences during the Crimean War can be seen. Now that nursing has become one of the female professions par excellence it is difficult to imagine the strength of character needed by a Victorian young woman of good family to go abroad to train as a nurse, which Florence did in 1851. At the time nursing had a poor reputation, that of a menial job done by women who could not support themselves in any more respectable way. She died in 1910, after a long career which embraced concerns of public health as well as the training of nurses, the first woman to be awarded the Order of Merit.

We next travel northwards, passing through the villages of **Addington**, clustered around its 17th Century Manor House, part of what was once a much larger building, and **Adstock**, with prettily thatched cottages and a small Church where examples of architectural styles from the Norman to the 14th Century can be seen.

The houses of **Thornborough** are spread out around a 13th Century Church, prized by experts on church architecture for the masonry laid in a herringbone pattern in the south wall. There is also a medieval bridge with three pointed arches.

BUCKINGHAM

We continue on to **Buckingham**, where the old centre is contained in a loop of the Great Ouse, here not very 'great' at all. Buckingham was the county town of Buckinghamshire in Saxon times, though many of the functions of a county town seem to have been performed by the more centrally-placed Aylesbury from quite an early date. It is a pleasant town, with many interesting old buildings. The **Town Hall** is on the south side of the Market Place and dates from the late 17th Century though the brick facade was added about 1780. It is a pleasingly simple building with a clock turret on top.

A disastrous fire in 1725 destroyed many of the houses in the town. Some of the replacements are very fine Georgian houses, especially in Castle Street. **Castle House**, which is in fact in West Street, is the best. It looks like a perfect Queen Anne house, with dormer windows, pediment and handsome doorway, but it is built around a much older medieval building in which Queen Catherine of Aragon once stayed.

The Church dates from the 1770s and was originally in a classical style, but it was virtually rebuilt and 'Gothicised' by George Gilbert Scott, whom we shall meet again shortly, from 1862. He also restored the Chantry Chapel, which is 15th Century but has a Norman doorway meaning that its origins must go much further back.

One notable addition to the town is the **University of Buckingham**, which was granted its Royal Charter in 1983, seven years after it first opened to students. It is an unusual institution among British universities in that it receives no direct state funding. It also has a four-term year, in contrast to the usual three terms, which means that students can study a subject to degree level in two years rather than three.

Leaving Buckingham we set off for the village of **Gawcott**, to the south west. Gawcott was the birthplace of George Gilbert Scott, the architect whom we have met as a restorer of churches several times on our travels, most recently in Buckingham. His father Thomas was the vicar at Gawcott and designed the present Church in 1827. Parental example might have influenced young George's choice of profession, though not his affection for the Gothic style. Gawcott Church is classical, a simple Georgian building in stone with arched windows.

HILLESDEN

On the other hand, Scott was inspired by the neighbouring **Hillesden** Church, a wonderful example of the Perpendicular style set down in a hamlet lost at the end of a country lane. It was built in the15th Century, and, unlike most English churches, was completed in one phase of building. It is impressive from the outside, especially the openwork crown of flying buttresses perched on top of a tower above the vestry. Inside there is fine stained glass, a carved rood screen between nave and chancel, pews with linenfold panelling and a finely carved family pew of the late 17th Century. In the vestry hangs a drawing Scott made of the Church when he was fifteen.

Whatever the influences on the young George Gilbert, he was certainly the architect of the age. The Albert Memorial and St Pancras Station and Hotel in London are his work, as is the India Office, just to prove that he could work in a classical style when he chose.

The bullet holes scarring the north door of Hillesden Church are said to date from the Civil War. Certainly **Hillesden House**, which once stood next to the Church and was the home of the Denton family, was destroyed by the Parliamentary Army. Sir Alexander Denton had fortified the house and tried to hold it for the King. There are monuments to the Denton family in the Church.

Preston Bissett is a picturesque village to the south-east of Buckingham, and a short detour round the country lanes south of Preston Bissett brings us to **Twyford**.

Dennis and Joan are the owners and hosts of **The Crown**, where a friendly crowd gather from ages 17 to 80 to exchange views whilst enjoying a good pint of beer or other refreshment. Located in The Square, which used at one time to be called 'The Knob', The Crown is the focal point of the village of Twyford; some of the older villagers like to meet here for coffee, whilst members of the local cricket and shooting clubs regularly gather here. The pub, dating from the 1800s, has been extended over the years but retains interesting features such as the old timbers and two open fires.

En-suite bed and breakfast accommodation with TV and hot drink facilities is available throughout the year. The Crown has a restaurant and a comfortable bar where Whitbread ales and light snacks are served. A friendly social atmosphere. ETB registered.

The Crown, The Square, Twyford Tel 01296 730216

CHETWODE

We next make our way to **Chetwode**, where the Parish Church is a relic of an Augustinian Priory founded in 1245. In 1480 the chancel of the Priory Church was taken over for the use of the parish and the narrow west tower added to it. In the lancet windows of the chancel is some fine early stained glass, including two figures in almond-shaped lozenges of about 1250, and some others of the 14th Century. Notice also that the squire's pew has its own fireplace, which must have been a comfort through many a long sermon on winter Sundays.

We now turn north, passing through **Tingewick**, dominated by the tall perpendicular west tower of its Church. Between the village and the river Ouse is the site of a Roman villa which was excavated in 1860-62, when 4th Century coins were found.

WATER STRATFORD

Between the A421 and A422 roads west of Buckingham lies the village of **Water Stratford**, which probably grew up here originally because this was the point at which a Roman road crossed the Great Ouse. It is a picturesque place on a slope above the river. The Church tower is 14th Century but the rest of it was rebuilt by a local architect in 1828, using some interesting fragments including the Decorated and Perpendicular style windows. The most interesting example of this recycling is a Norman tympanum, a semi-circular carved panel, over the south door. It shows Christ in majesty, supported by two angels, carved in a very lively manner with detailed drapery. A doorway in the chancel has a lamb and cross carved in the tympanum and Viking dragons on the lintel.

A little to the north is **Stowe School**, a leading Public School which occupies an 18th Century building, once the home of the Dukes of Buckingham, open to the public during the school holidays. It was built in several stages, starting from a late 17th Century house which was there when the new building started about 1710. This now forms part of the north front, with subsequent additions including stucco over the whole building and, in 1770, colonnades and pavilions. The south front was designed by Robert Adam and executed, with some alterations, in 1774, making a handsome facade, best seen from across the lake, with a columned and pedimented portico as a centrepiece.

The famous landscape gardens, on which even more time and money were lavished, are now in the hands of the National Trust and have more generous opening times. They are of the utmost importance partly because some of the most important people in the history of landscape gardening were engaged on them, but also because they epitomise one of the two approaches to landscape gardening associated with the 18th Century. Pevsner characterises these as the 'evocative' and the 'natural'. The evocative required the scattering of temples, alcoves, rotundas and so on around the landscape in order to evoke in the onlooker a romantic and poetic frame of mind. In these buildings Stowe is incomparably rich. They were designed by the best architects of the day, including Vanbrugh, architect of Blenheim Palace. William Kent, whose work we also saw at Rousham House, contributed, among others a 'Temple of British Worthies', built in 1733. The Gothic Temple is a fascinating early example of the 18th Century Gothic style, all the more so because it was designed by James Gibbs, usually thought of as being firmly in the Wren tradition.

It is not that this style of landscape gardening was seen as not being natural. It was, after all, a reaction against the formal style of gardening epitomised by the parterre, like the one at Cliveden. Alexander Pope, who was a frequent visitor at Stowe, cast the philosophy into rhyming couplets. He advised his audience to 'Consult the Genius of the Place in all,' that is to bring out the best in what is there already so that 'Spontaneous beauties all around advance' and then 'Nature shall join you, Time shall make it grow, a Work to wonder at - perhaps a STOW.' The grounds have not lost their 18th Century glory even though the name has gained and 'e' over the years.

It is one of the more intriguing quirks of fate that Lancelot Brown, always known as 'Capability' supposedly because of his habit of telling his clients that their park had 'capabilities', was head gardener at Stowe

216

for ten years. He was to become the chief exponent of the 'natural' style of landscape gardening which took over where gardens like those at Stowe left off. He arrived there in 1741 and began to work out his own style, one in which the landscape element in landscape gardening - belts and clumps of trees, natural-looking lakes, vast lawns - took on a new importance which has influenced ideas about what a beautiful stretch of English countryside should look like to this day.

After exploring Stowe and its wonderful gardens we continue north and east. We make our way through the charmingly-named villages of **Lillingstone Dayrell** and **Lillingstone Lovell**, both of which have some attractive buildings, pausing to see the Church at **Leckhampstead** which contains several examples of Norman architecture, the most important being a tympanum over the south door. This is carved with two intertwined dragons. It does not exactly fit the doorway, and so may be even older. The Church contains an effigy of a knight dating from about 1325.

STONY STRATFORD

The town of **Stony Stratford** dates back to pre-Roman times, and was later a popular staging post on the Roman Road of Watling Street. The town has long since been completely by-passed by the A5.

However, don't miss out on a visit to 'the pub that likes to be different' - the Fox and Hounds on Stony Stratford's High Street. This is a good fun place to visit, providing free membership to the Society of Stony Stratford International Junketers Club known as the SOSSIJ Club which holds regular meetings open to all.

Fox and Hounds, 87 High Street, Stony Stratford Tel 01908 563307

At lunchtimes the pub offers typical 'pub grub', whilst in the evenings, as well as traditional food, special Meal Nights are featured with menus based on the cuisine of a particular country or part of the world, typically Korean, Mexican, Malaysian, Russian, Basque, West African and North American. You can phone in advance to find dates and menus. Real ale is always featured with guest ales changing each week. Live music is provided on most Saturday nights featuring Blues and Jazz bands. Large beer garden and car park. Children welcome. Join in the fun!

The Bull Hotel on the High Street with its neighbour **The Cock** were in their heyday during the stage-coaching era. Together they provided accommodation and refreshment for the weary travellers. From the many lurid tales that were related here, often of questionable origin, the phrase 'a cock-and-bull story' is thought to have been coined.

A disastrous accident had its beginnings here. One windy day in 1742, while sheets were drying in front of the fire, one caught alight. Terrified of being found out, the maid stuffed the burnt sheet up the chimney. This caused a terrible fire which burnt down half the town - 146 houses and the church.

The Cock Hotel is one of the most famous hotels in England, having been in operation for over 600 years. Despite the spelling of its name, and indeed the sign hanging outside, the name comes from John Cok, who was landlord at the end of the 15th Century. The hotel features in several of the novels of Charles Dickens, who is believed to have stayed here, and is also mentioned in the nursery rhyme 'Ride a Cock horse to Banbury Cross'. Much of the hotel burnt down in the great fire, but when re-built had a new frontage, a magnificent doorway from Stowe Palace and some excellent wrought-iron work projecting over the High Street.

Please Don't Forget...

To tell people that you read about them in

The Hidden Places

The Swan, 1 London Road, Old Stratford Tel 01908 563654

The Swan at **Old Stratford** was originally an old stagecoach house, as many were on the London road, offering a rest to travellers on their long and bumpy journey to the city. It has been a pub for around 200 years

Stowe School

...at one time was partly taken over by the Home Guard. The Swan is
...od local pub sporting a large collection of water jugs hanging from
...e ceiling and offering real ales with regular guest ales. The furnishings
...re cottage style and the pub supports pool, darts and domino teams.
This is not a pub serving food but does offer two rooms self catering bed
and breakfast.

MILTON KEYNES

Studies carried out in the early 1960s favoured the dispersal of the
population concentrated in London out into new towns, of which **Milton
Keynes** was one. The Development Corporation which was charged
with bringing it into being was set up in 1967 and since then the
population of the borough has gone up from 60,000 to about 180,000. It
is a modern town, proud of its new housing, high-tech industries,
modern leisure facilities, and its shopping centre with over 140 shops, a
creche, 12,000 free parking places, public transport facilities and racks for
cycles.

However, Milton Keynes has not turned its back on the past. A
fascinating **Museum of Industry and Rural Life**, with a large collection
of industrial, domestic and agricultural bygones, is devoted to the lives
of the people who lived in the area in the 200 years before the new town
was a gleam in a planner's eye. Exhibitions on art, crafts, local history and
social life can be seen at the **Exhibition Gallery**, next to the library.

Much of the life of the area before 'MK', as the locals call it, was
concerned with transport. Wolverton Works was at one time one of the
largest railway works in the world and the Grand Union Canal runs
through the eastern part of the town. At Fenny Lock on the canal, at
Fenny Stratford, is the Fenny Lodge Gallery, where exhibitions of arts
and crafts are held. If you actually want to take a canal trip then day trips,
weekends or longer holidays can be arranged at Linda Cruises of
Cosgrave, just on the north-western outskirts of Milton Keynes.

The new town of Milton Keynes absorbed several older villages,
taking its name from one of them. In another, **Bradwell**, is a fine example
of a Tower Mill. In **Willen** is the **Church of St Mary Magdalene**. This is
an elegant jewel of a Church, built 1679-80 to designs drawn up by Robert
Hooke, who worked closely with Christopher Wren. He used a pleasing
red brick with details highlighted in stone. Many of the original furnishings
have survived. Also in Willen is the **Peace Pagoda and Buddhist Temple**,
opened in 1980. It was built by the monks and nuns of the Nipponsan
Myohoji, the first in the western hemisphere It is a place of great peace
and beauty. A thousand cherry trees and cedars donated by the ancient
Japanese town of Yoshino, famous for the beauty of its cherry blossom,
have been planted on the hill surrounding the Pagoda, in memory of the
victims of all wars.

In the centre of the picturesque village of **Simpson** on the outskirts of the city of Milton Keynes stands **The Plough**, a 400-year-old inn that offers its visitors plenty of real ales and good home-cooked food. The canal passes the end of the very sizable beer garden and in the summer months the pub is much frequented by local boatsmen and tourists alike. The inn itself is warm and friendly, with attractive decor and plenty of traditional furniture, with a great selection of old farming tools hanging from the walls and ceiling.

There is a separate restaurant with attractive tiled floors and candlelit tables that give the room an intimate feeling. Your hosts are Paul and Brona, who lived and worked in Spain for 12 years previous to running The Plough, so the cooking, which is undertaken by Brona, often has a Spanish influence. In addition to the bar menu there is also an A La Carte menu, which is available lunchtimes and evenings. You could start with an appetiser of Mussels with Garlic and Cheese, for main course you might try Authentic Spanish Paella, which is large enough to satisfy two people, and follow this with Mississippi Mud Pie if you have any room! All the dishes are home made by Brona using only the finest local ingredients and are freshly prepared to order at all times.

The Plough, Simpson Road, Simpson Tel 01908 670015

STOKE BRUERN

We continue northwards for a brief excursion into Northamptonshire to **Stoke Bruern**, for a museum and an historic building. The **Stoke Bruern Canal Museum** is on the Grand Union Canal and uses the site admirably in telling the story of 200 years of canal history and traditions. It includes the Blisworth Tunnel and a flight of seven locks, and there are guided tours, a shop, restaurants, a pub and plenty of opportunities for walks.

Nearby are **Stoke Park Pavilions**, two of them, linked by a colonnade. They are particularly significant in the history of British architecture, as

ideal stopping point for the family. The Globe is a comfortable pub with old features such as the stone walls and tiled floors. There's a games room, pool table and dartboard which gets everyone together for a friendly game or two.

The restaurant serves up big meals which are great value and the choice is varied indeed; choose for example the Deep Fried Camembert or Mussels Bonne Femme to start, followed by Swordfish Steam, Chicken in Cheese & Cider Sauce or perhaps a substantial Grilled Steak. If you still have room, the sweets will finish you off!

The Watts Arms is just half a mile from Milton Keynes Eventing Centre at **Hanslope**, where for one week each year the nearby Church spire is opened to the public and from where can be seen seven counties of England. This is a 'local' with real log fires, flickering lights, wood panelling and lots of brass and copper displayed. Don't miss the large mural painting of the village over the fireplace. The Watts Arms is a homely pub where the atmosphere is very friendly and all the cooking is done by Julie whose speciality is her recipe for Lasagne! The menu is certainly comprehensive and offers poultry, meats, fish dishes, vegetarian and continental selections. On Sundays there's a choice of traditional roasts with fish offered as an alternative. Senior citizens are catered for with a special of fish and chips available every day except Sunday. After the delicious food and drink you can always choose to stay overnight in one of the family or single rooms. Children are welcome and there is a large garden and play area.

The Watts Arms, Castlethorpe Road, Hanslope Tel 01908 510246

The village of **Haversham** has some stone cottages and an early 18th Century Rectory near the Church, which has a Norman nave, some interesting brasses and an alabaster effigy of a lady in an elaborately carved tomb of about 1390.

NEWPORT PAGNELL

We continue to **Newport Pagnell**, which, in spite of having expanded a good deal in recent years, retains in its centre the atmosphere of a market town. At first sight the name is a bit of a puzzle - by no stretch of the imagination can this ever have been a 'new port', so far from the sea, and even though it is sited where the river Lovat meets the Great Ouse it seems unlikely that water-borne traffic here could ever have been important. The answer is that 'port' sometimes mean 'a place to which goods are transported and where they are sold' - that is, a market town. The Pagnell part refers to a 12th Century Norman Lord of the Manor, Fulc Paganel, paganel being a nickname meaning 'little pagan', whose family had a castle here at the junction of the two rivers. In spite of the pagan association of the name, Newport Pagnell's **Church** is a fine building, a large and impressive, mostly of the 15th Century. The west tower is late medieval, built 1542-48 but the pinnacles date only from the 19th Century restoration.

The town has been known for many years as 'the town that built the M1', later famed for the motorway service station with its unique cuisine. Newport Pagnell's famous car manufacturer, Aston Martin, must have welcomed the new highway back in the days when there was no speed limit, and today they still hand-build cars that would test the mettle of the most law-abiding driver.

Just to the east of Newport Pagnell is **Chicheley Hall**, a beautiful baroque house built in the early 18th Century for Sir John Chester. His curious library is in the attic storey, with all the bookshelves hidden away behind mock panelling, which must reduce the problem of keeping the books dusted. It is an extremely attractive house with corinthian pilasters decorating the front, the centre part of which projects and has round headed windows, whereas the others are square-topped. This makes for a charming variety in the facade.

Inside is a museum devoted to Admiral Lord Beatty, hero of the 1914-1918 War which contains memorabilia of his naval campaigns. He was the son of a cavalry officer who joined the Navy as a cadet at the age of 13. In the opening days of the Great War in 1914 he commanded a battlecruiser squadron which sank two German cruisers and went on to show equal initiative in the most important naval battle of the war, at Jutland in 1916, though the losses to his battle cruiser squadron were heavy.

Chicheley Hall is one of the finest and least altered 18th Century houses in England and has examples of superb craftsmanship in its brickwork, carving, joinery and plasterwork.

From this delightful and interesting house we make our way south, skirting Milton Keynes and exploring 'the Brickhills', the three villages of **Bow**, **Little** and **Great Brickhill**, in wooded sandy country along the border with Bedfordshire.

Bow Brickhill has a pleasant Church, mostly19th Century, built of ironstone and perched on a wooded hill above the end of the village.

Little Brickhill suffers from heavy traffic, but the little **Church of St Mary Magdalene** is an attractive building with details of about 1600. **Great Brickhill** has some charming Georgian houses and a Church, again in the local ironstone, with a 13th Century central tower and chancel.

SOULBURY

The road to **Soulbury** from Great Brickhill crosses the Grand Union Canal, providing an ideal opportunity to renew acquaintances with this historic waterway with a canalside pub and a fascinating landscape of locks and humped-back bridges. The three locks here were built in 1800. Soulbury itself is a pleasant village. There is a school which was given to the village in 1724 by the Lovett family who used to live in the extensive **Liscombe Park** estate to the south. In the Church are monuments to the Lovett family, the one to Robert Lovett, who died in 1690, being carved by Grinling Gibbons, the best-known carver of his age, in white marble, with an urn, little angels and Gibbons' characteristically elaborate bands of flowers.

STEWKLEY

A little further west is **Stewkley**, a long village strung out along the road, with several attractive old houses. In the garden of the Manor House is a dovecot of the 18th Century with 800 nesting places. The Church, of about 1150, is a splendid example of Norman architecture with a massive central tower. It is decorated with zigzag patterns, including a string course which runs all round the Church. The tympanum over the west door is carved with dragons and surrounded with three layers of decorated arches.

WING

In our next destination **Wing**, however, the Church is even older in origin although it has undergone more alteration in the intervening centuries. The very rare Anglo-Saxon apse and crypt remain, dating from about 970, making it one of the most interesting Churches of its period left in England. There are also many brasses and monuments, including one to Sir Robert Dormer dated 1552, in a very pure renaissance classical style and reckoned to be the finest contemporary example in England.

In the village is the **Dormer Hospital**, founded in 1569 though the building was much remodelled in the 19th Century, and the 20ft mound where a Norman castle once stood.

226

Also at Wing is **Ascott House**, another Rothschild house containing Anthony Rothschild's collection of fine pictures, including works by Hogarth, Gainsborough, Stubbs and Rubens, as well as French and Chippendale furniture and exceptional Oriental porcelain. The house was mostly built in the late 19th Century around the core of a timber-framed building dated 1606. It was bought by Leopold Rothschild in 1874.

The gardens extend over 12 acres forming part of a 260-acre park, and include a fountain sculpted by the American artist Waldo Story. They contain many rare plants and trees, and there are thousands of naturalised bulbs as well as formal gardens.

Nearby is the first of the Rothschild mansions, **Mentmore Towers**, built for Mayer Rothschild between 1852 and 1855 to designs by Sir Joseph Paxton, architect of the Crystal Palace. It is an unusual Victorian version of Jacobean and Elizabethan styles, but with many details which were technologically advanced at the time, such as central heating and, as might be expected of Paxton, large sheets of glass and a glass roof to the central hall. it was packed with superb antique furniture and paintings. Unfortunately, when the house and contents were sold by the Rosebery family in 1977 insufficient money was available to buy them for the nation. The collection was therefore dispersed and the house was bought by the Transcendental Meditation movement. It is now open to the public on Sunday afternoons.

Our road south passes through **Cheddington**, where the church has a richly carved Jacobean pulpit, to **Pitstone Green**, where there is a fully restored post mill. The age of the mill is unknown, but the earliest documentary reference to its existence was made in 1624. Also in the village is a **Farm Museum**, with farm and barn machinery and domestic bygones.

After this fascinating glimpse of life in the rural past we join the road eastwards, which here follows the line of the Icknield Way, and pass below **Ivinghoe Beacon**, topped by its iron-age hill fort, before coming to the village of **Edlesborough**. Here the large Church stands battlemented and turreted on a little hill, commanding the surrounding plain. Inside it has some fine woodwork, including an outstanding 15th Century screen, and some fine brasses and monuments. The village also has a magnificent barn, some 180ft long, built in the middle of the 16th Century which has a timber frame filled in with brick.

We now leave Buckinghamshire for Bedfordshire.

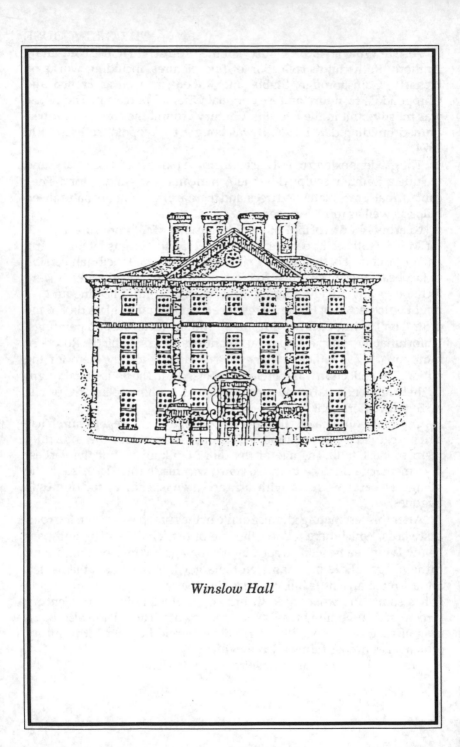

Winslow Hall

CHAPTER ELEVEN

South Bedfordshire

Luton Hoo

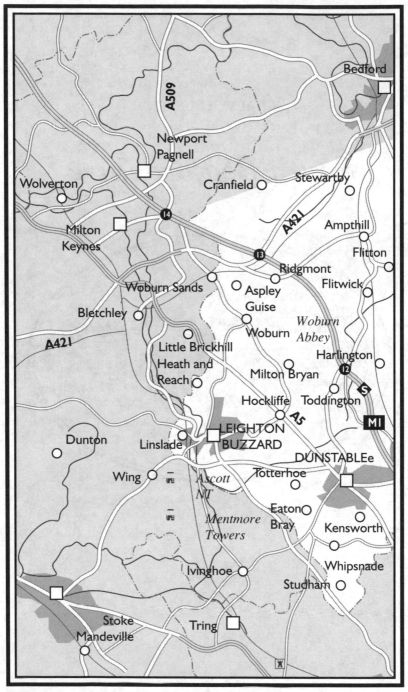

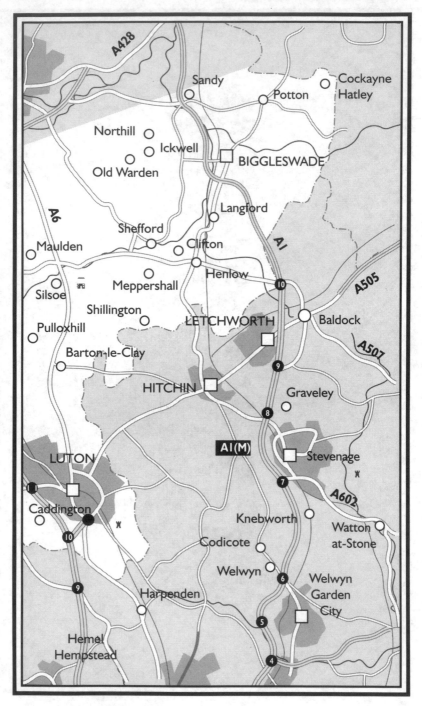

A428

Sandy

Potton

Cockayne
Hatley

Northill

Ickwell

BIGGLESWADE

Old Warden

A6

Langford

Shefford

Clifton

A1

Maulden

Henlow

A505

Silsoe

Meppershall

Shillington

LETCHWORTH

Baldock

Pulloxhill

A507

Barton-le-Clay

HITCHIN

Graveley

8

A1(M)

Stevenage

LUTON

7

Caddington

Knebworth

A602

Watton
at-Stone

10

Codicote

Welwyn

9

Welwyn

6

Garden

Harpenden

5

City

Hemel
Hempstead

4

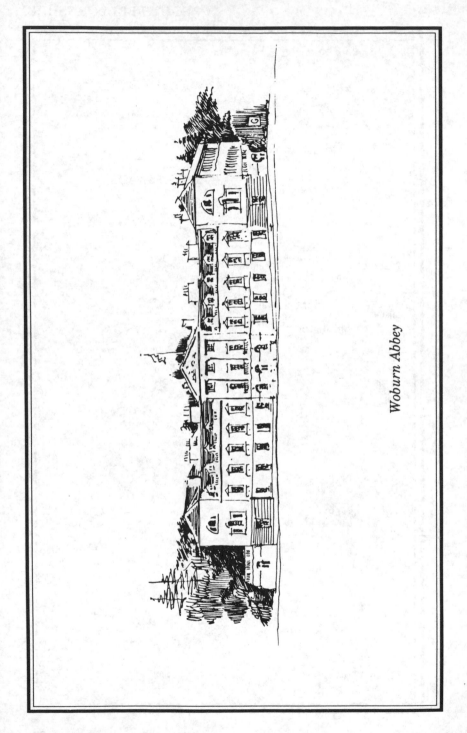

Woburn Abbey

CHAPTER ELEVEN

South Bedfordshire

This chapter brings us into a new county, Bedfordshire. Initially we are back in Chiltern country, for the southern part of south Bedfordshire, around Luton, Dunstable and the south-eastern fringe of the county are chalk hill country, similar to that with which we have become familiar in Oxfordshire and Buckinghamshire. The character of the countryside covered by this chapter, in fact, depends on three geological bands running diagonally north-east to south-west - first chalk downland, then, to the north, a layer of gault clay and finally, north again, the low wooded hills characteristic of greensand.

The last chapter ended with a fine Church and this begins with one, when we visit the village of **Eaton Bray**, just over the border from Edlesborough. The **Church of St Mary** is mostly in the Perpendicular style characteristic of the 14th and 15th Centuries and externally not particularly striking. But inside there are two richly carved arcades of about 1200 and 1235-40. It also has a fine late Perpendicular-style stone reredos and a fine screen, also Perpendicular. Don't miss the carved tomb of Lady Bray, a member of the family which gives the village the second part of its name. She died in 1558 and her tomb has an interesting mixture of motifs typical of Gothic and Elizabethan monuments.

Bellows Mill, Eaton Bray Tel 01525 220548

Attractive bed and breakfast accommodation can be found in idyllic surroundings at **Bellows Mill** set in 21 acres of picturesque grounds on the outskirts of Eaton Bray. The proprietor Mrs Hodge has created lovely en-suite bedrooms from tastefully converted stables,the original outbuildings to the old mill. The rooms are attractively decorated and furnished with antiques. All have remote control TV and direct dial telephones. There is a breakfast room, a sun lounge and a covered courtyard area with pool and table tennis.

Dinner is by arrangement and is served in the main house. Trout fishing may be arranged with the local private fishing club and many famous places to visit are easily arranged from this delightful house. Easily accessed from the M1 at junctions 9 or 12.

A little to the east is **Totternhoe**, an attractive village below **Totternhoe Knolls**, a steeply sloped spur of chalk topped by a motte and bailey Castle dating from Norman times from which the views are wonderful. The Knolls are a nature reserve, nationally known for orchids and insects, though the latter may be of less interest to the non-specialist than the former, with a picnic site and pleasant paths over the downs and through the woods.

Just outside the village is a combined wind and water mill for which restoration is planned. The local stone is a particularly hard form of chalk which was quarried here from the Middle Ages. Apart from being used in local buildings, such as the Church we have just seen at Eaton Bray and, on a more grand scale, at Woburn Abbey, it is found as far afield as Westminster Abbey and Coventry Cathedral.

Our eventual destination will be Whipsnade and the famous Wild Animal Park, which celebrated its Diamond Jubilee in 1991. On the way we pass through **Dunstable Downs**, a marvellous area of open country open to public access, where you can watch gliders from the London Gliding Club based at the foot of the Downs.

Towards another extreme of the time scale are the **Five Knolls**, a group of Bronze Age burial mounds, the finest examples in the Chilterns. They date from between 2000 and 1600 BC, but pagan Anglo-Saxons also buried people here. The **Visitor Centre** will provide you with all the information you need about this 130-acre 'breathing space'.

WHIPSNADE

We pass through **Whipsnade** village, surrounded by common land on which stands a **Tree Cathedral**, property of the National Trust. This is a curiously moving place. After the Great War of 1914-18 a local landowner named Edmund Kell Blyth planted a plantation of trees covering 20 acres in the shape of a Cathedral, with nave, transepts, chancel and cloisters. It is now in the care of the National Trust, and Services are held there in the summer.

Whipsnade itself has a charming small Church, very simple and dating mainly from the 18th Century, though the brick tower is two centuries older and the chancel a century later.

The white silhouette of a lion cut into the green hillside, a modern example of the tradition we met on the downs above Uffington and at Whiteleaf near Princes Risborough, is a magnificent landmark and advertisement for **Whipsnade Wild Animal Park**. The park is set in 600 acres of beautiful countryside and is home to over 2800 animals. It is the country home of the Zoological Society of London, specialising in the breeding of endangered species, such as cheetahs, rhinos and the scimitar horned oryx.

When it was opened the idea of keeping animals in as near natural conditions as possible was an innovation, and its record as a breeding centre is a tribute to the success of the policy. This serious purpose does not get in the way of providing a really enjoyable family day out to suit most tastes. Many visitors travel round the parkland on the free road trains which are provided, though you can drive yourself if you choose. Some of the animal houses are interesting for their architecture, as they were built by the famous firm of B Lubetkin and Tecton in 1934-5 in what was then an uncompromisingly modern style.

After leaving Whipsnade we take a detour through the attractive villages of **Studham**, the most southerly in Bedfordshire, and **Kensworth**, one of the highest, with an early Norman Church, one with quite a spacious nave, though the tower is later and Perpendicular in style.

DUNSTABLE

Our destination for this part of our journey is the town of **Dunstable**, now a bustling modern place though its roots are ancient. It grew up at the crossing point of two ancient tracks - the Icknield Way, which we have touched on a number of occasions on our recent travels and Watling Street, the Roman road followed by the A5 for much of its route. Dunstable was an important centre in Roman times - named Durocobrivae - and has been a market town for about 1000 years.

In the centre are a number of interesting buildings including the **Cart Almshouses**, built about 1723 and **Chew's House**, a fine Georgian building of 1719 with a pediment and a little tower and cupola rising from the roof. Jane Cart, who founded the Almshouses, was the daughter of Thomas Chew who had the house built.

The finest of Dunstable's buildings is the **Priory Church**. The Priory was founded in 1131 by Henry I as a community of Augustinians. The current Church, which is only the nave, less the eastern end, of the original building, dates from the 12th Century. The west front is all the more appealing for being asymmetrical, with a massive Norman door somewhat off-centre, and rich arcading on one side but not the other, likewise a single tower. It was in the Lady Chapel of this Church, in May 1533, that Archbishop Thomas Cranmer pronounced the marriage between Henry VIII and Katharine of Aragon null and void after 24 years of marriage.

The town has some attractive parks and coaching inns, dating from the days when it was an important stage for coaches running to and from London.

South from Dunstable we travel through the village of **Caddington** set on top of the evocatively named **Blows Downs**. The Church at Caddington contains Norman work, and some parts of it may even be Anglo-Saxon. The west tower has been much repaired over the years with flint, stone and brick and the result is surprisingly picturesque.

LUTON

We are now on the outskirts of **Luton**, another modern town. It does, however, have a very fine Church, a large and handsome building in the Perpendicular style, the different types of stone (flint and limestone) used in its construction giving it a checked appearance.

There are not many towns as lucky as Luton which have not only a superb museum, but one in such a splendid setting. **Luton Museum and Art Gallery** is housed in Wardown Park built in 1875. It is built of Luton brick and red Mansfield stone. At the time it cost £10,000 to build, but you could only guess at the value of this charming house and grounds today.

In 1903 the Council were offered the house and land but they hesitated to buy it. Fortunately two Council members, Edwin Oakley and Asher Hucklesby saw its value to the town, bought it for £16,250 and were philanthropic enough to sell it to the town for the same price. Two years later the estate was formally opened to the public. At first the house was used as a restaurant and during the 1914-18 War it became a hospital for officers. It was not until 1931 that the house became the home of the Museum and Art Gallery, which had previously been in the Library, in Williamson Street.

The Archaeology section was the billiard room, Applied Arts the Library, the drawing room and morning room are now the Art Gallery and the adjoining gallery was once the dining room. The house is reputed to have a ghost, and grouped round the entrance, are portrait heads of famous figures, Palmerston, Cobden, Bright, Gladstone and Disraeli, an interesting cross section of the nation's Parliamentary history, together with one of Dickens.

We cannot possibly describe all there is to see but you will find that the Museum has produced an excellent booklet which is very informative. A students' study room is available where access can be gained to the large Library and Archives Collection.

In the Decorative Art Gallery delight in the small collections of objects

236

mostly of functional purpose but designed with aesthetic feeling rather than purely for utility. They include examples from the collections of metalwork, glass, pottery and porcelain. Of special interest is the group of 17th and 18th Century drinking glasses and an amusing collection of stoneware gin bottles of the types that were produced in the early 19th Century.

The Art Gallery with its views from the south side of the building is reserved for continuous series of exhibitions usually changed each month. The work of local artists as well as nationally known figures is shown but exhibitions are not entirely limited to the arts, and subjects beyond the scope of the usual museum collections are included. There are displays of Social History.

Archaeology and Natural History, together with a range of household and kitchen items from farmhouses and cottages in Bedfordshire, are set out in what was the kitchen, where meals were prepared for the owner of the mansion and his family. You can look at centuries of cooking aids ranging from spits large enough to roast a complete sheep down to a tiny lark spit (skylarks were a local speciality). Until the spread of central heating the hearth was the focus of the whole household and such items as warming pans, linen press, boot jack and fire bellows are reminders of a way of life shared by many generations which is now completely gone.

Toys, Dolls and Costume are all beautifully displayed. In one small showcase are displays of underwear, costume accessories, fans and umbrellas. A beautiful example is the superb ivory fan with a handpainted design on silk and delicate silver repousse work. This very rare item was made for the ill-fated Marie Antoinette in about 1780 and bears her monogram.

Lace making was one of the two main cottage industries in Bedfordshire and, since the Luton collection is the largest of any museum outside London, a whole gallery is devoted to the crafts. The cottage interior has a lacemaker which is seen at the end of the landing when one enters the Lace Gallery, a reconstruction of a scene which was extremely common in the rural areas of the East Midlands. The farm worker's wife is shown sitting at the lace pillow which rests on a 'horse'. She is making a flounce or wide border of Buckinghamshire Point Ground Lace using more than 150 bobbins. The Lace Gallery illustrates the traditions and methods of the East Midlands lacemakers who, since the end of the 16th Century have produced fine lace in competition with such Continental lace making areas as Brussels, Mechlin and Lille.

Luton has undergone an expansion almost unrivalled by any other town growing from a market town of little more than 3000 people in the early part of the 19th Century to a major industrial centre with the skills capable of attracting engineering and car manufacturing firms. It has also undergone two major redevelopments since the mid 19th Century and many once familiar features have disappeared. **The Luton Life Gallery** includes reconstructions of some of these aspects of life which were familiar to Lutonians in the last century. It is a fascinating and fitting climax to our visit.

Just outside Luton is the magnificent house at **Luton Hoo**, originally designed by Robert Adam. It is set in 1500 acres of parkland landscaped by Capability Brown, who began work in 1764. Construction of the house began in 1767, though it was extensively remodelled in 1827 and again in 1903, when the interior of the house was remodelled in the French style for Sir Julius Wernher. It now contains his art collection, superb examples of jewellery by Faberge, porcelain and china, furniture, tapestries and paintings, including the work of Rembrandt and Titian. One unexpected touch is an exhibition of robes worn at the court of the Tsars before the Russian revolution and momentoes of the Imperial family.

The chapel has recently been restored, bringing the stained glass, wall paintings and colourful floor tiles back to their original glory. In the grounds are two lovely lakes, formed during Capability Brown's remodelling of the grounds by damming the river Lea. The stables remain as designed by Adam. The gardens include a restored Edwardian rose garden and formal gardens laid out at the turn of the century with wonderfully colourful herbaceous borders. The azaleas and rhododendron of the rock gardens are particularly fine if you have the good fortune to be there at the right season.

South of Luton and just off the B653 is **Someries Castle**, the remains of a fortified medieval Manor, dating from the middle to late 15th Century. It is the earliest surviving brick building in the county. The gatehouse and chapel survive and are very impressive. A castle on this site belonged first to the de Someries family, then to the Wenlocks, and the house of which we see can see only a romantic ruin may have been built for the Lord Wenlock who died at the battle of Tewkesbury in 1471, when the Yorkist victory ended the Wars of the Roses.

Leaving Luton and its outskirts we head northwards.

Originally built over 400 years ago, **The Old Sun** is located next to the old Methodist chapel, south west of the village of **Harlington** on the Sundon road. It was first used as a pub in 1783 and had a half timbered construction which was later converted into a brick frontage, but the original construction of the property can still be seen by the rear wall that divides the old pub from its extension. Originally known as Sun Cottage, it ws bought and converted into a pub by John Robinson, and aptly named The Sun Inn.

The main bar at the front of the pub still has all its original timbers and beams, and a large inglenook fireplace gives the Inn a comforting glow on those long winter nights. The serving bar itself is made from the slats of old beer barrels and is a real feature. On the subject of beer, the Old Sun serves three cask real ales that are kept at the perfect temperature for you to enjoy at your leisure. In the rear extension there is another bar area, complete with darts and a raised room that is used for pool.

Lunch and evening meals are served every day and they range from the usual sandwiches for a quick snack to the larger evening menu that includes some terrific steaks, all meals being cooked on the premises using only the freshest local produce. Owned and run by Sue and Roger Kemsley, The Old Sun really is a superb place to stop for refreshments and a meal after that long journey.

The Old Sun, Sundon Road, Harlington Tel 01525 872417

Next, pause for breath at the delightfully named **Sharpenhoe Clappers**, a wooded chalk hill with beech trees and an iron-age fort on top. It is owned by the National Trust, and is a favourite place for walks. This is a good area, a sort of northern outrider of the Chilterns, in which to spend some time in the open air.

Barton Hills, south of the village of Barton-le-Clay are a national Nature Reserve, managed by the Nature Conservancy Council. There are many public footpaths in the area, including one which follows part of the Icknield Way.

BARTON-LE-CLAY

Barton-le-Clay itself has an attractive Church with an impressive Perpendicular west tower. The roof has carved bosses and the figures of angels and apostles.

Located in the very centre of Barton on the Bedford road, **The Bull Hotel** offers the visitor a step back in time. Originally built in the 1600s, it was once two one-up-one-down cottages which were then extended and turned into butchers before finally becoming the pub that you see

239

before you now. It is believed to be haunted by the ghost of Polly Hook, the sister of the gentleman who ran the butchers, who died in the pub many years ago. The Bull Hotel was once used by John Bunyan the poet and was even mentioned in one of his poems, so you will be treading the path of a famous person when you walk through the front door. The inn is at present being restored to its original timber-lined interior. It has a large brick fireplace that is always burning brightly in the winter months and is a very popular spot for locals and visitors alike.

Food is served all day in the 32-seater restaurant, all made using only the freshest local ingredients and presenting excellent value for money. Don't miss out on the 'sizzling steaks' selection, it's a must. There is a super beer garden at the rear of the establishment which has a very well equipped play area for the kids, perfect for keeping the little darlings occupied while you indulge in one of the superb real ales that the bar keeps in tip top condition.

The Bull Hotel, 77 Bedford Road, Barton-Le-Clay Tel 01582 881218

PULLOXHILL

If you are partial to a decent glass or bottle of wine, then we can recommend an establishment reputed to have a wine list second to none in the Bedfordshire area. **The Cross Keys** is situated just two miles from the A6 Luton to Bedford road in **Pulloxhill** north of Barton. The Cross Keys not only has a superb wine list but also an atmosphere which is extremely pleasant and friendly. Our former statement can, we believe, be attributed to the age of the building and the fact that the present licensees have resided there for over 20 years.

The well stocked bar is complemented by a superb catering facility providing an extensive range of varying dishes. The average price of a meal ranges from £2.50 to £5 and represents excellent value for money. Credit cards are acceptable and the disabled have easy access to the

240

dining room and bars. Children are adequately catered for and as well as providing a children's menu there is also a play area in the garden. If you happen to be travelling with children The Cross Keys is an ideal place to stop and allow the children to stretch their legs.

The Cross Keys, High Street, Pulloxhill Tel 01525 712442

Located in this charming village you will come across the large farmhouse which is called **Pond Farm**. This rustic bed and breakfast style accommodation offers the traveller three bedrooms, each with all the usual facilities that would be expected.

Pond Farm, 7 High Street, Pulloxhill Tel 01525 712316

This working farm is owned and run by Judy Tookey and is situated in the village centre, offering the guest an insight into farmhouse and country living that few can match. If you are a dog lover, then Ponds Farm's two Great Danes will be delighted for you to find time to make a fuss of them in the house or garden. Or you can amble through the fields and enjoy the idyllic scenery of beautiful Bedfordshire. The atmosphere is a friendly and welcoming one, whilst the furnishings are typical of a traditional farmhouse, comfortable and homely.

SHILLINGTON

A few miles to the east is the village of **Shillington**, which is worth a diversion for its **Church**, a substantial ironstone building overlooking the surrounding countryside, and an excellent place for views. The Church itself is mainly 14th Century and inside are some interesting screens and benches, plus a large brass monument to Matthew Asscheton, a canon of Lincoln cathedral, who died in 1400.

MAULDEN

A short diversion north via **Clophill** brings us to **Maulden**. Located on the Ampthill Road in the centre of Maulden you will find **The White Hart**. Built in the 16th Century and originally used as a hat factory, the Inn is set back from the road with gardens at the front and rear of this beautiful property. Inside there are low ceilings, exposed wooden beams and timbers throughout, with the pub rambling over many different levels.

The main front bar leads upstairs and around to the large attractive dining area at the rear of the property, which is decorated with traditional 'country life' paintings, a selection of china and some wonderful brass items giving the room a definite sense of history. The windows overlook the pretty rear garden backing onto acres of fields that make for a spectacular view of the surrounding scenery. The food is superb with generous portions for a very reasonable price, Cajun chicken being the most popular dish on this very comprehensive menu. Also on offer are such culinary delights as the home made 'Pie of the Day', 'Mixed Grill' and the 'Fresh Fish of the Day'. There is also a wonderful selection of bar meals, from huge doorstep sandwiches to filled Jacket Potatoes and Quiches, not to mention the astonishing 14 different desserts that are served every day! If you are lucky enough to visit in the warm and sunny summer months there are BBQs some evenings in the large gardens of the inn.

There are four real and three regular ales served every day including one special guest ale, which are all kept in tip-top condition by the very able cellarman. The White Hart also has its own Pram Race Team; each village pub puts forward a two-man team and they race from pub to pub taking a pint in each one, an annual event that is clearly not for the faint hearted!

The White Hart, Ampthill Road, Maulden Tel 01525 406118

SHEFFORD

From here we travel on minor roads to **Shefford** - sheep ford in Old English, for here a Roman road, ancestor of the A600, crossed the river Ivel. In this small town Robert Bloomfield lived the last years of his life in great poverty and died in 1823. He was of humble origin and worked as an agricultural labourer and shoemaker, but also wrote a poem called 'The Farmer's Boy', published in 1800. Perhaps he was describing himself when he wrote 'Strange to the world, he wore a bashful look, The Fields his study, Nature was his book.' It was an enormous success, selling 26,000 in less than three years. His talent has been compared to that of John Clare, who lived in the neighbouring county of Northamptonshire and whose circumstances were somewhat similar.

Nearby is **Chicksands Priory**. It is not often open but it is a fascinating place, now the property of the RAF and actually part of a USAF base, and in the process of being restored to its former grandeur by an Anglo-American group of Friends. The Priory was founded in 1154 for 120 nuns and 55 brothers of the Gilbertine Order, the only Order which was created in Britain. Neither did it spread abroad. When the Order was dissolved, the buildings and land became the property of the King who sold them in 1540 for £810.11s.8d. After one more sale the Priory became the home of the Osborne family in 1576, remaining in the family until 1936, when it was sold to the Crown.

Some elements of the original buildings remain, but the house was extensively remodelled by James Wyatt in 1813. In spite of his reputation for rudeness and unreliability Wyatt was the most successful architect of his day, a rival of the Adam brothers, though, unlike them, he specialised in the neo-Gothic style. Most of his work has been destroyed. There is perhaps a certain rough justice in this as he was such a ruthless 'restorer' of genuine Gothic buildings that he was nicknamed 'Wyatt the Destroyer'. In spite of this the existing buildings apparently support the usual complement of monastic ghosts. The landscaped gardens boast an orangery and grape vines.

One member of the family, Dorothy Osborne, born in 1648, while on her way to St Malo in France, met William Temple and they fell in love. William Temple was a diplomat and writer of several books, mostly essays. But the families did not approve of the match - this was, after all, an age when parents expected to choose marriage partners for their children. So it was not until 1654 that they were finally able to marry. In the meantime she wrote to him letters telling of her quiet life at Chicksands, and waited for his replies. The letters were published more than 200 years after they were written.

BIGGLESWADE

Our next destination is **Biggleswade**, which lies on the Great North Road, the Roman Road linking the settlement which was the ancestor of London with the north. The slightly comic name comes from the Old English 'Biccel's ford', Biccel being a person and 'wade' derived from 'waed', a place where people and animals could wade through a river, here the Ivel. In the 14th Century the three-arched bridge we can still see was built.

Its position on the Great North Road (now the A1) made Biggleswade an important coaching centre. It has another link with the history of transport in that Dan Albone, one of the inventors of the modern bicycle, lived there. He was one of the designers of the first practical tandem, and also designed a machine for ladies to use, with a low cross-bar and skirt guard on the rear wheel. But he is most remembered for his racing cycle, named the 'Ivel' in honour of the local river, on which a hardy rider named C P Mills established two records in October 1888 - the fastest ride of 50 miles (in two hours four minutes 45 seconds) and longest distance covered in 24 hours (295 miles).

DUNTON

We continue eastwards on minor roads to **Dunton** where, standing in front of the historic Dunton Church in the centre of this peaceful village **The March Hare** is a terrific example of an unpretentious and unspoiled local village pub. The Inn was rebuilt many years ago on the site of the original Ale House, and has been extended over the years using the original timber supports from what had been the village blacksmiths. This extension is now used as the bench-seated dining room, where lunch and evening meals are served daily. All the food at the March Hare is made using only the freshest local ingredients and including the fine Scottish Rump Steak that has proved to be the Inn's most popular dish.

The pub interior is half-panelled in wood throughout and has plenty of pictures of Lewis Carroll's March Hare and some old caricatured golfers. This is probably due to the fact that the 'Dunton Old Boys Golf Club' use this splendid pub as their local meeting place, along with the local diving team, so you can see this Inn is very popular with locals and visitors alike. There are always three excellent real ales on pump from the brick and timber bar, not to mention the lagers, ciders and spirits that are also available to the thirsty traveller.

The March Hare, 34 High Street, Dunton Tel 01767 313852

WRESTLINGWORTH

Orchard Cottage, formerly the village bakery, is situated in the quiet, peaceful village of **Wrestlingworth** with easy access from the A1 and M11. This 16th Century thatched cottage with period extensions providing much character, offers comfortable bed and breakfast accommodation throughout the year. All rooms are pleasantly decorated and furnished, having views overlooking open countryside and the large secluded garden also with central heating, hot and cold washbasins, tea/coffee/chocolate making facilities and radio/alarm. A lounge with television is available for guests to relax in.

Orchard Cottage, 1 High Street, Wrestlingworth Tel 01767 631355

The charming tea room is in the original part of the cottage with its inglenook fireplace, oak beams, rebuilt Tudor oven and ash floor, an ideal setting, providing visitors with a selection of teas and coffees, including home made cakes, some delicious snacks and light lunches for those who are a little more peckish. Hours of opening are between 11am and 5.30pm Thursday to Sunday. The Orchard Cottage probably got its name from when it was built in Tudor times on the village fruit orchard.

The village of **Cockayne Hatley**, a little further to the north east, has a very fine **Church**, built of brown cobbles and dedicated to St John the Baptist. Inside there are magnificent furnishings, woodwork in the Baroque style and of very high quality, brought from Belgium in the 1820s by Henry Cust, the Lord of the Manor. The nave floor has several brass monuments to 15th and 16th Century members of the Cockayne family who gave the village its prefix. So much for hopes that this double-barrelled place name might have something to do with the Kingdom of Cockaigne which was, according to medieval legend, a land of luxury and idleness, where houses were built of cakes!

Cockayne Hatley is in an eastern corner of Bedfordshire and we now turn westwards, pausing first to look at **Potton**, which has an attractive Church with parts built in the 13th, 14th and 15th Centuries. It also has an attractive market place.

From Potton a short diversion north-west along a quiet road brings us to **Tempsford**. Located opposite the village Church in Church End, **The Wheatsheaf** is an attractive Coaching Inn dating from as far back as 1575. An Ale House only from the late 1700s, this Grade II listed building stands on what was once the Great North Road but has since been bypassed and is now locally known as the longest lay-by on the A1!

Your hosts are Kerry and Christine who have been running The Wheatsheaf for the past two years and offer their guests a friendly and jovial atmosphere in which to enjoy a drink or a meal. There are two bars at this inn, the Public and the Lounge bar, both offering the visitor a unique brand of hospitality.

Lunch is served in the Lounge bar or dining room and comprises a bar menu and a children's menu with all the daily specials and vegetarian dishes being displayed for your perusal. If an evening meal is what you are after, then look no further than the spacious restaurant at the rear of the property. This attractive room seats up to 28 under its beamed ceilings and timbered walls and serves a wide selection of freshly-prepared dishes including various curries and special cut steaks which are very popular.

There is a large garden to the rear of the inn which has a great children's play area and in the summer months there is a bouncy castle

Luton Hoo

at the weekends and delicious BBQs take place on a regular basis. There is also a converted stables bar which serves as a function room for wedding receptions or parties and comes complete with its own bar and dance area so everyone can enjoy themselves in fine style.

The Wheatsheaf, Church End, Tempsford Tel 01767 640226 Fax 01767 640723

SANDY

Sandy's name does, as you might expect, relate to the type of soil it stands on, a slight rise of sandy soil suitable for market gardening. However, the 'y' refers to the Old English word for island so the whole name means 'sandy island'. Immediately to the west runs the River Ivel, and the countryside around must formerly have been more of a swamp than it is now. In spite of this it is an area of ancient settlement, and Roman remains have been found, though no evidence of actual buildings.

The headquarters of the Royal Society for the Protection of Birds is at **The Lodge**, Sandy, and the Nature Reserve is set in 104 acres of open heathland and woodland. It is a fascinating place to visit for anyone with even a passing interest in birds.

On what was once the old Great North Road is sited **The Kings Arms,** a traditional 17th Century Coaching Inn. Still standing on the original cobbled walkway, this splendid Inn still has many of its original features including exposed wooden beams and low ceilings. Run by the very charming couple Ken and Jean Parry, The Kings Arms extends to all its visitors a warm and welcoming greeting.

The main dining area is comfortable in its appearance with a huge wooden lintelled feature fireplace that burns brightly in the colder Winter months. The food is superb and ranges from a comprehensive Bar Snacks Menu to an extensive A La Carte style Evening Menu for those who wish to take some time over their dinner. You could start your meal

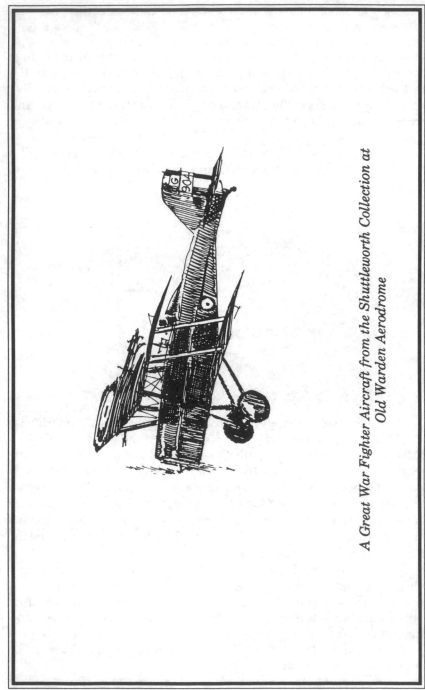

A Great War Fighter Aircraft from the Shuttleworth Collection at Old Warden Aerodrome

with 'Six Golden Butterfly Prawns' served with a choice of dips, move on to a main course of 'Kings Arms Speciality' Fillet Steak topped with Stilton cheese, wrapped in bacon and served with a port wine sauce. And if you have any room left finish with a delicious sweet from the trolley. The food really is gorgeous with all the meals cooked using only the freshest ingredients and charged at a very reasonable and competitive price. Why not relax in the light and airy Saloon Bar after your meal and enjoy one of the many Greene King real ales that are kept in excellent condition by Ken.

Also available is accommodation in self-contained chalets that offer en-suite facilities, television and tea and coffee makers in all rooms.

The Kings Arms, 27 London Road, Sandy Tel 01767 680276

On the east side of Sandy, in Cambridge Road, you will come across **The Queens Head**. This inn is over 300 years old and was originally two cottages that have been sympathetically extended and refurbished. The main bar area has a traditional wooden floor whilst the ceiling is low with exposed timbers and beams. There is a large inglenook fireplace where logs are burnt throughout the colder months and the warming smell envelops the bar on those winter evenings. The walls are half panelled with beautiful brass lamps glowing throughout the whole bar, giving the bar a snug and cosy appearance.

Run by the very capable Clair Ryan, this pub has a terrifically welcoming air to it the moment you walk through the front door. Friendly chatty and vibrant, The Queens Head is very much a community pub with a pleasant mix of locals and visitors alike. Good wholesome and traditional pub food is served every lunchtime in the bar area or on the patio and you can choose from Ploughmans, Cottage Pies, Curries, Pies and other delicious country fayre.

The patio area at the rear of the pub is home to a magnificent willow tree, which gives some pleasant shady relief to clients on those long, hot and sunny days. Also leading off from the patio is a large, well appointed garden with its very own play area for children where they can go and let off a little steam.

The Queens Head, 4 Cambridge Road, Sandy Tel 01767 681115

NORTHILL

We continue westwards then turned south for the pretty village of **Northill**, where we pause at the Church to look at two splendid stained-glass windows dating from 1664. They are, as Sir Nicholas Pevsner puts it 'bold, rich and very secular'.

The Crown, Ickwell Road, Northill Tel 01767 627337

It is always interesting to find in many English villages the local pub or hostelry in close proximity to the Church. In the village of **Northill**, **The Crown** is just such a place with its history dating back to the 16th Century, and in this case was formerly the vicarage. The pub stands in three and a half acres and was first an inn in 1780; its old visitors' book was signed by such famous dignitaries as Pitt and Thomas Walpole.

The Crown is well known locally for its excellent food prepared fresh each day from local produce. The menu is changed daily, one of the most popular dishes being a local sausage in bacon, mushroom and red wine sauce. Game is available in season and there is plenty of choice for all tastes. Food is available Tuesday through Saturday in the evenings and lunchtime seven days a week.

The pub is divided into three areas with traditional pub games played in the front bar. Plenty of old world hospitality is here with real ales, large inglenook and lots of original old beams. There is also a large children's play area with climbing frames, swings etc set well back from the car park. Recommended by Egon Ronay.

Northill's next-door-neighbour **Ickwell** is another attractive place, with houses grouped around a spacious village green.

OLD WARDEN

Just to the south is **Old Warden**, another pretty village, given a Swiss air through the influence of two local families, the Ongleys and the Shuttleworths. The Church contains some interesting woodwork, much of it Belgian, collected by Lord Ongley in the middle of the last century. The effect is a little overwhelming but attractive in a somewhat eccentric way. Some of the individual pieces are very fine.

If you are in the village of Old Warden we suggest you look for the Post Office and Village Stores. There are two other reasons for visiting Old Warden. One is the famous **Swiss Garden**, a romantic fantasy garden dating from the early 19th Century with a tiny thatched Swiss cottage, ironwork bridges and arches of creepers, all part of the original design. There is a superb collection of ferns, a grotto and a picnic area which has been laid out in the woodland beside a lake.

The second is an unlikely neighbour of this charmingly exotic garden, the **Shuttleworth Collection** of historic aircraft. The aerodrome is on the estate of the Shuttleworth family, whose firm developed and produced steam-driven farm machinery from the 1840s. The beginnings of this most original museum lie in tragedy. In 1932 the 23-year-old Richard Ormonde Shuttleworth inherited the estate. He was a keen motor racing driver who had already taken an interest in the then rather short history of motor cars. In 1932 he bought a De Havilland Moth plane and soon became passionately interested in aviation, laying the foundations of the historic aircraft collection in 1935 with a 1909 Bleriot and 1920 Deperdussin. He joined the RAF when war broke out in 1939 but was killed in a flying accident in 1940.

After the war Richard's mother founded a trust which had among its objectives the 'Promotion of education and training in the science, practice and history of aviation and automotive transport'. The collection, which includes a 1941 Spitfire in flying condition, opened to the public in 1960 and is now a fascinating place where the history of flying is brought to life. Many of the aircraft are the sole surviving examples of their type. Shuttleworth retains an interest in the general history of transport with cars, cycles and horse-drawn vehicles and runs a full programme of special weekend events.

SILSOE

We now make our way on minor roads to the A6 and turn south for the village of **Silsoe** and another wonderful garden at **Wrest Park House**. Although the manor of Wrest had been held by the de Grey family since the late 13th Century, the house we see now was built for the first Earl de Grey in 1834-6, designed by a French architect following faithfully the style of a French chateau of the previous century. It is a much more restrained and classical affair than, for example, Waddesdon Manor, which drew in a much looser fashion from earlier types of chateau.

Parts of Wrest Park are open to the public, but the real glory is the garden. They are a living history of English gardening from 1700-1850, including work by Capability Brown. In spite of his influence, the layout remained basically formal, including a full range of 'garden furniture' in the grand manner - Chinese bridge, artificial lake, classical temple and rustic ruin, statues and so on. Two buildings of particular interest are the Baroque **Banqueting House**, designed by Thomas Archer, which forms a focus of the view from the house across the lake, and the **Bowling Green House**, dating from about 1740 and said to have been designed by Batty Langley. If this is so it is indeed a rarity, for Langley was mostly known as a writer of architectural books for country builders and built little himself. Immediately beside the house is an intricate French-style garden, with flower beds, statues and fountains.

FLITTON

In the nearby village of **Flitton**, adjacent to the 15th Century Church, is the **de Grey Mausoleum**, a series of rooms rather more like a museum than part of a church, which contain the monuments of the de Grey family of Wrest Park. The earliest is a brass to Henry Grey who died in 1545. It is worth a stop even for those who don't have much of an interest in such things, for, if nothing else, you are unlikely ever to see so many monuments at the same time again!

1919 to a 2ft gauge for carrying sand, Now it has been metamorphosed into a successful tourist attraction, carrying passengers on a 65-minute, 5-mile round trip through very varied scenery around the town. It has an interesting collection of some thirty steam, petrol and diesel engines, including examples from India and the French Cameroon, all lovingly restored.

If your interest in means of transport extends to walking, you will be interested to know that Leighton Buzzard is at one end of the **Greensand Ridge Walk**, which will take you diagonally across Bedfordshire to finish some forty miles away at Gamlingay, just over the border in the county of Cambridgeshire. The name Greensand comes from the geology of the area, the belt of greensand which stretches from Leighton Buzzard up to Sandy and beyond.

From Leighton Buzzard we travel northwards for the village of **Heath and Reach**, which must be one of the more original names for a village anywhere. It achieved unfortunate notoriety as the place nearby which the Great Train Robbery took place, but is itself a charming place, with old cottages around the village green, and a village pump which looks like a church complete with clock tower. The 15th Century **Heath Farm** is a 'country living centre' where demonstrations of traditional cookery and country crafts are held, with goods for sale. It is also an ideal place to enjoy morning coffee, lunch or afternoon tea.

Nearby is the **Stockgrove Country Park**, 74 acres of parkland with woodland, a small lake and stream.

MILTON BRYAN

Our next destination is Woburn, but we make a short diversion to the east to see the church at **Milton Bryan**, whose tower is claimed as the loftiest point in the county, from which it is even possible to see the sea on a clear day. The nave and chancel are Norman, though drastically 'restored' in the last century. It contains a memorial window to Sir Joseph Paxton who was born in the parish. He began life as gardener for the Duke of Devonshire, but he is best known for his skill as an architect, his most famous work being the Crystal Palace, epoch-making in its time. He designed the mansion at Mentmore which we visited in the last chapter. In 1854 he became a Member of Parliament, a Liberal sitting for Coventry.

Situated at the very south end of Milton Bryan, at the end of a quiet winding lane opposite the Red Lion Pub stands **Town Farm**. The original farmhouse has been extended over the years and is sited on a 35-acre farm with a suckler herd of cattle and sheep. The attractive bed and breakfast accommodation is entered through the beautiful clematis-covered porch into the original brick and tile floored hallway. There are two light and airy twin guest rooms, each with its own private bathroom, tea/coffee making facilities and television.

Town Farm, Milton Bryan Tel 01525 210001

Downstairs in the dining room is where guests of Town Farm can sit and enjoy a generous full English, continental or vegetarian breakfast, before deciding to explore the beautiful countryside that surrounds the farm. There is a designated public footpath which runs through the farmland and on towards Toddington, the local town centre, and is the perfect way to walk off that wonderful breakfast, breathing in the fresh country air and watching the local wildlife. Although Town Farm is located in such a quiet and peaceful area you might be mistaken for thinking that it is miles away from civilisation, but this is not true. It is very convenient from both Woburn and the M1 and provides the perfect spot to relax and wind down from the stresses of everyday life.

WOBURN
Woburn (pronounced Wooburn) is a worthy overture for the very stately classical mansion of Woburn Abbey. The village has retained many Georgian houses and attractive shop fronts, built in warm red brick which gives the streets a cheerful air. The Church is a grand Victorian building beside the entrance to the park, built in a 12th Century French style in 1868. Part of the old Church still stands in Woburn High Street, used as a centre for visitors.

The Abbey from which **Woburn Abbey** takes its name was a daughter community of the Cistercian Abbey at Fountains in Yorkshire, founded in 1145. After the dissolution of the monasteries under Henry VIII it was granted, in 1547, to the first Earl of Bedford. Elements of the present house go back to about 1630, but what we see is almost all 18th Century.

The house contains an extremely important art collection including paintings by Canaletto, Van Dyck, Cuyp, Teniers, Rembrandt,

Gainsborough, Reynolds and Velazquez. There is also English and French 18th Century furniture and a famous dinner service, made at Sevres, which was presented to the 4th Duke by King Louis XV of France, enough to intimidate any guest and petrify anyone inclined to be clumsy.

In a lighter vein, and more than most stately homes Woburn caters for a wide range of tastes with its 'shopping centre', a forty-shop antiques, gift shop, pottery and garden centre.

The 3000-acre deer park was landscaped by Sir Humphrey Repton. Within it 300 acres are set aside as a **Wild Animal Kingdom and Leisure Park**. There is a large collection of animals to see including eland, zebra, hippos and rhinos, lions, tigers, bears, monkeys, sea lions, parrots and elephants. Should you be travelling with children, then the leisure complex will keep them amused for some time with a variety of rides. There is a boating lake for more delicate stomachs.

As part of the Woburn Abbey Estate, the attractive Georgian-built village of Woburn has retained much of its quiet character, yet is convenient for Milton Keynes, Bedford, Dunstable and London, and it is in this quiet village that you will find **The Bedford Arms Thistle Hotel**. The Hotel itself, originally named The George Hotel, dates as far back as 1724 and quickly gained the reputation of being one of the best Coaching Inns outside London. In 1802 it was granted the Sign of the 'Arms of the Bedford Family' and renamed 'The Duke of Bedford Inn'. In 1909 it was renamed again to 'The Bedford Arms Hotel', underwent extensive rebuilding then and again in 1971 to produce the general splendour that you can see around you today.

The Bedford Arms Hotel, George Street, Woburn Tel 01525 290441

Tastefully decorated and retaining much of its olde-worlde charm and elegance, the Hotel has 53 en-suite bedrooms. All bedrooms come complete with colour television and sky channels, radio, direct-dial telephone, trouser press and tea/coffee maing facilities. There are also

258

several Executive rooms available, including one with a four poster bed and luxurious suite, perfect for that honeymoon couple. The Bedford Arms Thistle Hotel also has a superb eating house called Holland's Restaurant named after the architect who built both the hotel and much of the Abbey, and it has a local reputation for its high standards of cuisine and service.

The age of coaching brought prosperity to the village and inns such as **The Black Horse** served coaches on a countrywide network. The earliest reference to The Black Horse is in 1824 and the coach arch is still a feature of this attractive and well-presented inn. Inside the inn is also very traditional with oak panelling to some walls which also display pictures and china; padded benches and beamed ceilings.

Food plays an important part of a visit to The Black Horse and you are invited to enjoy exceptional quality food at sensible prices. Fresh fish and the inn's famous prime steaks are cooked on the open grill to your individual taste. You are welcome to enjoy a single course or a three-course meal in the restaurant accompanied by fine wines and traditional ales. Children are welcome. Ask for details of interesting walks in the area.

The Black Horse & Forge Grill, 1 Bedford Street, Woburn Tel 01525 290210 Fax 01525 290050

Located in the very centre, only 200 yards from the famous Abbey, **Serendib** is a gift shop with a difference. The name itself means 'finding the unusual by chance', and this is definitely true of this hidden gem. Originally built in the 1700s, Serendib has an incredible selection of very unusual and bizarre gifts and memorabilia, ranging from a wonderful selection of original inglenook fireplaces in the cellar to walking sticks and candles.

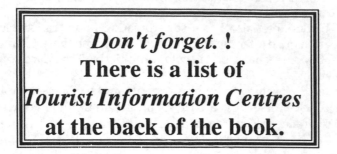

Don't forget. !
There is a list of
Tourist Information Centres
at the back of the book.

Serendib, 15 Market Place, Woburn Tel 01525 290464

The selection of collectors' dolls is superb and offers something for even the most avid collector; there are also lots of china cats and dogs, pots and brasses, with a good assortment of family tree kits which are usually very hard to find. Some of the pieces of silver jewellery that Serendib sell are quite unique and beautifully crafted. Also sold is a large range of artists' materials, from hand-made papers to pencils and paints. To complete your gift to a loved one you are going to need some wrapping paper - look no further, for there is a large supply of stylish gift paper and cards for every occasion. Open seven days a week (from 10am until 5.30pm Monday to Saturday and on Sundays 11am until 5.30pm) there really can't be a larger selection of unusual and incredible gifts in the whole of the Milton Keynes area.

To order other books in the series
see the order form at the back of the book
any 5 titles for only £ 20

Copperfields, 16 Market Place, Woburn Tel 01525 290464

Next to Serendib stands **Copperfields**, a traditional Tea Room. Owned and personally run by Shirley Droy and built in the 1700s, Copperfields is full of olde worlde charm and character. The rooms have all the originally exposed wooden beams and a small patio at the front of the establishment which is named 'The Pitchings' is the original cobbled part of Woburn. Inside the tea room culinary delights abound, from freshly made sandwiches using home-cooked beef and locally-cooked ham, to delicious salads using only the freshest local produce; though no hot dishes are served at Copperfields you won't be lacking in choice. The Specials are freshly toasted teacakes dripping with real butter or the clotted cream teas, with their delicious preserves, home-baked scones and a pot of tea - absolute heaven. Copperfields is also a guest house with a single, double, family and twin en-suite rooms.

Just a short distance from Woburn is the village of **Milton Bryan**, where stands **The Red Lion** village inn where 'tis rumoured Dick Turpin did court a lady of the village and did stay in this very inn on his way to London'! Built in the 17th Century as a private home, brewing was started on the site and in the 18th Century it became an ale house.

Today Bob and Jenny will extend a warm welcome whether you call in for a little liquid refreshment or a taste of their excellent country fayre. The Red Lion is fitted with air purification units ensuring that you are not surrounded by smoke - what a real benefit!

Traditional home cooking can be enjoyed in the rustic Tap and Spile bar or the cosy Bacchus Bar. A full a la carte menu is offered in the dining room where a really pleasant evening can be enjoyed. Children are welcome and will enjoy the play area provided. The inn offers easy access for the less able callers and a first class selection of cask ales, continental lagers and quality wines can be enjoyed in the very friendly bars.

The Red Lion, Toddington Road, South End, Milton Bryan Tel 01525 210044

After Woburn, we make tracks on minor roads, crossing the M1 to the village of **Steppingley** and a new chapter.

North Bedfordshire

Harrold Village

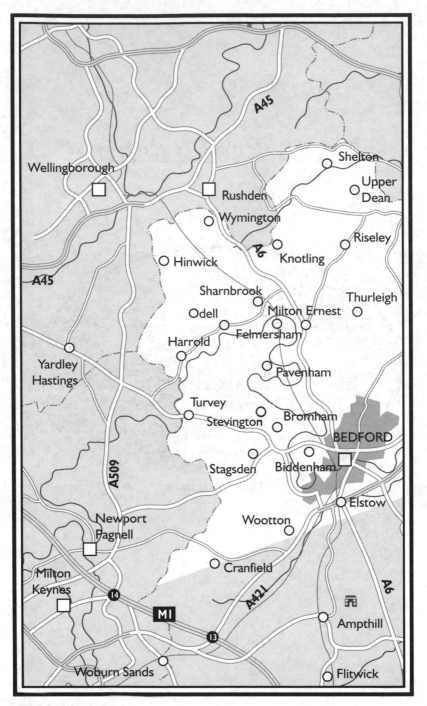

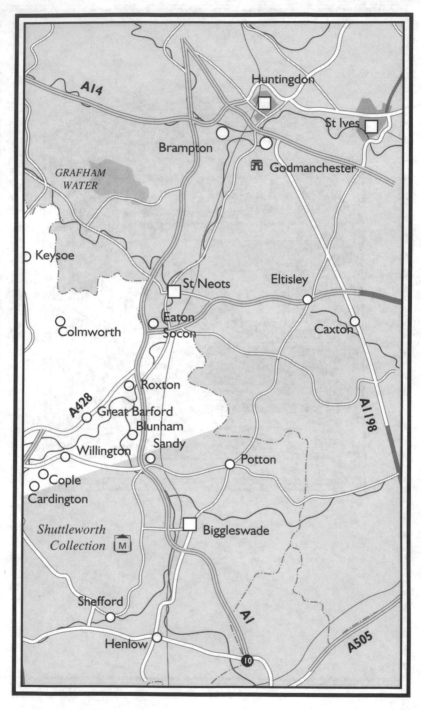

Bunyan Window

CHAPTER TWELVE

North Bedfordshire

In this chapter we explore the northern half of Bedfordshire. We travel through gentle countryside dominated by the Great Ouse river, the county town, Bedford, and a history which includes a man with a good claim to be the greatest religious writer in the English language. It is a countryside which has suffered unfairly from mineral extraction, but it is heartening to see that so much has been done to reclaim and improve what the despoilers have left behind, while the towns and villages have a quiet charm which is hard to forget.

AMPTHILL
Our first stop for this new chapter is **Ampthill**, a pleasant market town with a number of interesting buildings. The largely Perpendicular Church has a fine west tower. Inside are 15th Century brasses and a 17th Century monument to Richard Nicholls which includes the cannon ball which killed him, in 1672, during the battle of Sole Bay. This was an indecisive engagement at which a combined British and French fleet under the Duke of York, later James II, met the Dutch Fleet.

Katherine's Cross, in Woburn Road, was erected to commemorate the fact that Katherine of Aragon lived at Ampthill Castle while the hearing to end her marriage to Henry VIII was in progress at Dunstable. The castle has gone but its replacement, **Ampthill Park**, can still be seen. It was built on the site at the end of the 17th Century and enlarged about a century later.

Just to the north of Ampthill our footsteps cross those of someone whom we will meet again in this chapter, John Bunyan, who lived from 1628 to 1688. He was a man whose religious convictions were formed in the ferment of ideas which were the background to the Civil War, an unlicensed preacher who spent years in prison for his refusal to remain silent. It was in prison that he wrote many of his religious works, and began his masterpiece, 'The Pilgrim's Progress'.

In Bedfordshire there is something of a minor industry in spotting real places which correspond to descriptions of the allegorical places which Bunyan's Pilgrim, Christian, encountered. One which does seem convincing is where, after climbing the 'narrow way up the side of the hill which is called Difficulty', Christian is in danger of being benighted because he has slept on the way and spent time looking for his lost luggage.

Seeking a lodging for the night, he lifts up his eyes 'and behold there was a very stately palace before him, the name of which was Beautiful'. Tradition has it that this was **Houghton House**, which is indeed on a hill, and was begun in 1615 for Mary, Countess of Pembroke. Inigo Jones is thought to have had a hand in the design. In Bunyan's time, therefore, it would have been a new and startling addition to the landscape. Records show that Bunyan visited the house to repair and make cooking utensils. Perhaps he met with a generous welcome in the kitchen, for his House called Beautiful 'was built by the Lord on the hill, on purpose to entertain such pilgrims in'. When Christian leaves, on a clear morning, he is shown, far away to the south, the Delectable Mountains, 'a pleasant mountainous country, beautified with woods,' from which, Christian was assured, he would be able to see the gates of the Celestial City.

Houghton House no longer offers hospitality to the traveller, for it is now a ruin. It eventually became the property of the Dukes of Bedford, one of whom had it partly demolished in 1794. However, if you are lucky enough to be there on a clear day you will be able to see, away to the south, the line of the Chiltern Hills, which are indeed delectable.

RIDGMONT

We leave Ampthill to travel west to a village which provides another example of the influence exercised in this area by the Bedford family. **Ridgmont** was part of the Woburn Estate and is a typical example of an 'estate village', that is one where the owners of the land, which by definition meant, in most cases, being the employer of the inhabitants, provided the houses and other buildings. Here the estate's workers were provided with gabled houses in red brick.

The Church was also built, in 1854-5, at the expense of the estate, and was designed by G G Scott, whose birthplace at Gawcott we visited in a previous chapter. It is in a late 13th Century style.

Nearby, just off the road leading to **Eversholt** is the ruined Church of **Segenhoe**, a lost and romantic place, unexpected so close to the M1. It is architecturally interesting, with an early Norman chancel and other details, though the tower and windows are 18th Century.

STAGSDEN

Our next destination is **Stagsden**, where the **Bird Gardens** are a breeding centre for owls, flamingoes, cranes, pheasants, a variety of waterfowl and many other species of birds, including talking mynahs and parrots. Altogether there are about 1300 birds here, from 150 species, including many old and now rare breeds of poultry. The collection of

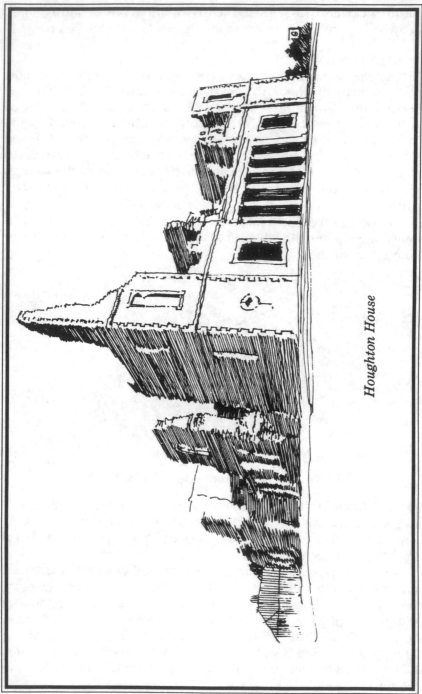

Houghton House

shrub roses is also magnificent. There is a 13th and 14th Century Church in the village, containing a rather fine Perpendicular style screen.

STEVINGTON

Our next stop is the pretty limestone village of **Stevington**, one of the prettiest villages in Bedfordshire and here you will find **The Royal George**. The building dates from the late 1600s and the original pub is now used as the dining area; the main bar was previously the living quarters and the former saddlery now serves as a games room. Good food is served throughout the day, all freshly prepared from local produce, one of the most popular dishes being the village cured ham, chicken and asparagus pie. The menu certainly represents good value for money. The pub serves real ales and a range of other beers, wines and spirits.

The keys can be obtained here for a visit to Stevington Windmill, the only restored windmill in the county and certainly well worth a visit after your satisfying meal.

The Royal George, Stevington Tel 01234 822184

The **Windmill** is a post-mill built in 1770. It is an impressive sight with its graceful sails. It is a popular attraction for visitors and by obtaining the key from the Royal George for a deposit of 50p it is possible to view it from the inside as well as out.

The Church is also interesting, with an Anglo-Danish base to the west tower. Under the wall of the Church is a 'Holy Well' whose waters are said never to fail, however dry the season. The village is a 'Bunyan Village', one of several places where John Bunyan used to preach when he was prohibited from preaching in Bedford. The **Bunyan Meeting Church** at West End is still in use and remains in excellent condition. Rumour has it that the Cross in the centre of the village was featured in Pilgrims Progress.

270

PAVENHAM

We continue through **Pavenham**, another pleasant village with an attractive riverside site. The traditional craft associated with Pavenham was the making of rush matting. The village Church is 13th Century, with a collection of Jacobean woodwork inside, 'recycled' from a variety of sources and given to the Church in 1848. The oldest parts of the bridge across the Ouse are 13th Century.

FELMERSHAM

Our next village, **Felmersham**, is also beside the river and has what is probably the finest Parish Church in Bedfordshire. It was built in the short timescale between 1220 and 1240, so it is unusually all in the same style. Why this village Church should have had so much beauty lavished on it is something of a mystery, but the result, both inside and out, is very harmonious.

To the south of the Church is a late medieval barn and just to the north-east of the stone bridge, built in 1818, evidence of an iron age settlement has been discovered with artefacts which dated from the 1st Century AD. An excavation of the site revealed an important collection of bronze utensils and pottery.

MILTON ERNEST

We come back to the A6 at **Milton Ernest**. The Church here has an early Norman chancel and work of other periods. It was restored from 1864-5 by William Butterfield, best known, perhaps, as the architect of Keble College, Oxford, and other buildings, almost all churches, in his typical multicoloured brick style.

Butterfield was a follower of the 'High Church' faction in the Church of England, which stressed the importance of ritual and preferred a celibate clergy. Butterfield himself had a rather high church approach to life, being a rather aloof and studious man who remained a bachelor. His father is buried in the churchyard. Butterfield also designed **Milton Hall** in the village, which was built in 1856, this time using buff-coloured stone with his favourite red bricks confined to picking out details.

CLAPHAM

Now we take the road south towards Bedford, but pause at **Clapham** to see the church of St Thomas of Canterbury (the Thomas a Becket who is the subject of T S Eliot's poetic drama 'Murder in the Cathedral'), which is a very ancient building. The west tower is impressive, Anglo-Danish with a 'new' top added by the Normans.

Then we turn away from the Bedford direction temporarily to take the minor road to **Bromham**, where with the 17th Century watermill which has been restored there is an exhibition of milling history. There are displays of natural history, crafts and other special exhibitions and outside is an attractive picnic area by the river.

The oldest of the arches of the bridge date back to the 13th Century, though extensive repairs were carried out in the 15th and 19th Centuries. The Church is well worth a look, particularly for a fine brass monument to Thomas Wideville, who died in 1435, and his two wives. The figures show a knight in armour and the two ladies wearing simple robes but elaborate headdresses, each with a little dog appealing for attention at her feet.

We continue towards Bedford again, passing through **Biddenham**, an attractive place with some handsome houses.

BEDFORD
The bustling county town of some 130,000 inhabitants. **Bedford** has made the best of its riverside site with wide embankment gardens and the handsome bridge built from 1811-13. When the church tower at Clapham was being built, in the 10th Century, Bedford was already a thriving market centre. The **Church of St Peter de Merton** dates from this period, though it has substantial Norman additions, particularly a Norman central tower. The south doorway is also Norman and very fine, though it was not actually intended for this church. In fact it was brought here from the Church of St Peter in Dunstable.

Bedford's main Church, however, is **St Paul's**, a large town Church in the Market Place. The building is mainly 14th and 15th Century and has good, recently restored roofs and furnishings. The modern engraved doors at the east end are worth close inspection and there are interesting monuments and brasses. Don't miss the fine 18th Century gates and railings in the churchyard.

Bedford is very proud of its most famous son, John Bunyan, whose statue stands at the northern end of the High Street. Bunyan was born in **Elstow** just south of Bedford, the son of a tinsmith, a repairer of metal utensils and implements, and followed the same trade which offered him more opportunities to travel about his area than many people would have had at the time. During the Civil War he was drafted, at the age of 16, into the Parliamentarian Army and was very much affected by the ferment of religious ideas characteristic of those unsettled times. In the 1650s he met John Gifford, who had been appointed pastor of an independent congregation which met at St John's Church. After long discussions with Gifford Bunyan experienced a conversion and became a member of the congregation. Gifford is commonly taken to be the model for Evangelist in Pilgrim's Progress, who asks Christian, 'Do you see yonder shining light?' and sends him off to 'keep that light in your eye'. Similarly, 'the house of the Interpreter' whom Goodwill told Christian 'would shew him excellent things' has been identified with the Rectory of St John's, where Gifford lived.

Bunyan was baptised by Gifford in the Ouse and later became a preacher, travelling round the villages of Bedfordshire. This brought him into conflict with the authorities. He was arrested in 1660, while preaching near Ampthill and was in gaol at Bedford for twelve years, during which he began writing his religious works in the simple and noble English which has made them immortal. He began writing 'Pilgrim's Progress', during a second, shorter, period of imprisonment in 1673.

The successor of the barn in which Bunyan preached to his congregation is the **Bunyan Meeting House** in Mill Street. It was built in 1850 and the interior has been recently restored and remodelled. The bronze entrance doors are very impressive. In the Church buildings is the **Bunyan Museum**, which has a collection of Bunyan's personal belongings, relics associated with his life and a collection of some 200 copies of The Pilgrim's Progress in many translations.

Bedford has two other museums which are well worth a visit. The **Cecil Higgins Art Gallery** has a very fine collection of English water-colours and drawings. There are important collections of ceramics and glass and also lace, formerly a cottage industry in the East Midlands. A particularly imaginative part of the museum is the 'Victorian mansion' which has rooms furnished to create the impression of a 'lived-in' home belonging to a middle-class Victorian family.

The other, **Bedford Museum** in Castle Lane, has an interesting collection relating to the history and natural history of the area. A piece of wall on display as an example of wattle walls comes from the **King William IV** pub in the High Street, **Kempston**, which started life as a farmhouse in the 14th Century. You can still see the original timber frame today. Most of the building was virtually destroyed after a disastrous fire but it was rebuilt in 1830 when William IV was on the throne.

ELSTOW

The birthplace of John Bunyan was a cottage on the eastern side of **Elstow**. The cottage itself has now vanished, but a stone marks the site, which can be approached by a footpath off Old Harrowden Road. The **Moot Hall** in Elstow is a building Bunyan would have known, a handsome timber-framed brick construction with a projecting upper storey and a steep, tiled roof, built about 1500. Inside is a Museum with furniture and other items illustrating life in Bunyan's time, traditions associated with him and an impressive collection of his writings. Nearby are some recently restored house cottages, also half timbered, but this time with the infilling painted white, giving the traditional 'black and white' effect.

The Church, where John Bunyan was baptised and was a worshipper and bell-ringer before finding that the Established Church did not satisfy his religious needs, is dedicated to **St Mary and St Helena**. It is an impressive building, the remains of a Benedictine Nunnery founded about 1075, and part of the building is Norman. The windows are Perpendicular in style. The bell tower, which is detached from the rest of the building, dates from the 15th Century. There are two brass monuments, one of them to one of the Abbesses who ruled over the community here before it was dissolved. There are also two stained glass windows commemorating Bunyan, installed in 1880. Nearby is the ruin of **Hillersdon Hall**, built in 1616 using stone from the dissolved Abbey.

The A6 south from Elstow passes through a part of Bedfordshire destined to become a 'Community Forest', one of the many 'green' initiatives of the European Community. The idea is that between 30% and 50% of the area will eventually be covered with trees. This is an area where the countryside has suffered much from the brick industry, and the next generation will see a lavishly wooded landscape of the type swept away by modern agriculture.

CARDINGTON

We continue on to **Cardington**, where two huge hangars are the relics of an aeronautical adventure which ended in tragedy and disappointment. They were built in 1917 and 1927 to house the two great airships, the R100 and R101. At the time it seemed that the future of passenger aviation lay in airships rather than planes. But the huge cigar-shaped balloons were filled with highly inflammable hydrogen gas and the history of this form of transport is scarred by a series of horrific accidents; there are few who will not have seen film of the German Trans-Atlantic Zeppelin Hindenburg's pyrotechnic end.

After the R101 crashed mysteriously over Beauvais in France on its inaugural flight in 1930, the aeronautical industry lost confidence in airships, though they have retained a limited place ever since. There is a memorial to those killed in the R101 disaster in the churchyard, but the huge dark hangars offer a far more impressive reminder of the tragedy.

We continue to **Cople**, where we pause to look at the attractive buff and brown stone Church. It was built in the 15th Century and has the best collection of brass monuments in the county. The earliest of these date from about 1400, and the most recent commemorates Robert Bulkeley, who died in 1556.

WILLINGTON

Our next stop is **Willington**, which also has an important Church, all late Perpendicular in style. It was probably built at the expense of Sir John

Gostwick who was Master of Horse to Cardinal Wolsey and later rejoiced in the title of Treasurer of the First Fruits and Tenths for King Henry VIII. He bought the Manor here in 1529 and there is a monument to him between the chancel and the north chapel. In the chapel are also two helmets from suits of armour. One of them was worn by Sir John at the 'Field of the Cloth of Gold', the occasion in 1520 when, amid much pomp, jousting and feasting, Henry VIII met Francois I of France.

Of Sir John's **Manor House**, where he entertained the king in 1541, only two minor buildings remain. The most impressive is the dovecot, large and oblong-shaped, built in a warm creamy brown stone, with stepped gables and a double-decked roof, and shutters for the birds to fly in and out between the two parts. There are nesting places inside for 1500 pigeons.

From here we pass through **Great Barford** and set out on a tour of some of the villages of north Bedfordshire.

BLUNHAM

We begin in the nearby village of **Blunham** where the poet John Donne was rector from 1622-31, at the same time as being Dean of St Paul's in London. He spent part of every year here, staying in a house opposite the Church, which has a chalice given by him in 1626. The beginnings of his life gave no clue that he would later become a clergyman and preacher of sermons which are valued right down to the present day. He began his working life as a secretary to The 'Lord Keeper of the Great Seal', Sir Thomas Egerton, but annoyed his employer, however, by secretly marrying his niece. Donne also sailed with two of the expeditions of the Earl of Essex, favourite of Queen Elizabeth I, before being ordained in 1615.

The Church itself has a number of interesting features, including a west tower which appears to be from the late 16th Century, though it also contains Norman work. There are some interesting bosses - carvings placed where the ribs of a vault meet - in the chancel and a fine screen in the Perpendicular style.

ROXTON

Next to the Church in the pretty village of **Roxton** you will come across **Church Farm**. This superb Bed and Breakfast is beautifully appointed in a quiet setting at the centre of this unspoiled village. The Church that the farm is so aptly named after is well worth a visit as it is a most unusual shape and also has a thatched roof. The property is owned and very capably run by Janet Must, who keeps her charming house spotlessly clean and very comfortable with a friendly welcome guaranteed. Although there are only two bedrooms available you will find that once you have stayed you will want to return again and again to sample some of the excellent hospitality that makes Church Farm so popular with all its guests. The atmosphere is a warm and friendly one, with the decor and furnishings giving the farm a traditional and cosy feel. Although Church Farm is no longer a working farm, you will still find plenty of things to do locally, such as golf, long river walks, stately homes to visit and museums to explore.

Church Farm, Roxton Tel 01234 870234

Now we make our way to **Bushmead Priory**, just north of **Colmworth**. The original Priory was founded about 1195 as a community of Augustinian canons. Canons were clergy who were attached to a Cathedral or Collegiate Church rather than being responsible for a parish. As such they were not monks in the usual sense although they sometimes, as here, adopted the monastic, communal way of life and the rules which went with it. All that is left of their buildings is the Refectory, a very fine building with a timber roof of the crown-post type of construction, build about 1250. Some wall paintings and stained glass have also survived.

This is quiet, undramatic, countryside, with villages embedded among rich farmlands, sometimes the church an architectural gem lost in this unsung part of England, and it is a relaxing area to be explored gently, savouring here a church, there a genuine country pub.

In the northern corner of Bedfordshire is the village of **Upper Dean**, which has a Church built mainly in the first half of the 14th Century. Outside there is a selection of entertaining gargoyles and inside a fine roof is decorated with carved angels. It also has some finely-carved screens, and interesting benches, stained glass and monuments. Its neighbour **Shelton**'s Church is interesting because it has escaped restoration by a tidy-minded Victorian church architect. The resulting unspoilt interior is mainly in the decorated style. There are also wall paintings, including one of St Christopher.

276

The village of **Riseley**'s church has a rather odd look. This is because the south aisle was built in the 13th Century as the nave. The whole building was given a root and branch rearrangement in the 15th Century.

Knotting has a Church with a Norman nave and is dedicated unusually to St Margaret of Antioch. Part of its attraction is its isolated setting. Pevsner characterises the tower arch as 'parabolic and barbaric and quite undateable' and it is interesting to try and work out what he meant. The west tower itself dates from 1615. The chancel gates were installed in 1637, after a scandal caused when cock fights were held in the Church, attended by the rector and churchwardens! This episode needs to be set in the context of the time, when some of the more extreme Protestants believed that the relationship of the individual to God was so important that too great a reverence for buildings - churches - got in the way of true religion. This was the climate in which John Bunyan grew up.

We once more cross the A6 heading for **Wymington**, where there is a Church, dedicated to St Lawrence, built in the style more characteristic of the churches of Northamptonshire -which is not, after all, far away. It is mainly in the decorated style, built in the late 14th Century, has a spire with crockets and gabled lucarnes (windows) which make for a very attractive ensemble. The monument to the man who paid for the church to be built, John Curteys, who died in 1391, is between the chancel and the south chapel.

Nearby **Podington**'s church is partly Norman and partly 13th Century, also in the Northamptonshire style, with a fine collection of monuments. There are the remains of a motte-and-bailey Castle behind **Manor Farm**.

HINWICK

In the village of **Hinwick** is **Hinwick House**, built between 1709-14 for the Orlebar family, whose descendants still live in it. It is a Queen Anne style house, the front decorated with corinthian pilasters and topped off with a pediment showing the goddess Diana. It is built in an attractive brown stone decorated with details picked out in a stone of a lighter colour. The house is sometimes open for visitors. Inside, the spacious entrance hall is particularly pleasing and there is an interesting collection of furniture and paintings.

Nearby is **Hinwick Hall**, with its oldest parts dating back to about 1540. The house was given a new front in the early 18th Century, with motifs which are very similar to those of Hinwick House.

We now head south, back to the River Ouse and the country park between the two villages of **Odell** and **Harrold**. Bedfordshire as a county has suffered very much from the extraction of minerals, notably gravel and clay for bricks.

The county has been particularly imaginative in converting these areas back into assets for the region, making a virtue of the flooded pits by turning them into landscaped areas where land and water complement each other.

The **Harrold-Odell Country Park** has some 144 acres of landscaped lakes, river banks and water meadows and 55 species of birds have been recorded there. People are also made welcome with an excellent visitors' centre and a clearly marked circular walk.

ODELL

The two villages are attractive in themselves, too. **Odell** has a spacious Church in the Perpendicular style with an impressive tower, and inside, in the tower arch, a fine screen dating from 1637. It also boasts a fine 16th Century thatched Inn, **The Bell,** a delightful riverside pub and eating place standing opposite the Church on the village green in a quintessential English setting. Created when three cottages were knocked together over two centuries ago, it retains a wonderful atmosphere with low-beamed ceilings, log fires and traditional decor.

Proprietors Doreen and Derek Scott have built up an enviable reputation for their food, drink and hospitality. They serve a mouthwatering range of home-cooked dishes, including traditional lunch on Sunday, all freshly prepared and surprisingly modestly priced. Egon Ronay reocmmended. The Bell was recently listed in The Independent as one of the top twenty pubs in the UK.

The Bell, Horsehair Lane, Odell Tel 01234 720254

Across the country park **Harrold** has some attractive buildings, including a house of about 1600 in the High Street and, on the village green, a circular lock-up for local malefactors and an octagonal wooden Market Cross. The bridge is partly 14th Century.

TURVEY

Our last call in Bedfordshire is at **Turvey**, where the county meets Buckinghamshire at the river Ouse. It is a good place to finish touring Bedfordshire. The interesting **Church of All Saints** is large, parts of it, such as the tower and the walls of the nave, dating from before the Norman conquest. The roof is Perpendicular in style, that is from the 14th or 15th Centuries, decorated with carved angels and bosses. The chancel, on the other hand, is Victorian, designed by Scott, with whose work and life we have become quite well acquainted on our travels.

Turvey Abbey is a Jácobean House built 1603-1608 and **Turvey House** is of 1794, with corinthian pilasters and an entrance porch complete with Tuscan columns and a pediment. The bridge has parts which date from the 13th Century, but major alterations have been made since, notably in 1795 and 1820. Beside it are two 18th Century sculptured figures, alleged to be Jonah and his wife.

From here we bid farewell to the county of Bedfordshire

Harrold Village

West Hertfordshire

Ware Village

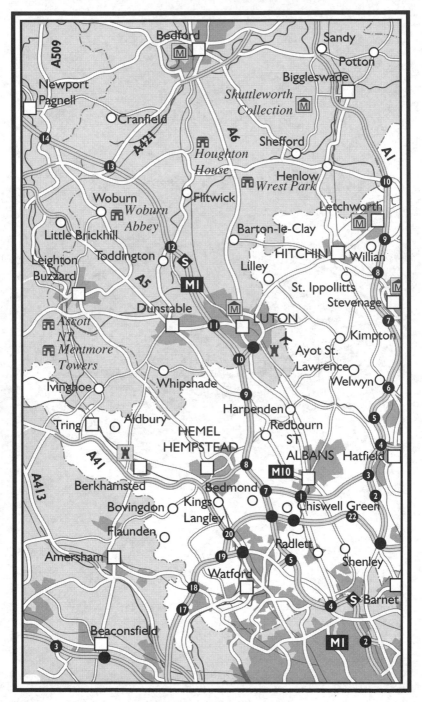

West Hertfordshire

HEMEL HEMPSTEAD

We now find ourselves in West Hertfordshire where we begin our travels at **Hemel Hempstead**. Although described as a new town, Hemel Hempstead has developed on the site of an existing town, the picturesque High Street of old Hemel Hempstead leading north towards Piccotts End and Ashridge. To the west the River Gade wends its way past the old and new town centres on its way south to meet the Bulbourne.

The delightful **Spinning Wheel Restaurant** stands on the High Street in the heart of old Hemel Hempstead. This excellent establishment is housed in a 15th-Century Grade II listed building which was originally part of a row of artisans' cottages. It is full of historic character, and even has an exposed section of its original wattle and daub wall encased behind glass.

Spinning Wheel Restaurant, 80 High Street, Hemel Hempstead Tel 01442 64309

Seating up to 55 people, it is the perfect setting for a reception or party, that special dinner for two or lunchtime treat with friends. Proprietors Kirsty and Ken provide the finest food and service in an atmosphere which is wonderfully relaxed and intimate. Their menu features, for example, tiger prawns in filo pastry and mushroom and coriander hot pot for starters, main courses of fillet stroganoff, or hazelnut chicken and salmon with tarragon, as well as a wide variety of steaks served with a

St. Mary's Church, Hemel Hempstead

choice of special sauces. There is also a selection of vegetarian, pasta and seasonal entrees on the chalkboard, and a comprehensive range of desserts, liqueurs and malt whiskies to round off the meal. An ideal place for that special meal out.

Journeying from here towards Aldbury we pass **Ashridge Park**, formerly part of the estate of Lord Brownlow and now owned by the National Trust. With grounds and woodland extending to some 4000 acres, this is a lovely place for walking and on afternoons between April and October you can visit the **Bridgewater Monument**, an impressive tower erected in memory of the Duke of Bridgewater who was famous for his pioneering work in the development of canals. The monument is the focal point of the park and affords wonderful countryside views. The National Trust Shop and Information Centre are also open at these times.

And so on to **Aldbury**. This picturesque village dates back to Saxon times and is an unspoilt haven of tranquillity. Traditional features such as the village green, the stocks and the village pond are still visible.

First mention of the grand house that is now Stocks Country House Hotel appeared in 1176 and since then it has been home to some famous names, including Walter de la Mare in 1273 and Phillip de Aylesbury in 1318. Most people assume that the house was named after the road on which it stands, but local historians say that it was probably named after a man called Stokkis who owned all the surrounding land during the Middle Ages.

If you're looking for peace and tranquillity, you need look no further than **The Greyhound Inn** at Aldbury. Whatever time of year you visit you will find it an idyllic setting with a pace of life you would think had all but disappeared. Overlooking the delightful duck pond and ancient stocks in the heart of the village, this welcoming inn will help you unwind the moment you cross its grapevine-covered threshold. Each of its charming rooms have been individually decorated and furnished with old pine, period pieces and antiques, to retain all the character of a bygone age. However, for your comfort and convenience, things are very much in the 20th Century, each room having its own colour satellite television, tea and coffee making facilities and private bath or shower room.

Proprietors Martin and Sue Roberts and their staff go out of their way to make you feel at home, whether your stay is for just one night or a week-long holiday - the welcome is even warmer in the winter when the huge inglenook is piled high with blazing logs. Optional continental or full English breakfast can be taken in the cosy, oak-beamed restaurant which in the evening serves the kind of food that brings folk flocking from far and near! The bar snacks are also a local legend, perhaps even more enjoyable in summer, when they can be eaten 'al fresco' beside the fountain and under the honeysuckle-covered pergola in the beer garden, enjoyed all the more when accompanied by one of the several real ales available or a traditional local ale brewed especially for the inn.

Being a conservation area the surrounding countryside is a haven for ramblers and nature lovers. Aldbury is also the ideal base for touring the beautiful counties of Hertfordshire, Bedfordshire and Buckinghamshire. There is no shortage of things to do and see during your stay at The Greyhound Inn - more than just a pub!

The Greyhound Inn, Stocks Road, Aldbury Tel 01442 851228

TRING

A few miles west of Aldbury lies **Tring**, a bustling little market town with a narrow winding High Street that leads past little alleyways and courtyards, all inviting exploration. Between 1873 and 1938 a large part of the town formed part of the Tring Park and Estate, which was then owned by the famous Rothschild family, great benefactors of the town.

Once in Tring a visit to the **Walter Rothschild Zoological Museum** is a must. Housing an amazing collection of animals and insects, now part of the Natural History Museum, it is the largest single collection of animal species in the country.

There are many places of interest within easy reach, such as **Tring Museum** and **The Grand Union Canal**.

BERKHAMSTED

To the south of Tring we come to the historic town of **Berkhamsted**, where in December 1066, two months after the Battle of Hastings, the Saxons submitted to William of Normandy. It was shortly after this that building work began on the Norman Castle close to the river, the ruins of which can still be seen.

Although not many of the original buildings of the town remain, one that is particularly attractive is Dean John Incent's jettied house, an impressive black and white timbered building situated in the High Street opposite the Church. Dean Incent was the founder of the original Grammar Gchool built in 1554 which has since been incorporated into Berkhamsted School.

In the south west corner of the county, close to the Buckinghamshire border, the villages of **Bovingdon** and **Flaunden** are well worth a visit, containing some wonderful examples of medieval hall-houses and cottages. The Church at **Bovingdon** contains an impressive effigy of a 15th Century knight in armour, although the Church itself only dates from 1845.

Travelling south-east out of Bovingdon towards **Chipperfield** you will come across signs for the pretty little village of **Flaunden** and then stumble across the intriguingly-named Hog Pits Bottom on the edge of the village.

In Flaunden the medieval chapel follows the plan of a Greek Cross, the building having four equal arms, with an adjoining curate's house. Left to decay since 1838 when a new village Church was built, all that remains of the chapel are overgrown ruins.

KINGS LANGLEY

Alongside the A41 is **Kings Langley**, where one of the best eating places in the area can be found in High Street. **La Casetta** is a first-class restaurant serving the finest traditional Italian cuisine. Housed in the oldest building in Kings Langley, the structure was originally built in 1509 and is now Grade II listed. Indeed, the date of construction and the builder's initials can still be seen upstairs on the inner front wall. With its exposed timbers, wood panelling, inglenook fireplace and crooked doorways the restaurant is full of original character. Even the floorboards creak as the staff and customers move around.

La Casetta, 18 High Street, Kings Langley Tel 01923 263823

287

Proprietor Carlo Petitto offers a remarkably broad and imaginative a la carte menu. The choice of fifteen starters includes scallops cooked in white wine and pancakes stuffed with chicken and asparagus, and there are a dozen pasta dishes which can be eaten as a starter or main course. Entrees include beef, chicken, duck, veal and fish dishes, as well as seafood specialities such as squid and king prawns. La Casetta enjoys an outstanding reputation, with diners returning again and again to enjoy the superb food, excellent service and charming atmosphere.

We next discover the delightful village of **Bedmond** which lies on the Hemel Hempstead to Abbots Langley road. This was the birthplace of the only British pope, Nicholas Breakspear who was crowned Adrian IV in 1154.

WATFORD

Watford is the industrial centre of Hertfordshire. Originally a country market town, the arrival of the railway brought new business, creating huge expansion and what was once a one-street town is now a vast hive of industrial activity. Among the few surviving buildings of the original town are the five-gabled **Bedford Almshouses** to the west of the Church, which date back to 1580. On the High Street, the splendid Mansion House which was once used as the offices of the local company Benskin Brewery, now contains the town's **Museum** where you can discover the industrial and social history of the area.

Whippendell Wood covers some 200 acres and offer a wealth of scenic walks, with attractively appointed picnic areas and two nature trails which start from the car park in Grove Mill Lane, Watford. Alternatively you can reach the woods on foot from **Cassiobury Park**.

SHENLEY

The pretty village of **Shenley** lies a few miles to the east of Watford and is a traditional country village with, at its centre, two inns, a pond, the site of a former pound for stray animals and a 'cage' or lock-up. One of several in Hertfordshire, the 'cage' is a brick-built beehive-shaped construction where drunks and petty criminals would be locked up overnight before facing the magistrate the next day. On either side of the door is the warning sign: 'Be Sober, Do Well; Fear Not, Be Vigilant'.

The Queen Adelaide at Shenley is a first-rate pub and eating place which stands in a delightful location next to the village pond. Constructed as an inn in 1924, this handsome red brick building continues to provide a warm welcome to visitors and locals alike. The interior has an inviting atmosphere with half-panelled walls and a collection of traditional brasses and china.

Proprietor Ann Harper serves an impressive selection of real ales and freshly-prepared bar meals. Outside there is an attractive patio and beer garden and the curious circular building, once the old village lock up, referred to earlier.

Queen Adelaide, 120 London Road, Shenley Tel 01923 856234

The White Horse is a delightful roadside inn which stands beside the B5378 at the southern end of Shenley. Parts of the building date back to the 17th Century, and it has a relaxed welcoming atmosphere, with exposed timbers, half-panelled walls and traditional prints and brasses. The extensive bar incorporates a games area and a first-rate restaurant which offers a superb range of steaks - everything from 5oz to 32oz. Other specialities include steak and kidney pie in Tetley bitter gravy, tortellini ricotta and jambalaya. A varied lunchtime menu includes baguettes and jacket potatoes, and there is also an attractive patio and beer garden to the rear.

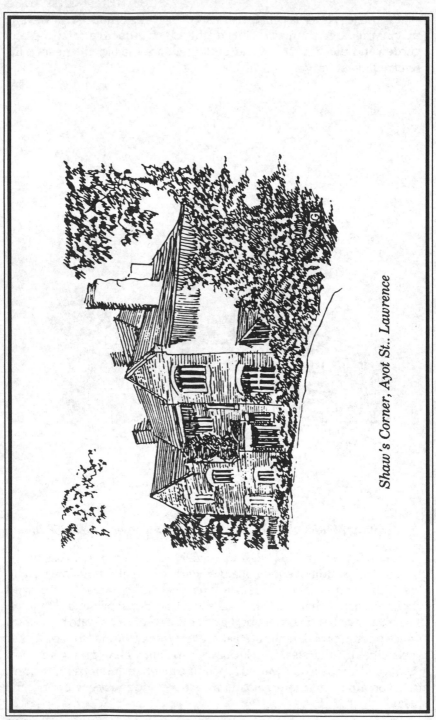

Shaw's Corner, Ayot St.. Lawrence

The White Horse, 37 London Road, Shenley Tel 01923 856315

A mile south of London Colney and just half a mile from junction 22 on the M25, aircraft enthusiasts will find a real haven at the **Mosquito Aircraft Museum** which is run by the De Havilland Aircraft Museum Trust Ltd. It was here in 1940 that the first Mosquito aircraft was built and then taken by road to the De Havilland airfield at Hatfield. In addition to the prototype Mosquito, there is a collection of 16 other De Havilland aircraft plus various engines and displays of all kinds of aeronautical memorabilia.

ST ALBANS

Travelling north we head for the historic Cathedral City of **St Albans**. Dominating the skyline from every direction, the magnificent Norman **Abbey** stands proudly above the city. A wonderful blend of the old with the new, it was built on the site of a Saxon Abbey and was designated as a Cathedral in 1877.

There is so much to see and do in this lovely city. **The Verulamium Museum** stands on the site of one of Roman Britain's major cities and provides a fascinating insight into life during Roman times, with ceramics, mosaic walls and personal possessions displayed in an authentic Roman setting.

On Hatfield Road, the **Museum of St Albans** relates the fascinating history of the city from Roman times to the present day. Among the exhibits is the famous Salaman Collection of Trade and Craft Tools, considered the finest of its kind in Britain.

At **St Albans Organ Museum** on Camp Road you can enjoy the stirring sounds of an amazing collection of working mechanical musical instruments including two theatre organs, musical boxes and reproducing pianos all lovingly restored and cared for.

Verulamium Park is a beautiful tranquil oasis where you can see the remains of Roman Walls, the hypocaust and the site of the London Gate to the city. A popular place with locals and visitors alike, on summer days there is a small fun fair for children to enjoy and refreshments are available in the café/restaurant.

Fishpool Street in the centre of St. Albans is a road with a long history. Standing in the shadow of the city's cathedral, it was on the original main stagecoach route from London to the West of England and until the early 19th Century as many as 40 coaches a day would be seen clattering past.

Probably one of the biggest attractions in Hertfordshire is **The Gardens of the Rose** at **Chiswell Green**, a 20-acre site which is run as a Charitable Trust and contains one of the most important collections of roses in the world. It is not necessary to be a horticultural enthusiast to appreciate the sheer natural beauty of beautiful displays such as The Presidents' Walk or The Queen Mother Rose Garden, named after the gardens' Patron, which contains some of the oldest varieties of rose. With the model gardens, the miniature roses and the breathtaking Pergola, it would be impossible to list the endless beauty of this place which really has to be visited to be appreciated.

Leaving St. Albans behind and travelling north we make our way to the village of **Redbourn** which during the stagecoach era was an important staging post as nearby Watling Street became the main London to Holyhead road.

HITCHIN

Another place well worth visiting is the medieval market town of **Hitchin** which still retains many old buildings among the newer developments. One such building is **The Priory** which stands opposite the end of Sun Street and was built in 1770-7 by Robert Adam for the Radcliffe family.

Also worthy of a mention is **The Biggin** in Biggin Lane, a building erected during the 17th Century on the site of a Gilbertine Priory. Having been successively a private residence and a school, in 1723 it became an almshouse for 'poore auncient or middle aged women', a function which in modern terms it still performs today.

During medieval times Hitchin had a vast market area where straw was purchased for the local cottage industry of straw plaiting and where completed plaits were sold. Gradually the area was reduced, giving way to more permanent premises and today only a small market place west of the Parish Church remains.

Set in the beautiful Hertfordshire countryside at **St Ippollitts** and surrounded by farmland is **The Greyhound**, a most appealing traditional country inn owned and run by Roy Pearce. Notwithstanding the country location, it is ideally placed for business travellers and weekend tourists on the B656 one mile from Hitchin and close to Stevenage, Luton and Welwyn Garden City.

A Public House has stood on this site for 300 years, the present building having been built in 1900. The Greyhound stood derelict for many years before Roy spotted its potential and created the very attractive inn that it is today. This is a place where people enjoy meeting, talking and socialising; you won't find juke boxes or fruit machines here! The cosy bar has two open brick fireplaces where logs are burned in the wintertime.

Four real beers are offered rather than keg beers. There's a small dining room where a full menu offers a good selection of home-cooked food including game and vegetarian dishes. Snack meals and blackboard specials are available and the Sunday Lunch is outstanding. Roy has four well-appointed guest bedrooms with en-suite facilities, TV and hospitality tray. Indeed, hospitality is the key word at the Greyhound. Roy's staff are his friends and his personal attention is guaranteed. ETB 3 Crowns Commended, AA 3-QQQ.

The Greyhound, London Road, St Ippollitts Tel 01462 440989

Follow the winding country lanes through **Little Wymondley** to **Willian**, where well-hidden in the village is **The Three Horseshoes**, a part-Queen Anne ale house that was extended in Victorian times and is now a first-rate pub and eating place. The interior has a friendly traditional atmosphere, with exposed timber beams, two inglenook fireplaces, and an interesting display of antique tankards and firearms.

Proprietors Jane and John Harvey serve an excellent pint of Greene King ale and an imaginative range of home-cooked dishes, including such traditional English specialities as bubble and squeak. There is also a delightful secluded beer garden which is a sun trap in summer.

Three Horseshoes, Willian Tel 01462 685713

In the nearby village of Halls Green, near Weston, **The Rising Sun** is a former 18th Century cottage that was owned by a family named Dimsdale. Baron Dimsdale was an 18th Century physician in Hertfordshire and later went to Russia where he inoculated Catherine the Great against smallpox. The Empress rewarded him with his title and considerable wealth, enabling him to become one of the leading landowners in Hertfordshire.

The pub has kept its traditional dark stained wood panelling and the main bar is dominated by a large central fireplace that burns a huge, roaring fire in the chill of winter. Much of the original timber and beams are still present throughout the bar area and this in turn leads off into the richly carpeted and curtained south facing conservatory that overlooks the 120ft garden. The grounds of the inn have been used for many purposes over the years including a menagerie, but now you are more likely to see a group of children kicking a ball around the 5-a-side football pitch that has been incorporated into the garden. The quality of food is excellent and the service superb, with such culinary treats as Shellfish Platter and Spicy Sausage Grill available, with a kiddies' menu available for the little ones.

St. Albans Cathedral

The Rising Sun, Halls Green, nr Weston Tel 01462 790487

LETCHWORTH

The attractive country town of **Letchworth** is renowned for the quality of its early housing and the consideration given to tree planting in its streets. Indeed this was the first 'garden city', where the ideals of Ebenezer Howard were put into practice. The idea was to create a comfortable and attractive living environment where residential, industrial and rural areas could co-exist in harmony. The history of Letchworth's development as a 'garden city' is related in detail in **The First Garden City Heritage Museum** which can be found at 296 Norton Way South.

Author George Bernard Shaw lived in the village of **Ayot St. Lawrence** from 1906 until his death in 1950. His house, **Shaw's Corner**, is preserved as it was in his lifetime, and his ashes were scattered in the garden.

WELWYN

In the historic town of **Welwyn** you will find the famous Welwyn **Roman Baths** which were excavated during the construction of the A1(M) and preserved in a steel vault within the motorway embankment. They formed part of a villa which was built at the beginning of the 3rd Century and occupied for over 150 years.

The centre of Welwyn is the meeting point of four streets: High Street, Church Street, Mill Lane and Prospect Place. In the past the Great North Road ran through the High Street and Church Street, but today with the A1 motorway half a mile to the east, Welwyn is relatively traffic-free.

On the north side of The Wellington public house stands **Ivy Cottage** which dates back to around 1450 and during the 1870's was Miss Applegarth's school. During this time Ann Van Gogh was the French teacher here and stayed at **Rose Cottage** in Church Street, where her famous artist brother is believed to have visited her.

It Is from here, having discovered some wonderful Hidden Places, that we conclude our travels in West Hertfordshire and make our way across the A1 into the eastern half of this lovely county which takes us into the next chapter.

St. Albans Clock Tower

CHAPTER FOURTEEN

East Hertfordshire

Hatfield House

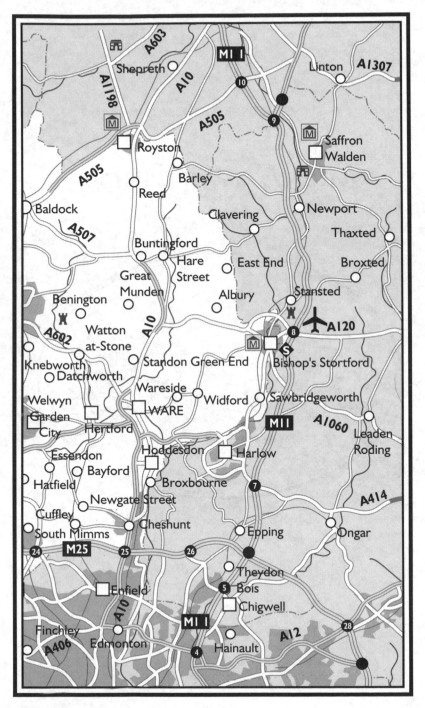

East Hertfordshire

HERTFORD

We begin this Chapter's journey in the delightful, unspoilt county town of **Hertford**. Dating back to Saxon times, it was founded on a ford across the River Lea (then called Lee), the boundary between Saxon and Viking England. Once an important waterway linking Hertford with London, the River Lea, which became the Lea Navigation Canal at Hertford, was used in the past to transport flour and grain, but today is a popular route for leisure cruises, riverside walks and fishing.

One particularly picturesque walk takes you through riverside meadows between the Lea and Beane, from the Hertford canal basin known as The Folly and St. Leonard's Church, Bengeo. The groves of willow on the banks of the Lea are a haven for wildlife and across the Lea Navigation at **Folly Island** there are some delightful 19th Century cottages as well as **The Barge**, a popular riverside inn.

With the growth of Hertford restricted by surrounding cornfields until about 1850, expansion was upwards rather than outwards, with extra storeys added to buildings creating the uneven rooftop skyline which is a familiar feature today.

The town itself is an interesting mixture of new and old with picturesque streets of attractive houses and cottages, some dating back to the 17th Century. Particular buildings of note are the beautiful Norman Church **St. Leonard's, Bengeo** which is Hertford's oldest building, dating back to around 1120, and the **Friends' Meeting House** in Railway Street, which has been in use since 1670 and is the oldest purpose-built Quaker Meeting House. Housed within a 17th Century building on Bull Plain discover **Hertford Museum** which through fascinating displays relates the archaeological, agricultural and social history of east Hertfordshire.

Following the road out of Bull Plain onto Maidenhead Street and down to The Wash, you will find the site of **Hertford Castle,** where the original Gatehouse still remains and is used as administrative offices by Hertford Borough Council. The castle grounds now form a public park where you can still see evidence of the castle's original motte and bailey plan, with the mound lying close to a wooden bridge across the River Lea and nearby, a short length of the massive Norman flint wall complete with 14th Century postern gate.

Knebworth House

The White Horse is a glorious and interesting inn in the oldest part of Hertford just opposite its Castle. A Grade II listed building, the pub dates back to the 16th Century and was built using timbers from the original castle of 1066. At first the bakery to the castle, the White Horse has been an inn for some 200 years. Owned by Janet and Ian Harvey and run with the help of Nigel the manager, the White Horse is full of character and olde worlde charm. A welcoming pub, with a lively and chatty atmosphere (and no piped music) this is the place to come for excellent ale that is brewed at the pub's own brewery (and an ever-changing selection from all over Britain), an interesting selection of fruit wines and equally delicious home-cooked meals (lunchtimes only).

The downstairs is divided into two bars separated by a large central fireplace which adds a warm glow in the winter. Upstairs is a third bar, open at weekends, which offers a cosy and relaxed atmosphere in lounge-style surroundings. This is a super place to stop for a pint and enjoy a good meal with warm and friendly company and perhaps buy some beer or wine to take home.

The **Dark Horse Brewery**, the pub's own brewery, is sited in the centre of Hertford near the river in a converted stables and welcomes visitors.

The White Horse, 33 Castle Street, Hertford Tel 01992 501950

Walkers will enjoy the delightful nature trail to the south of Hertford called the **Cole Green Way** which runs for about four miles between Hertford and the A414 near Cole Green. It follows the route of the now disused Hertford and Welwyn Junction Railway, passing through attractive meadowland with the former Cole Green station providing a pleasant picnic site en-route.

Just off the A414, we find our way to the picturesque village of **Hertingfordbury**, from whence the B158 leads to **Essendon** before a short diversion along the country lanes brings us to **Newgate Street**. **The Crown** in the centre of Newgate Street village is the place to come for those that enjoy the atmosphere of a real country pub. Recently completely refurbished by the owners, Jackie and Geoff Leigh, The Crown has once again become the centre of activity for the village and surrounding communities. Beautifully decorated and furnished, with tankards, jugs and china decorating the walls you can also see pictures of the original Crown that burnt down in 1930.

As well as enjoying a pint or two of excellent ale the delicious food served at the Crown, under Jackie's supervision, is wonderful and well worth travelling to sample. With meat supplied by Jackie's brother Richard Morris, a master butcher, you can be sure of something special and the home-made steak and kidney pies are out of this world. With a delightful large garden and a unique corral for horses the pub is also popular with the local riding community.

The Crown, Newgate Street Village Tel 01707 872107

The B158 links several delightful villages and we follow the road through the village of **Brickendon** to stumble across the picturesque 'hidden' village of **Bayford**.

South Mimms is a name familiar to most people because of the motorway services on the M25 motorway.

HATFIELD
Whilst in this area, it is only a short journey north to **Hatfield**, an historic town which grew up around the gateway to the Palace of the Abbots and Bishop of Ely. This is now the site of **Hatfield House**, an impressive Jacobean house built between 1607 and 1611 by Robert Cecil, 1st Earl of Salisbury who was Chief Minister to King James I. The elaborate architecture of the building is equalled by the exquisite interior, with a

world-famous collection of beautiful tapestries and paintings complementing ornate wood panelling and splendid antique furniture. The magnificent banqueting hall still hosts regular Elizabethan banquets throughout the year, and the intricately carved Grand Staircase is one of the finest examples of its kind in existence. The beautiful west gardens are open daily except Good Friday, and you can wander at your leisure, following nature trails through the woodlands and by the lake, with various picnic areas dotted about.

WATTON-AT-STONE

Further north, just off the A602 is **Watton-at-Stone**, where **The George and Dragon** is a wonderful example of the type of public house that this part of Hertfordshire is renowned for. The building was constructed in 1550, and was originally a row of terraced houses. In 1603 the middle house in the row was granted a licence and became a public house. In 1900 the next door property was added and the eventually the pub was extended to encompass the whole row. Today the George and Dragon has a wonderful rambling feel to it, with many different floor levels connected by steps leading up and down.

The pub is a popular one with both locals and visitors alike, the atmosphere always vibrant, yet with so many nooks and crannies quiet corners are easy to find.

The pub has won many awards; for the past three years it has been selected as Dining Pub of the Year by WHICH Good Pub magazine. The standard of the food is, as you would expect, of the very highest, with something on the menu to suit every taste. This is a great pub and a wonderful 'Hidden Place' - don't pass it by!

The George and Dragon, High Street, Watton-at-Stone.
01920.830285

DATCHWORTH

The Tilbury, the Inn off the Green, situated in **Datchworth,** is a good example of the type of public house that this part of Hertfordshire is renowned for. The building was constructed in the middle of the 16th Century and exhibits architectural detailing peculiar to the area. The pub is a popular one with both locals and visitors alike, the atmosphere always lively, yet it is easy to find a quiet corner with so many nooks and crannies.

A wide variety of unusual real ales are usually on tap, all in cask condition and well worth sampling. Two particularly fine beers are brewed by the landlord and there are plans to build a micro-brewery at the pub soon. The bar food is, as you would expect, of the very highest standard, with something on the menu to suit every taste. Don't pass by this great pub which is a wonderful 'Hidden Place'.

The Tilbury, The Inn Off The Green, Watton Road, Datchworth.
01438 812496

STEVENAGE

Stevenage which can be easily reached via the A1(M) was the first of Britain's 'new towns', a title which it was given in 1946, with the first houses being occupied in 1951 and the new town centre completed in 1957. Originally, however, what is now known as Old Stevenage, began as a settlement on the Great North Road which became its high street. There is still an annual street fair at the north end of Old Stevenage High Street and you can see the traditional 'middle row' of shops where once there would have been market stalls. There is a delightful tree-lined walk known as The Avenue which leads from the Bowling Green at the north end of the street to the Church.

Within the new town area beside the roundabout south of the railway station you can see the **'Six Hills'**, reputedly Romano-British burial mounds which formed a landmark on the Great North Road as it approached Old Stevenage from London.

BENINGTON

From Stevenage it is only a short distance to **Benington**, which is undoubtedly one of Hertfordshire's most attractive villages, with a splendid medieval Church and black and white timbered cottages surrounding the village green. Next to the church is **Benington Lordship** which at the time of the Domesday Book was the principal manor of Peter de Valognes. His Castle was demolished in 1212 and today only the dry moat and traces of the original flint walls remain. A large Georgian house now occupies the site and is surrounded by beautiful gardens which are open to the public throughout the summer on Wednesday, Sunday and Bank Holiday afternoons. Also within the gardens stands a beautiful folly built in 1832 which comprises two impressive stone-built towers forming a castle gateway and an adjoining summerhouse.

KNEBWORTH

Another popular place to visit to the south of Benington is **Knebworth**, a name which in modern times has become synonymous with open air rock concerts. A trip to **Knebworth House and Country Park** is a must, providing a full day of fun for the whole family. The Mansion House is a magnificent high Gothic structure created during the 19th Century by the Victorian statesman and novelist, Edward Bulwer-Lytton. Home of the Lytton family since 1490, Constance Lytton the suffragette lived here, as did Robert Lytton, Viceroy of India. A fascinating exhibition and audio-visual display vividly brings to life the story of Lord Lytton's viceroyalty and the great Delhi Durbar of 1877. The splendid great hall which was transformed into a Jacobean banqueting hall still remains and it was here that Charles Dickens is said to have taken part in amateur theatrical performances during a visit in 1850.

Within the park grounds there is wonderful herb garden established by Gertrude Jekyll and a lovely Victorian Wilderness area; herds of red and sika deer can be seen grazing the 250 acres of grassland. Children will find themselves absorbed for hours in the Adventure Playground which includes Fort Knebworth, a Monorail Suspension Slide, Bouncy Castle and many other attractions, and adjacent to the playground there is a Miniature Railway.

The 400 year old barn has been tastefully converted into a licensed café/restaurant offering welcome refreshments throughout the day and there is accommodation provided for visitors in the Novotel Stevenage which is situated at the Park entrance.

WOOLMER GREEN

We make our way south east of Knebworth towards the historic town of Ware, first though calling in at the village of **Woolmer Green**. A warm welcome awaits you at **The Chequers Inn**, where the traditional and informal atmosphere of the old country inn will make you feel at home the moment you walk through the door. The present Chequers Inn, built in 1927, stands on the site of the old Chequers Inn which was owned for some years by the Lytton family of Knebworth and literary fame.

The large open pub is renowned for its food and you are welcome to enjoy a single course or a full three course meal. The menu comprises traditional and continental wholesome food that is accompanied by fine wines from around the world and real ales. Why not try Chicken Breast cooked in a Lobster Sauce, or Pork Fillet in a Port and Basil Sauce, and for dessert how about Chocolate Torte or the delicious Zabaglione. Whatever you try on this outstanding menu, you will be impressed by the affordable prices and the incredibly high standard of food.

The Chequers Inn, London Road, Woolmer Green Tel 01438 813216

WARE

Situated at the point the Roman Ermine Street crossed the River Lea, **Ware** was the scene of a famous encounter between King Alfred and the Danes in AD895 and during the Middle Ages it became a trading rival to Hertford. The construction of a viaduct in the 1970s to carry the A10 across the valley has removed much of the traffic and despite development over the years, Ware still retains many of its original buildings.

Situated at the west end of the High Street next to the Public Library the conveniently placed car park makes an ideal starting point from which to explore the town.

Behind the High Street on its north side is West Street, where **Number 2**, a particularly old dwelling still retains some of its 13th Century timber frame partly visible from the pavement. In East Street, behind the east end of the High Street there is access to **Blue Coat Yard** where, on the right, you will find **Place House**, possibly one of Ware's two Domesday

Manor Houses, which was rebuilt during the 13th Century as a splendid aisled hall and in the 1680s was purchased by the governors of Christ's Hospital for use as a school for boys being fostered in Ware. Most of this building still remains and on the opposite side of the yard stand the cottages which were built in 1698 and provided accommodation for a foster mother and up to fourteen boys!

As you wander down the High Street to the point where it crosses the river at Bridgefoot you can still see some unique 18th Century gazebos many of which are being slowly restored to their former glory. The riverside footpath it will lead you back to the car park where a small gate leads into an attractive public garden behind what was once a Franciscan **Priory**, a few traces of which still remain. The fascinating history of Ware and its role as a major malting industry is related through detailed exhibits and displays at **Ware Museum** which is situated at Priory Lodge on the High Street and is open on Saturdays and Sunday afternoons.

No trip to Ware would be complete without visiting **Scott's Grotto** which is open on Saturday and Bank Holiday afternoons between April and September. Artificial caves such as this became fashionable garden features during the 18th Century and this particular one was built some time during the 1760s by John Scott of Amwell House, the son of a wealthy Quaker family. This small but elaborate construction consists of several passages lined with flints and beautifully decorated with shells. Its 'hidden' location, tucked away in a little hollow bordered by modern houses merely adds to its mystery and appeal.

Chapmore End is signposted off the B158. Follow a narrow winding lane past open fields and paddocks to this tiny hamlet. You will probably have to stop near to the village pond to allow ducks to cross the road. In this idyllic village setting you will find **The Woodman**.

The Woodman, Chapmore End Tel 01920 463143

The Woodman is a traditional public house, parts of which date back to the late 16th Century. First recorded as a pub in 1851, many changes and improvements have been made to it in the intervening years, yet it has lost none of its character. It is reputed to be haunted by an old landlady, but fear not, for the ghost is friendly, as is the atmosphere that pervades.

The Woodman features in The Good Beer Guide and serves a good variety of real ales including Greene King, Abbott, IPA and seasonal guest beers. Interestingly these are served directly from the cask, no pumps or taps are used. There is nothing that will detract from your enjoyment of these fine ales, no jukebox or rowdy background music. The Woodman has a large beer garden which has its own Mini Zoo, featuring Brian, an 11ft Burmese Python. Popular annual events such as the Summer Folk Festival and the Guy Fawkes Night Fireworks Display are always very well supported here and should not be missed.

The Chequers Inn in the centre of the village of **Wareside** on the B1004 between Hertford and Bishops Stortford, is a charming old inn dating back to the 17th Century. Retaining many original features such as oak beams and characteristic low ceilings, this old coaching inn has been added to and altered over the years.

Today the Chequers Inn offers plenty of character with a traditional decor and real fires in winter. Owned and personally run by Julie, Denise and Douglas Cook, this is a traditional country inn offering excellent food, drink and accommodation as well as a warm and friendly welcome to all who enter. There is always a wonderful range of real ales on tap and the delicious food is freshly prepared on the premises each day and served in a small and intimate restaurant area. With three comfortable letting rooms this is the perfect place to stay whether you are on business or holiday.

The Chequers Inn, Wareside Tel 01920 467010

In the neighbouring village of **Widford** is **The Green Man**. Originally known as the church house, The Green Man was used as the church court many years ago and was converted into a pub back in 1852. A coaching inn in those days, the old barn still stands at the rear of the pub, is classed as a listed building and can be viewed on request. The Green Man has been owned and run by Richard and Jan Marchant for the last two years and the friendly and lively atmosphere owes as much to this lovely couple as it does to the wonderful surroundings. The traditional pub benches and upholstered heavy bar stools add to the feeling of stepping into a bygone age, as do the dark stained half-panelled walls and the real fire that burns throughout the cold winter months.

Usually up to five real ales are served in the bar and this makes it popular with an assortment of musicians who come in to play the upright piano; every Sunday Traditional Jazz is played from 8pm by the resident band. Food is served all day and the blackboard menu proves very popular with at least one vegetarian special on every day, though Jan is very flexible and will try to cook whatever it is that you request.

The Green Man, High Street, Widford Tel 01279 842454

MUCH HADHAM

From here a short drive eastwards lead us to **Much Hadham**, a large, unspoilt village with a long main street lined with handsome timber and brick houses, the oldest of which dates back to the 15th Century. Following bombing damage to his London studio in 1941, the famous sculptor Henry Moore established a new studio and set up home in nearby **Perry Green** where he lived for many years.

Hall Cottage in this picturesque village, famed as having the longest village high street in the country, lies next door to **The Hall**, which you may have seen in various commercials and in the television series Lovejoy. A charming 17th Century building, Hall Cottage is owned by

Nicky Hawksley who has been running a bed and breakfast establishment here for the past 18 months. Retaining many of the original features such as oak beams, the cottage has a warm and cosy feel as well as plenty of character. Guest accommodation is in a choice of two en-suite comfortable bedrooms and guests also have use of the secluded walled cottage garden. Breakfast can be whatever you want ranging from the traditional full English to continental with plenty of choice for vegetarians. This is a charming, informal house in the heart of a beautiful village.

Hall Cottage, High Street, Much Hadham Tel 01279 842640

Originally built in 1840, **The Jolly Waggoners** is also situated in this lovely village, only a few miles from Bishops Stortford, Harlow and Ware. Set in two acres of grounds with a large paddock and safe play area for children complete with duck pond. Robert and Jacqui Oliver are on hand to offer you a warm welcome, along with their four children, Catherine, Anna, Bethany and Dominic and of course not forgetting Salt and Pepper the donkeys, Chloe and Ben the dogs and the sheep and goats, what a family!

The restaurant stands in what was originally two cottages that predated the pub itself and were integrated into the building in 1975. There is an extensive menu including a selection of home-made dishes, fish, steaks, vegetarian meals and much more as well as snacks and sandwiches. All this wonderful food can be enjoyed in front of the cosy open fire which is lit on winter evenings or if it is a balmy summer evening why not take your food and drink outside and enjoy the splendid views of the surrounding countryside.

*The Jolly Waggoners, Widford Road, Much Hadham Tel 01279
842102*

To the north of Much Hadham lies the vast parish of Standon which incorporates the delightful hamlets of **Puckeridge, Colliers End** and **High Cross**. The parish extends west beyond the A10 where at **Old Hall Green** is the Roman Catholic **St. Edmund's College**. A turning south from here leads to **Standon Green End** where in a field behind Great Mead you can see the **'Balloon Stone'**, a memorial erected in honour of Vincenzo Lunardi the pioneer balloonist who landed here having completed the first balloon flight in England on 15th September 1784.

The Plough, Great Munden Tel 01920 438335

The Plough is a traditional English pub in the village of **Great Munden**, just off the main A10 road. Built in 1880, the pub was modernised in 1962 and in 1967 its greatest feature, a Compton Organ was installed here. The organ had come from the Gaumont ci nema in Finchley where between 1938 and 1967 it had been played by some of the greatest theatre organists of the time. Beautifully maintained, the organ is played here every Friday, Saturday and Sunday evening and on Sunday lunchtime.

Today the pub is owned and personally run by Wendy and Peter Godwin and Elaine and Tom Whitear who, as well as providing a unique opportunity to see this great musical instrument offer wonderful real ale and a delicious menu of home-cooked food including home-made steak and kidney pie. Behind the pub is a caravan site which has often been the base for caravan rallies.

Continuing north from Puckeridge on the B1368 there is a delightful stopping-off point **Hare Street** Village. but take time also to explore the village of **Buntingford**, situated alongside the A10, which by-passes the village itself.

Barrallis, a popular restaurant at the north end of the High Street, is housed in a handsome Grade II listed building and serves high quality Italian food. This bistro style restaurant has a welcoming and relaxed atmosphere, the perfect setting to enjoy dishes which are second to none. Every dish is individually cooked to order using only the very freshest of ingredients, locally produced wherever possible. The most popular dishes are probably those with wild or stuffed mushrooms, but the Sole Ferrari (Sole in champagne and shrimp sauce) and Calamari Livornese (Squid with garlic and tomato in a white wine sauce) are particularly delicious, as indeed are the steak and veal dishes. Whatever you decide to try you will not be disappointed. An extensive wine list provides you with the opportunity to select the perfect wine to accompany your choice. This is an excellent restaurant, one that you will likely want to return to again and again.

Barrallis, 72-74 High Street, Buntingford Tel 01763 273951

Bourne Cottage is a charming restaurant standing on the main street. A wonderful 16th Century Grade II listed building that was originally two cottages, the restaurant is owned and personally run by Elaine and Les Saunders. Maintaining many of its original features, including two fireplaces and two chimneys, a 17th Century stone floor and a small minstrels gallery, gives Bourne Cottage a unique atmosphere.

Cosy and intimate, the simple but delicious menu features many favourites such as steak and kidney pie and liver and bacon that are all freshly prepared on the premises. The house speciality, Lample Pie, is based on an 18th Century recipe using lamb and apples, hence its name. This is a charming place, full of character, that will always serve you a tasty meal. Just in case you are wondering about the Isambard Kingdom Brunel memorabilia adorning the walls, the owners are fans of the engineer's work.

Bourne Cottage, 69 High Street, Buntingford Tel 01763 271341

A diversion north through the country lanes will be rewarded at **Barley**, where **The Chequers Inn** is a delightful pub and eating place which is renowned for its friendly atmosphere. Set within an attractive garden with its own children's play area, this lovely old building has been an inn for almost three centuries. The interior is traditionally furnished, with exposed timber beams, wood panelling and welcoming log fire. Proprietors Carol and Tony West serve a range of delicious home-cooked food, including such trditional English delicacies as steak and ale pie and sticky toffee pudding. They also provide a courtesy bus service for those wishing to leave their car at home.

The Chequers Inn, London Road, Barley Tel 01763 848378

From here, before returning south, skirt the large town of **Royston** to arrive at **Ashwell**, just off the main A505 between Baldock and Royston.

The Rose and Crown, a handsome timber framed building, was purpose-built in the mid 1800s and has served as a public house ever since. Situated in Ashwell's High Street, this traditional English pub is one that should not be missed. With its inglenook fireplace, horse brasses, exposed oak beams, beer garden and friendly atmosphere, this lovely 'hidden place' has everything that a good pub should have.

In addition to its good selection of cask condition ales The Rose and Crown also serves superb food in the dining area, which has a separate section for non-smokers. Tuesday and Thursday are Fresh Fish Days, and the pub gets very busy; be sure to make a booking in advance. Whether you call in for a refreshing drink or a delicious meal, you will not be disappointed, for pubs of this standard are few and far between.

The Rose and Crown, 69 High Street, Ashwell Tel 01462 742420

BISHOP'S STORTFORD

Returning south via Buntingford, he delightful rural town of **Bishop's Stortford** lies to the south-east of Puckeridge and during the 18th Century prospered as a market centre for this large rural area. A major coaching town on the route from London to Norwich, its two main industries were malting and brewing. Its name is believed to have derived from two sources: the River Stort provides the 'Stortford' part and the 'Bishop' was added in Norman times, the Domesday Book recording the Bishop of London as being Lord of the Manor here in 1087.

There is a wealth of history within the town and it was here in 1853 that Cecil Rhodes was born, who after leaving in 1870 went to South Africa where he found fame and fortune as the founder of the famous Kimberley Diamond Mines. One of Bishop Stortford's most famous inhabitants, his former home **Nettleswell House** has now become the **Rhodes Memorial Museum** with displays detailing his life story.

SAWBRIDGEWORTH

As you enter the delightful village of **Sawbridgeworth** which lies to the south west of Bishop's Stortford there is an air of timelessness. The streets are little changed over the centuries and relatively traffic-free with business traffic travelling past on the A1184 to the west of the village centre. You can leave your car in the Bell Street car park and stroll at your leisure, taking in the individual character of buildings such as **The Elms** and **The Red House**. Despite its size, Sawbridgeworth has a lot to offer the casual visitor.

And so here we reach the end of our journey through the Hidden Places of Thames and Chilterns, a journey which has been a treasure trail of discovery, and one which you will enjoy yourselves - Safe Travel.

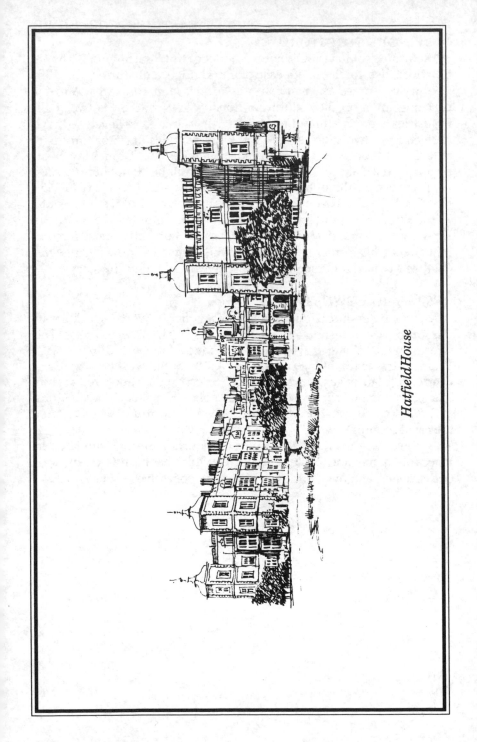

HatfieldHouse

TOURIST INFORMATION CENTRES

ABINGDON 25 Bridge Street 01235 522711

AYLESBURY 8 Bourton Street 01296 330559

BEDFORD 10 St Paul's Square 01234 215226

BISHOP'S STORTFORD The Old Monastery, Windhill 01279 652274

BRACKNELL The Look Out, Nine Mile Ride 01344 868196

BURFORD The Brewery, Sheep Street 01993 823558/590

CHIPPING NORTON The Guildhall 01608 644379/045

DUNSTABLE The Library, Vernon Place 01582 471012

FARINGDON The Pump House, 5 Market Place 01367 242191

HEMEL HEMPSTEAD Dacorum Information Centre, Marlowes 01442 234222

HENLEY-ON-THAMES Town Hall, Market Place 01491 578034

HERTFORD The Castle 01992 584322

HIGH WYCOMBE 6 Cornmarket 01494 421892

LUTON 65-67 Bute Street 01582 401579

MAIDENHEAD The Library, St. Ives Road 01628 781110

MARLOW Court Garden Leisure Complex, Pound Lane 01628 483597

MILTON KEYNES 411 Secklow Gate East, The Food Hall 01908 232525

NEWBURY The Wharf 01635 30267

OXFORD The Old School, Gloucester Green 01865 726871

READING Town Hall, Blagrave Street 01734 566226

ST ALBANS Town Hall, Market Place 01727 864511

SOUTH MIMMS M25 Motorway Services 01707 643233

THAME Market House, North Street 01844 212834

WALLINGFORD Town Hall, Market Place 01491 826972

WELWYN GARDEN CITY Campus West, The Campus 01707 390653

WENDOVER The Clock Tower, High Street 01296 696759

WINDSOR 24 High Street 01753 852010

WOODSTOCK Hensington Road 01993 811038

INDEX

THE HIDDEN PLACES SERIES

To order more copies of this title or any of the others in this
series please complete the order form below and send to ;
M & M Publishing Ltd.
118 Ashley Rd. Hale, Altrincham, Cheshire. WA14 2UN.

TITLE		QUANTITY
Scotland	£8.99	....
Ireland	£8.99	....
Wales	£8.99	....
Lake District	£5.99	....
Northumberland & Durham	£5.99	....
Yorkshire	£5.99	....
Lancashire, Cheshire, & I.O.M	£5.99	....
Peak District & Potteries	£5.99	....
Welsh Borders (Shrops, Here, Worcs.)	£5.99	....
Heart of England (The Midlands)	£5.99	....
East Anglia (inc. Cambs & Essex)	£5.99	....
Cotswolds	£5.99	....
Wessex	£5.99	....
Devon & Cornwall	£5.99	....
Dorset, Hants, & I.O.W	£5.99	....
The South East	£5.99	....
Thames & Chilterns (Berks, Oxon, Bucks, Beds, Herts.)	£5.99	....

NB. FREE POSTAGE & PACKAGING

I enclose Cheque for £..................... made payable to:
M & M Publishing Ltd.
NAME..
ADDRESS..
....
POSTCODE..